Do Apes Read Minds?

Do Apes Read Minds?

Toward a New Folk Psychology

Kristin Andrews

The MIT Press
Cambridge, Massachusetts
London, England

© 2012 Massachusetts Institute of Technology

All rights reserved. No part of this book may be reproduced in any form by any electronic or mechanical means (including photocopying, recording, or information storage and retrieval) without permission in writing from the publisher.

MIT Press books may be purchased at special quantity discounts for business or sales promotional use. For information, please email special_sales@mitpress.mit.edu or write to Special Sales Department, The MIT Press, 55 Hayward Street, Cambridge, MA 02142.

This book was set in Stone Sans and Stone Serif by Toppan Best-set Premedia Limited. Printed and bound in the United States of America.

Library of Congress Cataloging-in-Publication Data

Andrews, Kristin, 1971–.
Do apes read minds? : toward a new folk psychology / Kristin Andrews.
 p. cm.
Includes bibliographical references and index.
ISBN 978-0-262-01755-8 (hardcover : alk. paper)
1. Human behavior. 2. Ethnopsychology. 3. Cognitive psychology. I. Title.
BF199.A53 2012
150—dc23
                                                                    2011044397

10 9 8 7 6 5 4 3 2 1

Contents

Acknowledgments ix

I Identifying the Problem   1

1 Do Apes Read Minds?   3
Social Apes   3
Standard Views of Folk Psychology   7
A Pluralistic Folk Psychology   10

2 Baby Humans and Adult Chimpanzees: Propositional Attitude Attribution in Philosophy and Psychology   13
From Philosophy to Psychology   13
Belief Attribution in Philosophy   14
Belief Attribution in Psychology   18
Theory of Mind in Children   22
Infant Belief Attribution   25
Children's Changing Understanding of Other Minds   33

3 The Asymmetry of Folk Psychological Prediction and Explanation   37
Standard Folk Psychology Emphasizes Prediction (and Assumes Explanation Follows)   37
The Symmetry Thesis   39
Criticisms of the Symmetry Thesis   41
An Asymmetric Folk Psychology   43

II Prediction   45

4 How Do You Know What I'm Going to Do? You Know My Beliefs   47
Prediction and the Propositional Attitudes   47
Predicting Behavior   49
Accuracy of Predicting Behavior by Relying on the Attitudes   51
Propositional Attitude Attribution Is Not Sufficient for Accurate Predictions   52
Propositional Attitude Attribution Is Not Necessary for Accurate Predictions   54

Prediction in Theory Theory and Model Theory   56
Prediction in Simulation Theory   60
Leaving the Armchair   63

5 How Do You Know What I'm Going to Do? You Know Me   65
Mental Content and Intentionality   65
Methods of Prediction   67
Predicting from the Situation   70
Predicting from Self   75
Predicting from Stereotypes   81
Predicting from Traits   88
Other Factors Involved in Predicting Behavior   93

6 The Role of Propositional Attitudes in Behavior Prediction   99
Predicting Behavior and Mental Content   99
Does Trait Attribution Require Attribution of Mental Content?   101
How Accurate Is Standard Folk Psychology?   105
What Place Is There for Traditional Folk Psychological Prediction?   109
Predicting Behavior without Attributing Propositional Attitudes   111

III Explanation   113

7 What Is Folk Psychological Explanation?   115
A Preliminary Account of Folk Psychological Explanation   115
Explanation and Prediction   126
Four Questions about FP Explanation   128
Explanation in Theory Theory   129
Explanation in Simulation Theory   132
Explanation in Model Theory   138
My Answers to the Four Questions   143

8 The Science of Folk Psychological Explanation   145
Aspects of Explanation   145
Explanation Seeking in Children   146
Infants   146
Verbal Children   148
Explanation Generating in Children   151
The Purposes of FP Explanation   153
Explanation Types and Contents   156
Explanatory Pluralism   161

9 Worries about Explanation and Mental State Attribution   163
Explaining Behavior without a Theory of Mind   163
Nonverbal Explainers   164
Automatic Mental State Attribution   168

Explanations, Reasons, and Causes   175
Toward a New Way   178

IV   The Solution   181

10   Folk Psychological Pluralism: Reading People, Not Minds   183
The Principles of a Pluralistic Folk Psychology   183
Folk Psychological Pluralism   197
How Do the Traditional Accounts of Mind Reading Stack Up?   198
Reading People, Not Minds   206

V   Implications of the Account   213

11   Social Intelligence and the Evolution of Theory of Mind   215
The Social Intelligence Hypothesis   215
Deceiving without a Theory of Mind   218
Predicting with a Theory of Mind   220
Norms and Theory of Mind   222
An Adaptive Function of Explaining Behavior   224
Social Intelligence as Explaining Behavior   229

12   Being a Critter Psychologist   231
Problems with the Chimpanzee Theory of Mind Research Program   231
Chimpanzee Critter Psychology   234
Intentional Agency   234
Predicting and Coordinating   237
Explanation Seeking   240
Belief Attribution   243
Moving Forward   247

13   Conclusion   249
Seeing People   249

Notes   253
References   255
Index   289

Acknowledgments

The gestation period for this book was longer than I had ever hoped or even feared, and so I had plenty of opportunity to receive much-appreciated assistance on a number of fronts. Poppy was born in the middle of the writing, and though the delay in final product should be seen in that context, my pregnancy and her birth and development into a little person also taught me much. I'm lucky to have had social relationships with both little humans and little orangutans during the book's development.

This project was supported by a Social Science and Humanities Research Council Standard Research Grant, and because that funding permitted me to travel to Indonesia to learn about orangutan social cognition in a natural setting, this book would have been very different without the support of SSHRC. I also have to thank members of York University's Department of Philosophy for offering me a regular schedule of teaching releases so that I could write this book. I have also received financial assistance in various forms from York University, and that support provided me additional opportunities for travel and research.

Ideas that made it into the book have been presented in a number of venues, including meetings of the Society for Philosophy and Psychology, the Southern Society for Philosophy and Psychology, and the European Society for Philosophy and Psychology. I have also benefited from presenting to colloquiums around Ontario; thanks to Carleton University, McMaster University, Queens University, University of Guelph, University of Waterloo, University of Western Ontario, and York University for invitations to present at department colloquiums and for offering helpful feedback. I also thank Ron Giere, James Harold, Dan Hutto, Heidi Maibom, Bertram Malle, Karsten Stueber, and Peter Verbeek for helpful conversations about this project at its earliest stages and for looking at various drafts. My colleagues, especially Bob Myers and Claudine Verheggen, served as helpful critics.

Acknowledgments

As with any interdisciplinary project, I benefited from the expertise of many individuals. Without Ljiljana Radenovic, I would not have known nearly as much as I do about forms of autism and methods of intervention. Conversations in Toronto's Comparative Cognition in Context reading group provided me the opportunity to learn much about animal cognition research from local scientists and visiting scholars, especially Nathan Emery, Suzanne MacDonald, Tetsuro Matsuzawa, Susan Perry, Sara Shettleworth, and Frans de Waal. Thanks to York University for funding that valuable project as well. Anne Russon, co-organizer of the initiative, gets a very special thanks, for she also invited me to Indonesia to study her studying the orangutans, and I learned more during my weeks there than I could have reading at home for years. Getting dirty—really dirty—was invaluable. I could not have had that experience without the support of Borneo Orangutan Survival Foundation, who offered me a formal invitation to visit BOS-Wanariset Orangutan Reintroduction Project in Samboja Lestari, East Kalimantan, Indonesia, in 2007 and 2008. While I learned much in the forest from the orangutans (including Cecep, Gozgelek, Noel, Ciu, Sipur, Aggie, and Betty), I learned just as much in the evenings on the pondok porch in conversations with Anne, as well as Agnes Ferisa, Purwo Kuncoro, Wiwik Astutik, and Rafaella Commitante.

I must also thank everyone who helped with preparing the manuscript, including Nadia Halim, Olivia Sultanesco, and Hilary Martin. They spent hours wrestling with my tortured prose and tracking down missing references.

A number of people read and commented on drafts of the manuscript, including Ljiljana Radenovic, undergraduate and graduate students at York University (especially Sara Applebaum, Mike Carnevale, Rachel Dineen, Matt Ivanowich, Alex Kouramanis, Hilary Martin, Craig Roxborough, Serife Tekin, Ryan Tonkens, Chris Woolley, and Mark Zolotar), and three anonymous reviewers for MIT press. Brian Huss read innumerable drafts of the book over the years. The final product is much richer for the feedback I received from all these sources.

I could not have written the book without quite a lot of personal support as well. Thanks to Rosa Lima and later to the staff of Annex Montessori for taking good care of my daughter during the last two years of this project. Thanks also to my parents Phyllis and David Andrews, who have always supported me no matter how strange they found my choices.

Acknowledgments

My family deserves the biggest thanks—and an apology. Brian and Poppy, thanks for your enthusiasm about the book (even when you didn't know what you were happy about, Poppy), thanks for drawing me out of the project when I needed a break, thanks for your laughter and love—and sorry for responding impatiently to your interruptions. Without you both, I can't even imagine.

I Identifying the Problem

1 Do Apes Read Minds?

I know that you believe you understand what you think I said, but I'm not sure you realize that what you heard is not what I meant.
—Robert McCloskey, attributed

Social Apes

A dirty young orangutan named Ceceb wants his head cleaned off. He picks a leaf from the ground and hands it to a human named Anne, who uses it to brush away some dirt. But Ceceb isn't satisfied with the first brushing, because he picks up another leaf and hands it to Anne, as well. But now Anne does nothing. Ceceb decides to show Anne what he wants, so he takes the leaf away from her, rubs it on his head, and hands it back. This time Anne gets the message, cleans his head, and Ceceb walks away, satisfied (Russon and Andrews 2010).

Daniel Tammet, who has a form of Asperger's, writes, "I found it difficult to understand the concept that people had their own personal space that was not to be entered and that had to be respected at all times. I had no idea that my behavior could be irritating and intrusive and felt hurt when a brother or sister became angry with me for what I considered to be no reason" (Tammet 2006, 108–109).

Sherlock Holmes is searching for a respectable gentleman named Neville St. Clair, who was last seen in the window of an opium den, without collar or tie. Since St. Clair isn't the sort of man who takes opium, Holmes wonders what he was doing there.

A two-and-one-half-year-old child named Alexandra sees a fallen child in the park and asks, "Why is she crying?" Her mother responds, "Why do you think she's crying?" Alexandra answers, "Because she wants her mommy."

Here we have four examples of apes engaged in the practice of folk psychology. Ceceb's behavior is interpreted in terms of his wants or desires.

Daniel thought his siblings were angry with him for no reason. Sherlock is trying to explain a behavior that doesn't cohere with what he knows about a man. And Alexandra is explaining a behavior, though probably poorly. The social ape knows to various degrees how to engage with other agents, and the skilled apes can anticipate what others are going to do, understand their motivations, and read their feelings. Most verbal apes soon use language to explain why people do what they do, in terms of reasons and causes or sometimes just in terms of factors that make the behavior cohere with the other things we know about a person.

By the time the human ape reaches adulthood, it is typically an expert in human behavior—without needing to take a single university course. While skill levels vary, most adult humans are able to make sense of the myriad behaviors they find in their environments, from the shopping mall to the family dinner. We anticipate normal behavior, like going to the checkout counter before walking out of the grocery store; we make predictions in more uncommon situations, like concluding that he will accept if you propose marriage; we can explain someone's actions to others, like saying that the celebrity shaved her head because she lost it; and we can justify or condemn others' behaviors by presenting what we take to be their reasons for engaging in a behavior, like explaining the young adult's decision to get a tattoo as being intended to upset Mom and Dad.

We are also skilled at describing individuals in terms of their typical behaviors, moods, personality traits, skills, desires, and beliefs. While sister Heather is a creative, intelligent, fun, but moody person who loves to travel and learn new things, neighbor Lucia is a retired Italian meatpacker who believes in God and shares her lasagna with us.

In the philosophy of mind, our understanding of others has largely been explained in terms mindreading, or knowing others' beliefs and desires. It is true that we are skilled at offering descriptions of others' beliefs and desires—the farmer hopes it will rain, the politician believes the death penalty is wrong, the physicist wonders whether there is a grand unified theory. But this skill is only one part of a much larger story.

Descriptions of others' behavior in terms of the beliefs and desires associated with them are thought to form the core of what has come to be known as folk psychology, or the commonsense understanding of other people. This lay understanding of others has been given an important role in the philosophy of mind; the concepts of mentality that come from folk psychology are taken as the explanandum for work in the metaphysics of mind, and in some parts of action theory and neurophilosophy, and are arguably also implicated in philosophical research in ethics and epistemology. We have good reasons to start with folk psychology in the study of mind. Folk psychology allows us to individuate behaviors; without some sort of framework, we would not know how to divide the flow of movement into individual behaviors, and we would not know how to categorize the behaviors that we have identified. If we want to understand the nature of mind, we must have some conception of what the mind is, and starting with the commonsense view will at least assure us of studying something that the folk are interested in.

However, an analysis of the mental that begins with the commonsense understanding of the mind is a good method only insofar as it gets the commonsense understanding of the mind right. This is not to say that the commonsense understanding of the mind must be correct; the folk might be wrong about the mind just as early human folk astronomy was wrong. Two distinct questions arise here: What is the nature of folk psychology? And is folk psychology accurate? Both questions can be examined through appeal to empirical evidence. This book tackles only the first question, so my aim here is to accurately describe how the folk understand other minds in terms of how they engage in the practices associated with folk psychology. A common assumption in philosophy is that folk psychology is mindreading. From this it would follow that folk psychology is limited to attributions of propositional attitudes, things like the belief that snow is white or the desire that the ruling party fall. I challenge this assumption by appealing to research in developmental psychology, social psychology, comparative psychology, and social cognitive neuroscience. While humans do think about others' beliefs and desires, we more often think about other people in terms of their emotions, personality, moods, past behavior, and experiences, as well as our expectations about what the individual should do given her role in society, her group memberships, and her cultural norms. All these considerations are involved in our folk psychological practices of predicting, explaining, and justifying behavior.

Based on an investigation of the practices of folk psychology, I argue that the standard theories of folk psychology rely on an overly narrow understanding of other minds. Instead I offer a pluralistic account of folk psychology and suggest two necessary conditions for engaging in folk psychological practices: a folk psychologist must (1) be able to distinguish agents from nonagents and (2) be able to build and use models of individuals that include a variety of individual properties (including moods, propositional attitudes, emotions, personality traits, dispositions, typical behaviors, group memberships, socioeconomic status, social role, cultural background, and past experience). The practices of folk psychology constitute a social competence and include the ability to identify behavior, predict behavior, explain behavior, justify behavior, normalize behavior, and coordinate behavior. The social competence of folk psychology is subsumed by a number of different cognitive mechanisms, and one's degree of success as a folk psychologist is a function of the number of competences mastered and the degree of facility with the different competences. This view contrasts with standard approaches to folk psychology, according to which being a folk psychologist is a binary situation: either you can mindread or you cannot. In my view, to be a folk psychologist is to satisfy the two necessary conditions, which are jointly sufficient for landing somewhere on the folk psychology continuum. As will be seen, this means that some nonhuman apes can be folk psychologists, too, even if they can't attribute beliefs and desires.

Why is it important to correctly characterize the commonsense understanding of other minds? First, there are methodological implications for scientists. In both developmental psychology and animal cognition, researchers are trying to determine when children first start attributing beliefs and desires, and if any other animals do. I argue that these research programs have been investigating the wrong sorts of behaviors, because the standard accounts of folk psychology have mischaracterized adult human folk psychology. It has long been accepted in this field that correctly predicting or anticipating the behavior of someone with a false belief requires an understanding of belief and an understanding that people have beliefs different from one's own. I argue that appeal to belief is not necessary, and different methods could be used to accurately predict behavior even in false-belief situations. My conclusion is that researchers need to do different kinds of experiments to examine belief attribution in children and other apes; we need to examine whether individuals seek to explain behavior. By introducing the social psychology research on how normal adult humans predict behavior into the theory of mind research program, better experiments for studying theory of mind in humans and nonhumans can be devised.

We should also want to correct the characterization of how humans engage in their folk psychological practices if we want to identify some of the mechanisms involved in these practices, so this project is relevant to researchers engaged in the debate between simulation theory, theory theory, and hybrid theories. The current discussion has too frugal a view of the methods by which humans understand others; my claim is that many methods are involved in folk psychology, and the models being put forth leave out some essential elements implicated in our folk psychological practices. If I am correct, then the models of folk psychology put forth by philosophers such as Alvin Goldman (2006) and Nichols and Stich (2003) miss the mark by neglecting these elements.

Standard Views of Folk Psychology

But first things first. Folk psychology, understood most generally, is nothing more than the commonsense understanding of other minds. But in the philosophical literature, the term *folk psychology* has a more specific definition.

The topic of folk psychology is often introduced to students by using examples such as the following: "I might predict Mary's future behavior by saying, 'We cannot count on Mary's vote because she will almost certainly not turn up to the Faculty meeting, because she believes that Fred will be there and she just cannot stand Fred'" (Lyons 2001, 118). As the story goes, we attribute beliefs and desires to Mary (the belief that Fred will come to the meeting, the desire to avoid Fred), appeal to some general law (e.g., people act to fulfill their desires, ceteris paribus), and conclude that Mary will not attend the meeting. The process is straightforward: we attribute a specific mental content and attitude to the target, then use a folk psychological theory—or perhaps a mental simulation, or some combination of theory and simulation—and then generate the prediction. The claim of standard folk psychology is that the richness of our social lives, the ability to anticipate what others are going to do and to understand what they have done, is made possible by this ability to attribute propositional attitudes to others.[1] According to this view, the folk rely on propositional attitudes because they think that propositional attitudes are what cause behavior. For example, the student's belief that class meets at 3 p.m. and his desire to attend class jointly cause him to go to class at 3 p.m. His action was caused, as well as explained, by his belief and desire, and any intentional action will be caused by a similar set of mental states. The first principle of the general approach that I will label Standard Folk Psychology (SFP) reflects this commitment:

(SFP1) Propositional attitudes are the cause of all intentional behavior.

The next two principles of SFP are illustrated by two encyclopedia entries on the topic. Lynn Rudder Baker's entry for *The MIT Encyclopedia of the Cognitive Sciences* emphasizes the role of propositional attitudes when she describes folk psychology as "commonsense psychology that explains human behavior in terms of beliefs, desires, intentions, expectations, preferences, hopes, fears, and so on" (Baker 2001, 319). Barbara Von Eckardt emphasizes the functions of folk psychology in her entry to Blackwell's *A Companion to the Philosophy of Mind*, where she states that folk psychology minimally consists of "(a) a set of attributive, explanatory, and predictive practices, and (b) a set of notions or concepts used in these practices" (Von Eckardt 1995, 300). Together, these accounts suggest the second and third principles of SFP:

(SFP2) Folk psychology is the attribution of propositional attitudes.

(SFP3) One needs to be a folk psychologist to have robust success in predicting, explaining, and interpreting behavior.

These two elements of folk psychology are thought to be intimately intertwined, such that the attribution of mental content is what allows us to engage in the folk psychological practices. However, the ability to engage in social action—predicting, explaining, and so forth—is what is essential to folk psychology, and we can take (SFP3) as the central claim of folk psychology or part of the core definition of the term. If someone were unable to formulate predictions, explanations, or interpretations of human behavior, then they would lack a folk psychology.

Despite disagreements over the mechanisms that connect the attribution of content to the prediction of behavior, the notion of the unification of folk psychological prediction and explanation is almost universally shared, as we will see in chapter 3. Thus we can state a fourth principle:

(SFP4) The cognitive mechanism that allows us to predict behavior is also the cognitive mechanism that allows us to explain behavior.

That is, whatever the correct account of the cognitive mechanism we use to ascribe mental content to others, it will also be the mechanism we use to understand, predict, and explain others.

The principles of SFP suggest that two main descriptive questions are associated with our ability to understand other minds. The first question is "How do we attribute mental content to ourselves and others?" The second is "How do we predict and explain behavior?" Though many views of folk psychology assume that if you answer the first question, you get the second answer for free, I will argue that these questions are not parallel. The methods we use to predict and explain behavior need not be the same methods we use to attribute mental states, because we may be able to predict and explain without appeal to the content of others' beliefs and desires.

The commitments of SFP can also be seen in the discussion of the simulation theory and the theory theory. This debate focuses on the cognitive mechanisms used in the attribution of mental states to predict and explain behavior. Fundamentally the debate is between those who claim that our understanding of other minds is theoretical and those who deny that claim. According to the theory theory, we postulate beliefs, desires, and other unobservable theoretical entities and use a theory to predict and explain behavior. The theory may be partially innate or learned, but either way it consists of generalizations that connect mental states and behaviors to one another in a lawlike fashion. In this view, our understanding of others is inferential and indirect, mediated by our theories of behavior.

On the other hand, the simulation theorists argue that we understand other minds directly via a kind of mental simulation. We imagine being another person and use the same cognitive mechanisms that generate our own behaviors to understand what another will do. We do not need all the bulky machinery of a tacit theory of mental states, because all that information is available in the processes that lead to our own behavior.

In the 1980s and 1990s, the assumption was that theory theory and simulation theory were "the only two games in town" (Stich and Nichols 1995, 90), and the debate largely consisted of supporters of one theory citing studies that appeared problematic for the other theory. As this game proved less than productive, many participants in the debate came to accept some version of a hybrid model (A. Goldman 2006; Nichols and Stitch 2003). However, the hybrid models also assumed a central role for the attribution of propositional attitudes for predicting behavior.

My project takes the debate between simulation theory and theory theory to be ancillary to the larger questions about the nature of folk psychology. I focus on the assumptions behind these sorts of models. The four principles of SFP are descriptive claims about the causal nature of the attitudes, how we predict and explain behavior, and how we attribute propositional attitudes. I argue that if we take the core concept of folk psychology to be (SFP 3), or the notion that a folk psychologist enjoys success in predicting, explaining, and interpreting behavior, we will have to reject the other principles of SFP. The pluralistic account of folk psychology that I suggest as an alternative is meant to be an empirically adequate account of how we understand others and how we engage in the folk psychological practices of predicting and explaining behavior.

A Pluralistic Folk Psychology

The central goal of this book is to argue that the folk understand one another not primarily as receptacles of propositional attitudes but rather as whole persons embedded in time and in social and physical environments. Our understanding of others' beliefs and desires derives from a more basic understanding of others as intentional agents. We think about beliefs in particular kinds of situations, such as when a person deviates from expected behavior or violates the norms of society, but we don't need to appeal to beliefs to predict quotidian behavior.

I begin to defend this position in chapter 2 by discussing the research programs on theory of mind in human children and chimpanzees. I show how these research programs have been influenced by philosophical theories of the mind, and I argue that neither infants nor young children need a representational understanding of belief to predict or anticipate the behavior of an actor with a false belief. Because understanding of representational belief develops only later in life, children who predict behavior before they gain this understanding provide some evidence against SFP.

In chapter 3, I offer another argument against SFP's emphasis on belief attribution by challenging the psychological symmetry thesis. I argue that prediction of behavior and explanation of behavior are not both subsumed by a single process, so we should not expect a model of folk psychological prediction to also serve as a model of folk psychological explanation. I conclude that the methods we use in both prediction and explanation are pluralistic, and that the mechanisms of folk psychology can differ depending on whether one is predicting or explaining a particular event or action. Here too methodological implications arise for researchers studying theory of mind. This ends the first part of the book.

Next I turn to a detailed examination of the folk psychological practices of prediction and explanation. Chapters 4 through 6 deal with prediction, and chapters 7 through 9 focus on explanation. For both practices, I examine the philosophical commitments and the empirical data and argue for an account of how we engage in these practices. This investigation leads toward an acceptance of folk psychological pluralism. Take prediction, for example. Not all predictions are equal, and not all predictions involve the same reasoning processes. When I predict that my daughter will wake at 7 a.m., and when I predict that the taxi driver will take me home as I asked him to, I am using different kinds of information. I know my daughter's normal behavior, and I use that knowledge to form my prediction about her future behavior. But I have never met the taxi driver before, though I know quite a bit about the social role of taxi drivers, as well as the stereotype of a Toronto taxi driver, and this is the information I use to predict his behavior. The empirical evidence from developmental and social psychology helps to defend the claims that an individual need not be able to attribute propositional attitudes to predict or explain behavior, that behavior can be understood without knowing the causal processes that led to the behavior, and that a number of cognitive processes are involved in different folk psychological acts. We can no more generalize about the cognitive mechanisms that subsume one folk psychological practice than we can generalize about the cognitive mechanisms that subsume types of folk psychological practices. Thus we get pluralism both between prediction and explanation and within each category.

In the book's final chapters, I present my positive theory of folk psychology and examine two implications. In chapter 10, I conclude that what is central to folk psychology is seeing something as a person—or, if you prefer, as an intentional agent. Intentional agents or persons are unified creatures who are self-propelled, cognitively flexible, and differentiated in their personality traits and abilities. The folk understanding of a person, or agent, is what forms the core of folk psychology, while the cognitive architecture that allows a creature to act intentionally consists of a heterogeneous and interconnected set of mechanisms.

As a result of examining the practices of folk psychology, I propose replacing the principles of SFP with the following five principles of Pluralistic Folk Psychology:

(PFP1) One needs to be a folk psychologist to have robust success in predicting, explaining, and interpreting behavior.

(PFP2) Folk psychology is a social competence, which includes the ability to identify behavior, predict behavior, explain behavior, justify behavior, normalize behavior, coordinate behavior, and so on.

(PFP3) The social competences of folk psychology are subsumed by a number of different cognitive mechanisms, and one's degree of success as a folk psychologist is a function of the number of competences mastered and the degree of facility with the different competences.

(PFP4) Intentional behavior is seen as sometimes caused by any number of factors, such as moods, propositional attitudes, emotions, and so on, and sometimes influenced by other factors such as personality traits, dispositions, or historical facts.

(PFP5) The requirement for being a folk psychologist is the ability to recognize that there exist intentional agents and to fare well in discriminating intentional from nonintentional agents.

Pluralistic Folk Psychology is more empirically adequate than the alternatives, insofar as it reflects the development and the diversity of our folk psychological practices of prediction and explanation. This approach also has greater explanatory force insofar as it can account for folk psychological practices other than prediction and explanation, such as justifying and coordinating behavior, understanding others, and the more normative aspects of folk psychology.

Chapter 11 examines an implication of pluralistic folk psychology, namely, its challenge to the dominant view of the evolution of the concepts of belief and desire that we find in some versions of the Social Intelligence Hypothesis. According to this hypothesis, human cognitive abilities, including the ability to attribute belief, evolved as a result of our ancestors' complex social environment. I show that if our attitude concepts did evolve based on social pressures, these would not have been pressures to make better predictions of behavior. While the folk psychology and theory of mind literatures have emphasized agents' ability to predict behavior, I argue instead that it is in the explanation of behavior that we see a greater role for belief attribution. Any evolutionary pressures that made the development of the attitudes an adaptation would have to be based on the advantages associated with explaining behavior, rather than predicting it.

Finally, in chapter 12, I argue that my account of folk psychology also makes sense of nonhuman animals' social cognition. Some critters (a term I prefer to the unwieldy *nonhuman animal*), like humans, could form models of individuals, groups, and species that they use to predict behavior, make normative judgments about behavior, and even engage in explanation-seeking behavior. While this theory brings humans and nonhumans closer together in their folk psychological abilities, it does so by offering a deflationary theory of folk psychology that does not require the sophisticated cognitive machinery of second-order metacognition typically associated with having a representational theory of mind.

Folk psychology is less a causal theory of human intentional action than it is a means of individuating behaviors and constructing, modifying, and using models for persons and types of persons. As such, it is misleading to say that apes read minds. If they are reading anything at all, they are reading persons.

2 Baby Humans and Adult Chimpanzees: Propositional Attitude Attribution in Philosophy and Psychology

> Why is it we don't see skin-bags but husbands and wives and children—people with thoughts and feelings, beliefs and desires like ours. . . ?
> —Alison Gopnik, Andrew Meltzoff, and Patricia Kuhl

From Philosophy to Psychology

In the last chapter, I suggested that a common assumption of Standard Folk Psychology (SFP) is that folk psychology consists primarily of the attribution of propositional attitudes. A propositional attitude will take the form Person-Attitude-Proposition: Brian hopes that the Chiefs will win; Sam believes that he will visit the Giza pyramids; Anne hates that classes start on Tuesday. According to SFP, we use the attitudes to anticipate what others will do next and to explain why people did what they did, and the attitudes are seen as both a cause of behavior and a tool that we use to understand others and ourselves. Indeed, the ability to attribute propositional attitudes, and especially the ability to attribute belief, is taken to be necessary for understanding other minds.

I challenge the claim that the ability to attribute propositional attitudes and having the concept of belief are necessary for successfully engaging in our folk psychological predictive and explanatory practices. The emphasis on the need to attribute beliefs and desires to others, and to engage in a calculation to predict or explain behavior, is part of a larger trend in philosophy and cognitive science associated with information-processing models of mind, and its influence has also been felt in developmental and comparative psychology.

In this chapter, I first demonstrate that while it is widely held that a folk psychologist is someone who is skilled at the practices of predicting, explaining, and interpreting behavior, it is also generally assumed that folk psychology consists of the attribution of propositional attitudes. I then turn to the research on children's emerging understanding of belief to undermine the conjunction of these two claims. Since we are taking the practices of folk psychology to be central to the notion, a tension between the two claims should lead to a rejection of the assumption that a folk psychologist must also be a belief attributor.

Until recently, psychologists thought that children do not have the ability to attribute belief until around four years, because it is not until then that they have an understanding of belief as representational (Wellman et al. 2001). However, this view has been challenged based on the growing body of evidence that even young infants are capable of tracking an actor's false belief (Baillargeon et al. 2010). I argue that these studies do not offer compelling evidence that infants have a folk understanding of representational belief and that there are other methods they can use to make predictions and form expectations about how a person with a false belief should act. Further, I argue that even at four years, children do not have anything like a robust understanding of representational belief. I conclude that during childhood, children continue to develop and refine an understanding of representational belief, all the while acting as fully fledged folk psychologists who predict, explain, justify, and coordinate behavior with others.

The interpretation of the children studies owes much to the tradition in philosophy that emphasizes the role of belief and desire as a cause of action, and as the way of understanding others' actions, so let us begin there.

Belief Attribution in Philosophy

The view that behavior is both caused by beliefs and desires and understood through their attribution can be traced back at least to classical times. In looking to understand animal and human behavior, Aristotle (1987) postulated that desire is the fundamental cause of action. For Aristotle, it is desire in conjunction with the ability to perceive the world that leads humans and other animals to action. I desire to eat, so when I perceive food, I will move toward it; but when I desire to avoid a fight, I move away from my potential opponent. Desire alone will not lead to these actions, though, because if desires were the complete cause of behavior, the only thing that would stop us from acting on a desire would be a stronger, conflicting desire. But we sometimes avoid fulfilling our desires even while lacking a stronger desire in the other direction. Aristotle concludes that desire, while necessary for action, cannot be sufficient. Instead desire must be combined with practical reason. Even animals need practical reason along with desire to act, because sometimes their desires conflict as well.

Aristotle's causal model of action portrays desire as activating practical reason, which then takes over in determining how best to fulfill that desire. The action is the final output. Since both perception and desire are needed to move one to action, if we want to understand an individual's behavior, we need to know both aspects of the cause.

A similar line of reasoning is present in the writing of David Hume, who also insists that action rests on two aspects. In Hume's case, however, action is jointly caused by reason and the passions, or in current terms, by belief and desire. Hume, like Aristotle, emphasizes the role of the conative aspect of action: "Reason is, and ought only to be, the slave of the passions, and can never pretend to any other office than to serve and obey them" (Hume 1978, 415). While I may believe that I will get rich if I become a corporate lawyer, having that belief will not cause me to do anything, any more than having a desire alone can cause me to act. The question is whether getting rich is one of my desires. Hume's famous portrayal of reason as the slave of the passions shows that he, like Aristotle, takes desire to be fundamental. Reason—our beliefs—guides us in the fulfillment of our desires, but both are needed for action.

If beliefs and desires are the cause of behavior, then knowing what mental states an individual has should help us predict and explain behavior. This epistemic issue was of central concern to Wilfrid Sellars (1956), who argued that we do not have private and privileged access to our own mental states, much less to the mental states of others. Sellars is often credited with originating the idea that we understand other minds through appeal to a folk theory of psychology in his critique of the Myth of the Given, where he argued that little is epistemically given and much is inferred (Sellars 1956). To establish the idea that we understand mental states as theoretical entities that fulfill some functional role, he asks us to consider another myth—the myth of our Rylean ancestors. Sellars tells us that our Rylean ancestors had language that they could use to describe appearance, behavior, and so forth, but they lacked any way to refer to internal states, such as beliefs and desires. While this society worked quite well, one day a genius named Jones began to ask why people behaved as they did. While individuals would often articulate reasons for their actions, sometimes they engaged in behavior without saying anything. Jones reasoned that when people do not speak their reasons, they still have reasons. Being a genius, he realized that he could ask people why they engaged in the behaviors that they did, and they would respond by citing reasons. He realized that those reasons existed for an agent even before they were uttered, as a kind of unspoken utterance.

The unspoken utterances became the postulated beliefs and desires, unobservable entities that are useful when predicting and explaining people's behavior. Sellars thinks that with the introduction of mental-state vocabulary into human society, our Rylean ancestors acquired a new language that "contains an *explanation of*, not just a *code for*, such facts as that *there looks to me to be a red and triangular physical object over there*" (Sellars 1956, 116). Our ancient ancestors came to posit mental states as an explanation for human behavior much as they came to posit gods as an explanation for natural phenomena. That is, we became able to explain behaviors both anomalous and common by talking about the actors' beliefs and desires that caused the behaviors. The combination of Aristotle and Hume with Sellars provides the kernel of the theory-theory account of human folk psychology. We understand other minds by understanding the beliefs and desires that others have.

In contemporary philosophy, encyclopedia entries and top textbooks on the philosophy of mind continue to focus on the role of propositional attitude attribution in human folk psychology. For example, John Heil writes, "The practice of explaining behavior by reference to the propositional attitudes is sometimes labeled 'folk psychology'" (2004, 152). In E. J. Lowe's textbook, folk psychology is identified with our "propositional attitude vocabulary" or our "belief-desire discourse" (2000, 62). Jaegwon Kim also takes folk psychology to consist primarily of attributing attitudes to predict and explain behavior: "Much of our ordinary psychological thinking and theorizing . . . involves propositional attitudes; we make use of them all the time to explain and predict what people will do. Why did Mary cross the street? Because she wanted coffee and thought she could get it at the Starbucks across the street" (2006, 15–16).

The reliance on propositional attitudes as central to folk psychology is also seen in much contemporary philosophy of mind and language. From David Lewis's account of mental-state terms to Daniel Dennett's analysis of belief, attribution of attitudes, rather than attribution of emotions, sensations, or other nonpropositional mental states, has taken center stage.

Jerry Fodor is one of the staunchest defenders of folk psychology as using the propositional attitudes. He writes, "Folk psychology is primarily *intentional explanation*; it's the idea that people's behavior can be explained by reference to the contents of their beliefs and desires" (Fodor 1994, 292). Given Fodor's commitment to realism and representationalism, he believes that the propositional attitudes that we use to explain and predict behavior have three essential properties: they are semantically evaluable; they have causal powers; and they are linked together in lawlike generalizations in such a way as to resonate with our commonsense assumptions about the mind (Fodor 1987). In this view, to believe that *P* is to represent *P* in the right way, so that it is in the correct functional relationship with other attitudes and behaviors. The attitudes form the core of cognition for Fodor and are an essential aspect not only of social cognition but of cognition more generally. They are so central for Fodor that he says that if the eliminativist challenge were right, and we were to learn that beliefs, desires, and the other attitudes do not exist, it would be "the end of the world" (Fodor 1990, 196).

To be fair, Fodor does not claim that folk psychology exhausts mental representations; he wants his view to be consistent with subpersonal or unconscious processes. And he admits that the attitudes may not be the only kind of mental representation: "It's *not* also required that the folk-psychological inventory of propositional attitudes should turn out to exhaust a natural kind. It would be astounding if it did" (Fodor 1987, 26). However, Fodor emphasizes the attitudes, and other mental experiences, such as sensations, emotions, and perceptions, play only a supporting role.

Donald Davidson also focuses on the attitudes. On his account of reason explanations, we explain intentional action in terms of propositional attitudes to provide the agent's reason for the action, which in turn "gives the action a place in a pattern" (Davidson 1963, 692). Thus we begin with the idea that the propositional attitudes are entrenched in rational rather than logical relations that produce a holistic and normative description of human action. Mental events are propositional attitudes, and their content is determined by their relationship to all the other relevant attitudes.

Davidson takes the attitudes to include intentions, perceptions, memories, decisions, wantings, urges, and aesthetic, moral, and social norms, as well as the more mundane beliefs and desires. However, for Davidson these are all attitudes that take a proposition. A person *judges that* Africa is more interesting than Asia, *decides that* this year's summer trip should be to Tanzania, *desires that* the plane tickets are not too expensive, and so forth. We get this focus on propositional attitudes from Davidson's interest in accounting for mental causation. A belief and a desire (or what Davidson calls a pro-attitude or what Hume would call a sentiment) are jointly necessary to give an agent a reason for acting, and thus for intentional action itself. At the risk of oversimplifying, in Davidson's view, our attitudes toward those propositions serve to cause our behavior and are also the reasons—or explanations—for our action.

A third contemporary theory that endorses the standard view of folk psychology is Dennett's account of intentional agency. Like Fodor and Davidson, Dennett starts with the notion that our commonsense understanding of other minds primarily involves a set of propositions that are logically related to one another in such a way as to allow for predictability of behavior. In Dennett's view, to be a minded agent is to behave as if you have goals that are rational given your environment, and as if you have beliefs that allow you to fulfill those goals (Dennett 1978a, 1987a). For a third party to predict rational behavior, she must take the intentional stance; that is, she must determine the beliefs and desires the target ought to have given the assumption of rationality. Not only does the intentional stance have the pragmatic advantage of allowing us to predict behavior, but it also has epistemic value as a method for distinguishing between agents and nonagents, and a metaphysical value insofar as it provides an account of what belief is. "Intentional systems are, by definition, all and only those entities whose behavior is predictable/explicable from the intentional stance" (Dennett 1996, 34).

According to Dennett, the predictive power of folk psychology makes possible all our interpersonal projects and relations; without it, "we would be baffling ciphers to each other and to ourselves.... Our power to *interpret* the actions of others depends on our power ... to predict them" (Dennett 1991, 29). In this view, the primary role for folk psychology as the attribution of beliefs and desires is presented as the simplest predictive heuristic available for making accurate-enough predictions across different domains. Even to predict that a person will duck when a brick is thrown at him, we rely on the attribution of beliefs and desires (Dennett 1991).

While Dennett and Davidson certainly have influenced psychology, it is the representationalism in Fodor's view of belief, not the instrumentalism or interpretationism of Dennett and Davidson, that has had the most purchase. In both developmental psychology and comparative cognition, when researchers investigate the subject's understanding of belief, what they are really interested in is representational belief.

Belief Attribution in Psychology

In psychology, we can see the influence of such views of the mind in at least two different areas: theories about the function of our mental-state ascriptions, and research on human children and members of other species. Many evolutionary psychologists have been interested in the function of our mental-state ascriptions and have looked for the ultimate and proximate causes of this ability. Psychologists who are examining how the ability to attribute beliefs and desires evolved in the human species largely accept the principles of SFP. The dominant account of the evolution of propositional attitudes is known as the Social Intelligence Hypothesis, an idea developed independently by the psychologist Nicholas Humphrey (1976) and the primatologist Alison Jolly (1966).

According to the Social Intelligence Hypothesis, human cognitive ability evolved as a result of our ancestors' complex social environment rather than due to pressures of the physical environment. The daily battles and stresses that come from living among others created a need to become psychologists who are better able to make predictions of behavior, and these pressures led to the development of mental-state concepts and a corresponding logic (Humphrey 1978). The logic is nothing more than the platitudes of folk psychology that connect beliefs and desires to one another and to behavior.

Humphrey draws a picture of a cutthroat political landscape that emerged as a result of large social groups, and describes social intelligence as what allowed our ancestors to survive the subsequent challenges. This Hobbesian description of our social milieu has led some to describe Humphrey's thesis as Machiavellian (see, e.g., Byrne and Whiten 1988), because anyone who had the ability to attribute mental states, like Sellars's genius Jones, had a huge advantage over those who did not have the ability. Jones would be better able not just to predict behavior but also to manipulate behavior by deceiving others. In the Machiavellian intelligence view, Jones's insight was the beginning of an evolutionary arms race. Like the principle of SFP that this account largely relies on, this version of the Social Intelligence Theory is subject to criticisms that I discuss in chapter 11.

A second psychological beneficiary of the Aristotelian view of the propositional attitudes is the research program known as theory of mind. David Premack and Guy Woodruff introduced the term in 1978 during their investigation into whether chimpanzees are able to attribute propositional attitudes. They originally defined the term as follows: "An individual has a theory of mind if he imputes mental states to himself and others. A system of inferences of this kind is properly viewed as a theory because such states are not directly observable, and the system can be used to make predictions about the behavior of others" (Premack and Woodruff 1978, 515).

Premack and Woodruff's definition of theory of mind reflects Sellars's claim that our understanding of minds is indirect and mediated by theoretical inference. But it also reflects the Aristotelian and Humean views by suggesting that to predict intentional behavior, one has to understand the cause of that behavior. That is, one has to understand the belief and desire that led to the behavior. Premack later wrote that he and Woodruff were interested in the question "Does the ape do what humans do: attribute states of mind to the other one, and use these states to predict and explain the behavior of the other one? For example, does the ape wonder, while looking quizzically at another individual, What does he really *want*? What does he *believe*? What are his *intentions*?" (Premack 1988, 160). The implicit inference here is that to predict some class of behaviors, one must know the cause of the behavior, and since it is belief and desire that jointly cause behavior, we must attribute them.

In the theory of mind research program, the essence of the strategy used to determine whether someone has the ability to attribute belief is to examine her ability to predict what someone will do when she has a belief the subject knows to be false. Understanding false belief as the key arose from discussions of Premack and Woodruff's study of chimpanzee theory of mind. In their study, Premack and Woodruff asked a fourteen-year-old chimpanzee named Sarah to predict the behavior of a human who was confronted with a problem, such as acquiring out-of-reach bananas or warming up a cold room with a heater. Sarah rather easily accomplished this task by choosing from an array the photograph that demonstrated the best solution to the problem. Originally Premack and Woodruff interpreted Sarah's performance as requiring the attribution of "at least two states of mind to the human actor, namely, intention or purpose on the one hand, and knowledge or belief on the other" (Premack and Woodruff 1978, 518).

In commentaries on the paper, this interpretation was soundly criticized. Sarah could simply be solving the problem herself, not thinking about how the actor portrayed in the photographs was thinking. But what emerged were some novel suggestions for how to test for theory of mind. Three philosophers independently suggested that to determine whether a chimpanzee knows that others have beliefs, experimenters could present the chimpanzee with a problem where he would have to alter his own behavior in expectation of another's behavior (e.g., Bennett 1978; Dennett 1978b; Harman 1978). Predicting that another will act the same way you would may be relatively simple, but making predictions of someone's behavior when she would act differently from you is more of a challenge. Different behavior in the same environment cannot be predicted using an associationist strategy, because there would be no difference in the stimulus. The difference in the two cases must be conceptual, rather than environmental.

In Dennett's commentary, he argued that a good test of theory of mind will rest on a coordination problem that involves the subject responding to the actor's false belief. This will ensure that the anticipated action will be relatively novel, and that an associationist explanation is not possible. Dennett suggested modeling a test after a Punch and Judy puppet show. Children watching Punch and Judy squeal for joy when Punch is about to push a box over a cliff, because though Punch thinks that Judy is still in the box, the children know that Judy snuck out when Punch wasn't looking.

Dennett proposed constructing a similar situation for chimpanzees: First let the chimpanzee observe someone move a banana from one box to another. Then when the experimenter comes to retrieve the banana, the chimpanzee who has a theory of mind will predict that the experimenter will go to the wrong box. The only problem, as Dennett noted, is how to tease out the chimpanzee's expectation. In any case, the task requires that the subject understand that the actor has a false belief and will thus act in a way inconsistent with his goal.

These suggestions for testing chimpanzee theory of mind were taken up by the developmental psychologists, first with Wimmer and Perner's false-belief task (which I discuss in the next section), and later with other tests of false belief such as the unexpected-contents task (Gopnik and Astington 1988). The unexpected-contents task lets a child watch as a familiar box, such as a tube of Smarties candies, is filled with atypical objects such as pencils. The child is then asked what another uninformed child thinks is in the box. Older children will correctly say that the uninformed child thinks the box contains candy, but younger children will say that the child thinks the box contains pencils.

It is not always clear whether the focus on false belief reflects an epistemic or constitutive criterion. In some cases, passing the false-belief task is described as a method for determining whether a child has a theory of mind. This view is sometimes conflated with the constitutive claim that understanding belief requires understanding false belief. Premack, for example, sees understanding false belief as a methodological criterion: "False belief is pivotal to the claim that an individual is attributing states of mind" (Premack and Premack 2003, 148). But understanding false belief may be implicated in the concept of belief, and to understand belief, one must understand truth and falsity. This view is clearly associated with the representational theory of mind as developed by Fodor, and it is also defended by Davidson. Davidson argues that one cannot have a belief without having the concepts of objective truth, or of truth and falsity, and to have those concepts, one must have the concept of belief (Davidson 1982, 1991). This is because you can't understand the meaning of a proposition without joint attention, or what Davidson calls triangulation, and a successful triangulation involves two agents who can interpret each other's attitude toward an object in the external world (Davidson 1991). The act of triangulating leads to an understanding of truth and falsity, because it requires that the agent recognize whether the other agent's utterance correctly describes the external world. Thus it follows that you can't believe that P without believing that P is objectively true. All thoughts depend on having the concept of objective truth.

As part of the acceptance of representational belief, this constitutive view appears to be the one that has gained acceptance in the past twenty-five years. Alan Leslie writes, "The central dogma in the field quickly came to be that children attribute beliefs to other people only when they pass the 'standard' FB task at 4 years of age" (Leslie 2005, 460), and he cites Josef Perner's book *Understanding the Representational Mind* (1991) to back up the claim. That is, understanding false beliefs is thought to be necessary for understanding that others have beliefs.

We can turn now to the research on the child's theory of mind. I argue that the experimental results are consistent with the position that children do not have an understanding of representational belief until late childhood. Rather, infants and young children may have a dispositional understanding of belief, given that their ability to anticipate people's false-belief behavior can be explained in terms of other mechanisms.

Theory of Mind in Children

Humans are born into the social cognitive domain. Infants orient toward human faces, prefer to look at and listen to humans, and even imitate others when only a few days old (Wellman 2010). Infants are able to synchronize behavior with others from a very early age; as early as two weeks from birth, infants can imitate facial expressions (Meltzoff and Moore 1977). Toward the end of the second month of life, an infant begins to actively engage with the caretaker through an exchange of positive emotional actions (Lavelli and Fogel 2005). By six months, infants recognize that hands have agency (Leslie 1984), and by ten months infants already treat others as intentional agents with whom experiences can be shared (Desrochers et al. 1995; Legerstee and Barillas 2003). At this age, children engage in declarative pointing with adult caretakers, indicating objects of interest and checking to verify the partner's gaze (Camaioni 1993). They can also distinguish between adults who are unwilling to engage in an action and those who are unable to do so, and they get angry with unwilling partners (Behne et al. 2005). They can also identify and imitate someone's goal even when the actor fails to achieve it (Brandone and Wellman 2009). Between eight and eighteen months, infants' ability to differentiate self and other increases, and around twelve months prosocial behavior such as helping emerges (Roth-Hanania 2002). Just after twelve months, infants are able to differentiate between information that is new and old for another (Tomasello and Haberl 2003). By fourteen months, a child knows what others can and cannot see (Moll and Tomasello 2007).

Despite the rich social understanding demonstrated by human infants, until recently the consensus has been that children do not understand desire until about eighteen months and do not understand belief until about four years (Wellman et al. 2001). The evidence for belief comes from the traditional false-belief task, developed by Hans Wimmer and Josef Perner (1983). This task is often taken as a litmus test for understanding belief, insofar as anyone who passes it is thought to have a full understanding of the propositional attitudes, including the ability to recognize that others have beliefs and desires that differ from one's own. In the original version of this task, children watch a show in which a puppet named Maxi puts away a piece of chocolate before leaving the room. While Maxi is out, his mother finds the chocolate and moves it to another location. Maxi returns to the scene, the show is stopped, and children are asked to predict where Maxi will go to look for his chocolate. This experiment came to be known as the unexpected-transfer test or simply the false-belief task.

The result of Wimmer and Perner's original experiment is that children younger than four fail to predict that Maxi will search for the chocolate where he left it, and only 57 percent of children in the four- to six-year range make successful predictions (Wimmer and Perner 1983). This result has been widely replicated, and a meta-analysis of 178 studies concludes that children are able to pass this task as four-year-olds (Wellman et al. 2001).

The finding that children pass the false-belief task at four years is consistent with many other things we know about children of this age. It is not until this age that children begin to use contrastives to remark on any discrepancies between a mental state and reality; though they use mental-state language such as "think," "know," and "remember" from two and one-half years, they will not say things like "Before I thought he was mean, but he's nice" (Sabbagh and Callanan 1998, 492). They also begin to understand that people lie and deceive (Siegal and Peterson 1996, 1998), that thought bubbles show a person's thoughts (Wellman et al. 1996), that people control their facial expressions to mask their true feelings (Harris et al. 1986), and that appearance and reality can differ (Flavell et al. 1987).

If failing the false-belief task demonstrates that a child does not understand that others have beliefs, as is commonly claimed, then children younger than four cannot be using a full-blown folk psychology based on propositional attitude attribution. Yet even very young children are able to make accurate predictions. Infants at eighteen months are able to differentiate between their own desires and others' desires based on facial expressions and are able to predict what will please another person (Repacholi and Gopnik 1997). When given the chance to offer food to an experimenter, the infant could offer either food the infant herself prefers or a food the experimenter prefers. At fourteen months, infants tend to offer an experimenter the food that the infant prefers, but four months later will offer food that the experimenter expresses preference for, even when the infant herself does not prefer the food.

Another study that explicitly asks children to make predictions based on a person's desire was conducted with two-year-olds (Wellman 1990). Children were told a story about Sam, who wants to find his rabbit. Sam's rabbit is hiding in one of two locations. Sam walks to one of the locations, where he finds his rabbit, or finds a dog, or finds nothing. At this point the story is halted, and children are asked whether Sam would now go to school, or whether he would look in the other location. At two years, children are able to correctly predict Sam's behavior depending on whether he found the rabbit.

Nonetheless, at this age children do not have a perfect understanding of desires. Even four-year-olds have trouble attributing different desires to two people who are performing the same actions (Baird and Moses 2001), and have problems distinguishing intention and desire (Schult 2002). Despite these problems, children are able to successfully engage in many folk psychological practices at a young age. This raises the question about how children are accomplishing such behaviors.

There are two ways of resolving the tension: either children younger than four do understand belief, or children do not need to understand belief to engage in these practices. While the first response seems to be supported by a growing body of data about infant social cognition, I think the second response has more merit. To see why, we can turn to the research on infant belief attribution.

Infant Belief Attribution

With the publication of Kristine Onishi and Renée Baillargeon's study of infant false belief understanding in 2005, the claim that children do not understand false belief until four years came under attack. Since then, a flurry of studies on infant understanding of false belief has suggested that humans come to understand false belief by their second year of life (Baillargeon et al. 2010). Infants demonstrate their sensitivity to people's false beliefs through spontaneous response tasks, such as helping an adult with a false belief (Buttelmann et al. 2009), anticipatory looking (Clements and Perner 1994; Garnham and Ruffman 2001; Southgate et al. 2007), and violation of expectation paradigms (Onishi and Baillargeon 2005; Song et al. 2008; Surian et al. 2007; Träuble et al. 2010).

The violation of expectation paradigm is commonly used in studies of infant cognition, and in this context it is used to test whether infants will look longer at actions that are inconsistent with the actor's false belief than they will look at actions that are consistent with false belief. The interpretation is that infants look longer at unexpected events than expected ones; thus researchers believe they can determine what an infant expects before she can utter a word. In Onishi and Baillargeon's 2005 study, the structure of the task is modeled after the standard false-belief task: infants are first familiarized with a scene including an actor, an object, and two boxes. In the false belief condition of the test, the actor places the object in one of the boxes and then is removed from the scene by a screen that blocks her vision (and the infant can no longer see her). While the screen is down, the object moves from one box to the other box. When the screen is raised, the actor looks into one of the boxes. Infants stared at the scene longer when the actor looked into the box that now held the object, rather than the box where the actor had left the object. Onishi and Baillargeon also ran a true-belief condition and found parallel results. The infants were surprised, that is, they looked longer, when the actor's apparent belief and action were inconsistent. But when they were consistent, the infants were relatively uninterested. Onishi and Baillargeon interpret these and related findings as indicating that "even young children appeal to others' mental states—goals, perceptions, and beliefs—to make sense of their actions" (257).

While these experiments and subsequent related studies seem to indicate that infants have a theory of mind long before they are able to pass the traditional false-belief task, they raise questions about how children go about solving these tasks. If the understanding of belief is sufficient, and children understand belief at fifteen months, then we should expect children to pass the standard false-belief task as well. But of course they don't. How to explain this apparent conflict?

One answer is to claim that the false-belief task is too difficult and requires children to do much more than attribute belief. Even before the infant studies took off, many criticized the false-belief task for being difficult even for children who have an understanding of belief. For example, Bloom and German write, "To solve it, the child has to follow the actions of two characters in a narrative, has to appreciate that Sally could not have observed the switching of the chocolate, has to remember both where the chocolate used to be and where it is at the time of the test, and has to appreciate the precise meaning of the question (for instance, that it means where will Sally look, not where she *should* look)" (2000, B27). They conclude that having a theory of mind is not a sufficient condition for passing the false-belief task, but it is a necessary one.

Specific difficulties with the false-belief task include the act of making a prediction (Moses and Flavell 1990; Robinson and Mitchell 1995), counterfactual reasoning (Riggs et al. 1998), the necessity of controlling one's inclination to refer to reality (Carlson and Moses 2001; Mitchell 1994; Robinson 1994; Robinson and Mitchell 1995), the curse of knowledge, or inhibiting one's own true belief (Birch and Bloom 2003), and the need to ignore heuristics that have been successful in the past, such as the rule that people will generally act so as to fulfill their desires (Fodor 1992; Roth and Leslie 1998; Saltmarsh et al. 1995). To predict the behavior of someone with a false belief, the child must disregard the actual state of affairs. Children must be able to refrain from indicating where the object actually is, and young children are notoriously bad at inhibitory control; young children may find referring to the chocolate in the story irresistible (Carlson and Moses 2001, 1034). Other studies suggest that children are more likely to refer to the actual state of affairs unless the character's false belief has been given a physical instantiation (Mitchell and Lacohée 1991; Saltmarsh et al. 1995).

These criticisms of the traditional false-belief task can only explain the difference in performance if these features are not also involved in the infant false-belief tasks. Scott and Baillargeon (2009) suggest that this in fact is the explanation. They emphasize the difference between the spontaneous nature of the infant tasks and the more controlled nature of the traditional false-belief tasks, which they call *elicited-response tasks*. They claim that the spontaneous-response tasks involve only one process, the representation of false belief, whereas the elicited-response tasks involve three processes: representation, a response-selection process (which allows them to access the represented false belief), and a response-inhibition process (which allows them to inhibit their tendency to respond based on their own knowledge). However, the claim that only one process is involved in the spontaneous-response tasks is implausible; if the infant does first represent the target's false belief, then, in an information processing model of cognition, that representation is information that still needs to be activated and connected with other relevant information to cause the looking behavior. Other processes must be involved, and many of the difficulties associated with the traditional false-belief task are also implicated in the infant false-belief tasks. For example, infants still need to inhibit their own knowledge about the location of the object to accurately represent where the actor thinks it is, they are still prone to the curse of knowledge, and they are still engaged in an act of prediction when anticipating where the target will look for an object.

If task difficulties cannot explain why infants demonstrate theory of mind yet preschoolers do not, we need to turn elsewhere to look for an explanation. Let's look at two candidates. First, it may be that the infant experiments have been optimistically interpreted by researchers, and the infant behaviors can be explained in terms other than understanding belief. Second, it may be that the infants have some nonrepresentational understanding of belief. We will examine these claims in turn.

Given that the infant studies have challenged conventional wisdom, there has been no shortage of alternate explanations offered for the infants' success in these tasks. There are at least four alternative explanations for the infants' behavior:

1. Associations or behavioral rules. Infants might form associations between people and their actions on objects that guide their future actions (Perner and Ruffman 2005). Or infants might have a theory about how people behave in certain situations, and generate new rules from observed behavior (e.g., following Povinelli and Vonk 2004).
2. Reasoning from ignorance. Infants might expect that actors who are ignorant are more likely to make an error or be uncertain in their action (Southgate et al. 2007; Wellman 2010).
3. Explicit simulation or perspective taking. Infants might be able to ask themselves what they would do or desire if they were in the target's situation, or they might recognize that the target has her own unique perspective (e.g., following Gordon 1995b).

4. Teleological understanding. Infants can understand another's goals without understanding anything about belief. Knowledge of goals plus attribution of rationality might be sufficient for predicting behavior (e.g., following Csibra and Gergely 1998).

One potential problem with the association interpretation is that it would require infants to have a large set of associations or rules, which may be biologically implausible. Baillargeon and colleagues claim that the association explanation cannot be correct, given control conditions. For example, infants who habituate to an adult grasping object A will look longer at the adult when she grabs object B *only if* object B was present and visible to the adult when she was grasping object A. This, they suggest, indicates that the infants are not merely forming associations between the actor and an object but have some understanding of the actor's motivations and their inaccurate informational states (Baillargeon et al. 2010). However, this reply would only work if infants had the ability to make only very simple associations, and it may be that infants are able to make more robust associations that do not merely associate a person and her behavior with an object but instead associate a person, an object, and a context. So this interpretation largely rests on whether an infant's mind is capable of processing a large number of fairly complex associations or behavioral rules.

The reasoning-from-ignorance interpretation is based on a larger worry about the looking-time methods. Wellman (2010) points out that while this method tells us that infants have some expectations, it does not tell us what the content of the expectation is. The interpretation of the experiments is based on the assumption that an infant's expectation is an exclusive disjunction, such that the infant expects the actor to engage in either action A or action B. However, it is possible that the infant expected neither action; from the information that the infant did not expect action A, we cannot infer that she did expect action B. But it is just that inference that leads Baillargeon and colleagues to conclude that infants understand false belief.

However, Wellman's concern does not generalize to other spontaneous-response tasks, such as the Buttelmann study of infant false belief using an active helping paradigm (Buttelmann et al. 2009). In this study, eighteen-month-olds were encouraged to help an actor fulfill his goal by opening one of two boxes. During the initial setup, the child watched the adult play with a toy, then put it into a box, and then the child helped another adult lock the box. In the true-belief condition, the actor then tried to open the box without the toy, and the child helped the actor open that box. In the false-belief condition, the toy was moved from one box to another when the actor was out of the room. When the actor came back, he attempted to open the box that had previously held the toy (i.e., the box that the actor falsely believed held the toy). The child helped by opening the other box—the box with the toy in it. This result suggests that the children understood the actor's goal in the true-belief condition was not to get the toy but to look inside the other box, and that the actor's goal in the false-belief condition was to get the toy. But for the infant to determine the actor's goal in the false-belief condition, she would have to understand that the actor did not realize that the toy had been moved to the other box. The authors claim that the infants needed to actively imagine the actor's belief to usefully help the actor.

However, alternative explanations exist for the performance on the active helping paradigm as well. For example, it may be that the social nature of the interaction allows the infant to put herself in the actor's position and see the world from his perspective, or to run a mental simulation from that starting point. However, an explicit simulation may be too difficult for an infant, insofar as it requires counterfactual thought, quarantine of one's own beliefs, and perspective taking.

Alternatively, solving the task might involve teleological understanding rather than an understanding of belief. For example, the child may be considering the actor's goal, rather than his belief. In the false-belief condition, the child correctly tracks the actor's goal of retrieving the toy. In the true-belief condition, the actor changes games by switching from one box to the other, and the child's willingness to help the actor open the new box can be explained in terms of the child taking the actor to have a new goal associated with the new behavior.

Even if these alternative explanations are not immune to criticism, they are certainly no worse off than the explanation that infants have an understanding of representational belief. While compelling evidence shows that infants are able to track the behavior of people who have false beliefs in quasi-social situations, the claims that success in these tasks "require[s] the active imagining of others' beliefs" (Buttelmann et al. 2009), that infants "must imagine a thought bubble in [the actor's] head that has actual content driving his behavior" (341), and that infants "represented the agent's false belief and used this representation to infer what goal the agent was trying to achieve" (Baillargeon et al. 2010, 116) are too strong. These researchers think that tracking false beliefs requires having an understanding of representational belief, but as we will see, it could be that children are using a dispositional understanding of belief. This interpretation would help to make sense of the cognitive changes around age four; it may be that the development of a primitive understanding of representational belief allows children to begin passing the traditional false-belief task around this age.

Representationalism about belief is the dominant theoretical perspective about the nature of belief; when we believe something, we have a symbol—a representation—tokened in the head that has the same content as the proposition used to describe the belief. Thinking is the manipulation of these symbols, and a belief is a relationship between the belief attitude and its represented content. In this view, to understand that others have beliefs requires being able to represent a representation, and thus requires metacognitive abilities. Whether belief is representational or not, the infant's folk understanding of belief may not reflect representationalism. Instead infants might track false belief understood nonrepresentationally, and the infants' folk understanding of belief might be described dispositionally as a relation between a subject and a possible state of affairs (Marcus 1990). For example, Ruth Barcan Marcus presents her dispositional account of belief as follows: "x believes that S just in case under certain *agent-centered circumstances* including x's desires and needs as well as *external circumstances*, x is disposed to act as if S, that actual or non-actual state of affairs, obtains" (Marcus 1990, 133).

In Marcus's view, a belief is related to its content without being under a particular description, since states of affairs are ordered structures of actual objects, properties, and their relations. To represent someone's belief, then, would be to understand how a person would act in a certain state of affairs.

According to another dispositional account, belief is understood as a dispositional stereotype that consists of a cluster of behavioral and phenomenal properties that we are apt to associate together. In describing this view, Eric Schwitzgebel writes: "To believe that P, on the view I am proposing, is nothing more than to match to an appropriate degree and in appropriate respects the dispositional stereotype for believing that P. What respects and degrees of match are to count as 'appropriate' will vary contextually and so must be left to the ascriber's judgment" (Schwitzgebel 2002, 253).

The account is dispositional because it treats believing as being disposed to do and experience things, and it is phenomenal because the dispositional stereotype also includes emotions, moods, and other phenomenal states. Dispositionalism, like associationist explanations, plays up the nonlinguistic conceptual and categorization abilities that are a core feature of human cognition. According to such views, humans are able to engage in sophisticated behaviors without the need for representational or symbolic abilities.

The dispositional approach to belief is related to antirepresentationalism in cognitive science, such as Rodney Brooks's research in artificial intelligence and robotics (e.g., Brooks 1991). Some cognitive scientists and psychologists who accept a connectionist or dynamical approach to modeling cognition also argue that the human mind, and hence belief, is nonrepresentational (Thelen and Smith 1994). In philosophy, too, interest in the power of nonrepresentational models of cognition has been growing (Clark and Toribio 1994; Thompson 2007; Van Gelder 1995).

Whether or not such views begin to accurately describe human cognitive architecture, they may nonetheless accurately describe some part of the folk understanding of belief. Infants who track false belief using a dispositional understanding of belief do not require metacognitive abilities. Rather, in certain situations for which they have something like belief stereotypes, scripts, prototypes, or general rules, infants would be able to act in ways appropriate to the actor and her situation.

The difference between attributing dispositional belief and attributing representational belief may map onto the difference between *knowing how* and *knowing that*. *Knowing how* refers to procedural knowledge that allows one to act. We know *how* to speak English, to ride a bike, to get to work, to make an omelet. On the other hand, our *knowledge that* is propositional in form and takes sentences or propositions as objects. We know *that* January comes before February, and we know *that* Java is part of Indonesia. In knowing *how*, we may lack explicit awareness of the processes underlying the activity, and the ability may not be under voluntary control. In contrast, the propositions that we know can be made available to consciousness, and we can choose whether or not to consider them.

To make sense of the claim that the infant has implicit knowledge of the propositional attitude "Actor believes that the watermelon is in the green box," we would need to understand how we can "know how" a propositional attitude. To know a propositional attitude implicitly is to know how to act on propositional knowledge. But the infant does not have the propositional knowledge, in this interpretation of implicit knowledge. She only knows how to act *as if* she has this knowledge.

Consider a paradigmatic example of knowing how: riding a bicycle. The ability to ride a bicycle can be described in the language of physics by referring to concepts such as friction, center of gravity, inertia, and force.

Being able to engage in bicycle riding requires skill that is sensitive to these physical constraints. We have implicit understanding of these domains as we engage in the particular practices, but that knowledge is tacit, not explicit, and cannot be straightforwardly applied in different contexts.

The activities that we know how to do may be subsumed by rules—such as the rules of grammar—but these rules need not become explicit. The developmental story being suggested is that children begin with situated *know how* knowledge about social interaction. Only later do they develop an explicit understanding of those platitudes when they develop more general metacognitive abilities. The shift from implicit *knowledge how* to explicit *knowledge that*, or the shift from relying only on dispositional belief to also relying on representational belief, can be accounted for in terms of the developing general ability to engage in metacognition.

Note, however, that given these suggestions, we should expect differences in the understanding of belief in infants and preschool children. For example, a full-fledged understanding of representational belief requires an understanding of truth and falsity, and an understanding of the opacity of belief. It is unlikely that the infant has an understanding of the opacity of belief, given that even older children have difficulty understanding that while Frank might believe that Mark Twain wrote *Huckleberry Finn*, he need not believe that Samuel Clemens wrote *Huckleberry Finn*, even though "Mark Twain" and "Samuel Clemens" refer to the same person. Children are not able to make these sorts of inferences until after they pass the false-belief task, and according to some reports, they cannot handle such inferences until seven years (Apperly and Robinson 1998, 2001, 2003; Russell 1987; Hulme et al. 2003). Without understanding that others may lack relevant information about the different true descriptions of the same object, one cannot make accurate inferences about an individual's other beliefs, desires, and so on. Children who lack the ability to make such fundamental inferences about others' beliefs and desires de dicto and had only standard folk psychology to rely on to predict and explain behavior would be horribly flawed as human beings. They would be unable to understand much of the goings-on in their social environment. But this is not the case.

Rather, it seems that infants, four-year-olds, and seven-year-olds have different understandings of belief, and a full-fledged understanding of representational belief is not necessary for tracking or even predicting false belief. I believe that we must be cautious when we talk about belief, given the different theories and features associated with it. The term *belief*, like the term *theory of mind*, might be an umbrella term that involves a number of different cognitive processes, and having an understanding of representational belief might be only one of them.

Children's Changing Understanding of Other Minds

Despite the wealth of studies on children's developing understanding of mind, we still lack a model of the development of cognition that makes sense of the changes in children's abilities in these tasks during the first several years of life. By way of an easy explanation, we might say that children are developing a representational theory of mind. But that explanation might tell us more about the current theoretical framework under which researchers are operating than it tells us about the actual concepts or cognitive processes involved in children's folk psychological capacities.

The change in children's ability to pass the false-belief task may have more to do with developing an increasingly sophisticated and nuanced understanding of behavioral correlations, rather than with developing a belief concept. For example, four-year-olds may pass the false-belief task by appealing to a newly developed behavioral correlation, such as the "People look for things where they left them" rule that was suggested to explain infant performance. A general rule such as this would allow the child to successfully interact in a variety of contexts and is not specific to the experimental condition.

Children could pass the false-belief task in five steps:

(a) Subject observes Maxi putting her chocolate in a box and then observes Maxi leaving the room.
(b) Subject observes Mother coming into the room and moving the chocolate from the box to the cupboard.
(c) Subject observes Mother leaving the room and Maxi returning.
(d) Subject appeals to her database of behavioral generalizations and finds the matching "people look for objects where they left them" heuristic.
(e) Subject predicts that Maxi will look for her chocolate in the box. (Andrews 2005)

This explanation for children's performance in the false-belief task mirrors explanations given to undermine mentalistic interpretations of chimpanzee performance on related tests of mental-state understanding (Povinelli and Vonk 2004). If the existence of these kinds of alternative explanations undermines the claim that chimpanzees understand the relevant mental state, then it is prima facie sufficient to undermine the claim that children understand the mental state of belief. Of course, to back up this conclusion, we must consider related abilities. While children might have a concept of representational belief at four years, performance on the false-belief task cannot determine whether or not that is the case. Given the possibility that alternative mechanisms are at play in successful false-belief prediction, appeal to false belief cannot be used as the criterion for understanding belief or being able to attribute propositional attitudes.

Research on children's verbal behavior further undermines the notion that they have an understanding of belief at age four. If a child has an understanding of belief and is an able user of language, we might expect her to explain behavior based on people's beliefs. However, the ability to predict behavior that is the result of a false belief seems to appear before children begin to explain behavior based on a false belief (Hughes 1998; Perner et al. 2002). Perhaps it is more difficult for children to explain behavior than it is to predict it. However, several psychologists have argued that the task demands for explanation should be simpler than for prediction (Robinson and Mitchell 1995; Moses and Flavell 1990; Bartsch and Wellman 1989), and given such arguments, we should expect that children who can predict by attributing beliefs can also explain behavior in terms of beliefs.

We can give several reasons for the claim that explaining behavior based on a false belief should be cognitively simpler than predicting behavior caused by a false belief. If passing the false-belief task does indicate that the child has an understanding of belief, then prediction would be more difficult than explanation because the prediction tasks ask for more than just belief attribution; they ask the child to use the belief attribution to predict what others may do. It may be that to predict behavior is a more complex task than merely to recognize that one can have false beliefs. For example, if young children have a general difficulty with counterfactuals, as Riggs and colleagues argue (1998), it is possible that they have false-belief understanding yet are unable to make predictions based on this knowledge. If successful false-belief predictions rest on a familiarity with counterfactuals, then a child who has a rich belief-desire folk psychology may be unable to make predictions because of the conditional nature of the task.

Another reason given for the expectation that explanation is cognitively simpler than prediction is that children need not avoid referring to reality when explaining a behavior that has already happened (Mitchell 1994; Robinson 1994; Robinson and Mitchell 1995). In the traditional unexpected-transfer tasks, children have the opportunity to predict that the protagonist will look for the object where it actually is (Wimmer and Perner

1983). In an explanation task, the behavior to be explained has already occurred and is the actual state of affairs; thus it has been suggested that any bias children might have toward reality would not affect performance on explanation tasks (Robinson and Mitchell 1995). If this were true, then explanation would be intrinsically easier than prediction, and not simply an artifact of the experiment. In addition, Moses and Flavell (1990) have argued that explaining behavior is simpler than prediction because the false belief can be read off behavior. They claim that when children see an actor behaving contrary to the satisfaction of his desire, this is a clue to his false belief.

If children robustly understand representational belief, they should understand it, and use it, across circumstances and for different purposes. The evidence that children are not explaining in terms of others' beliefs until after they pass the false-belief task suggests that even at four years, children may not have a flexible and robust understanding of representational belief.

Instead of looking for litmus tests for a child's possession of representational belief, I suggest that we should instead investigate the folk psychological practices across situations. We can examine the changing understanding of other minds both in active social interactions and in more passive situations to better understand the relationship between the child's knowledge of how to behave in the face of actors' different epistemic states and her metacognitive theoretical understanding of the reasons why people act as they do.

Regardless of exactly when children begin to attribute propositional attitudes, it is clear that they are able to engage in folk psychological practices before this ability develops. Before young children are able to flexibly and robustly attribute beliefs in both situated social interactions like the active helping paradigm and in more spectatorial situations such as understanding how a character in a story would act, and before young children are able to use beliefs to explain others' behaviors, they are still folk psychologists. Since alternative accounts of the young child's folk psychological abilities are plausible, we have reason to be suspicious of SFP's emphasis on folk psychology as the attribution of propositional attitudes.

The claim that we understand other minds by understanding what others believe and desire is in one sense obviously true. Without knowing that a theist believes in god or that a capitalist desires to maximize profits, we cannot have a rich understanding of those individuals. The problem arises when one insists that knowing others' propositional attitudes is the whole story. People do not just have beliefs, desires, fears, hopes, and so forth. We also have intentions—goals that need not be expressed in propositional attitudes. We have emotions, moods, and other qualitative mental experiences, and scientists are learning about how some of these emotions are related to physiological states. Stress, for example, is associated with increases in the hormone cortisol in humans and other primates. We have perceptions, and these perceptions allow us to navigate the physical as well as social world. We also have sensations, of cold and warmth, comfort and discomfort. We have past histories, personality traits, social standing, and a host of other features that all work together with the attribution of beliefs in our understanding of the theist and the capitalist. While it is true that children do not understand people as bags of skin stuffed into pieces of cloth, it is also true that children do not understand people as bags of skin filled with propositional attitudes.

While it has already been hinted at in this chapter, in the next chapter I turn to an explicit examination of the SFP assumption that folk psychological prediction and explanation rely on the same cognitive mechanism. The assumption that folk psychological prediction and explanation are symmetrical has played an important methodological role in the theory of mind research program described in this chapter. I argue that because the assumption of symmetry is unwarranted, the methods that researchers use to investigate belief attribution require significant revision.

3 The Asymmetry of Folk Psychological Prediction and Explanation

The fact is that the average person is able to explain, and even predict, the behavior of other persons with a facility and success that is remarkable.
—Paul Churchland

Standard Folk Psychology Emphasizes Prediction (and Assumes Explanation Follows)

There is no doubt that we attribute beliefs and desires to others to a great extent, and for many reasons. We gossip about what others desire or believe, we condemn people simply by citing their beliefs ("He rejects evolution because he thinks that dinosaurs still exist and they're really good at hiding!"), and we ascribe propositions to manipulate our audience or as an act of celebration. However, the ubiquity of our belief and desire talk in our explanations of behavior should not be taken as evidence that we consider beliefs and desires when predicting behavior.

Despite this fact, it is a widespread assumption that psychological prediction and explanation are symmetrical. The general account of symmetry in folk psychology goes like this: When I predict what a person will do by appealing to initial belief-desire conditions C and the relevant information F, I can infer with some degree of probability that the person will engage in the behavior B. And when I explain behavior B, I look for appropriate initial conditions C and information F that implies B. For prediction, beliefs and desires are the inputs, and the behavior is derived. For explanation, the behavior is the input, and the beliefs and desires are derived. The slogan for the symmetry thesis is "No prediction without explanation, and no explanation without prediction." Because in folk psychology the symmetry of prediction and explanation is thought to be cognitive rather than logical, the psychological symmetry amounts to the view that prediction and explanation are accomplished by the same cognitive processes.

That is, the two folk psychological practices are subsumed by the same mechanisms.

If the psychological symmetry thesis is true, then any account of the structures underlying folk psychology must accommodate both our predictive practices and our explanatory ones. This view has been held either implicitly or explicitly by a number of philosophers of various stripes (Fodor 1987, 1991; Churchland 1989; Gordon 1995a, 2000; Stich and Ravenscroft 1996; Nichols and Stich 2003; Sehon 2005). This assumption appears also to be widespread in the research on theory of mind in apes and children, as reflected in the writing of developmental psychologists Elizabeth Robinson and Peter Mitchell, who describe explanations as nothing more than "backward predictions" (Robinson and Mitchell 1995).

Despite its popularity, I argue that we should reject the psychological symmetry thesis. If no symmetry exists between psychological prediction and explanation, then it cannot be the case that a single model of folk psychology works for both practices. A rejection of symmetry does not provide evidence that different cognitive mechanisms are at work *within* our acts of predictions or *within* our acts of explanation. It only implies pluralism between prediction and explanation.

Rejecting the psychological symmetry thesis has two implications. For one, it suggests that the current attempts to model folk psychology are flawed insofar as they presume a set of mechanisms that are implicated in both our predictive and our explanatory practices. In addition, rejecting symmetry has methodological consequences for practicing psychologists and animal cognition researchers. The experiments in these disciplines are designed to find evidence of folk psychological abilities by having participants predict behavior, and from their findings, researchers make inferences about participants' ability to explain behavior. Given the asymmetry of folk psychological prediction and explanation, researchers should develop experiments on belief attribution that examine the ability to explain behavior. The experimental paradigms designed to test for belief attribution in human children, especially in young infants, as well as those used to test for belief attribution in other apes, should be reevaluated.

Before we begin to examine the symmetry thesis, we need some understanding of what is meant by *prediction* and *explanation*. A prediction can be described as an expectation that some event will occur in the future. Understanding what is meant by *explanation* requires a little more work. An explanation may be of an event that will happen or of an event that has already happened. Explanations are not limited to events but may be given for states of affairs, capacities, functions, intentions, and so on.

Following Bas van Fraassen (1980), we can understand an explanation as an answer to a why-question. Explanations are responses to a desire to understand the explanandum, a need to make the world coherent and comprehensible, and why-questions express that desire. Two caveats must be made with regard to this initial way of understanding explanations. First, we should not limit explanations to linguistic or quasi-linguistic acts. It may be possible to seek or offer explanations in nonpropositional terms, as we will see. Second, we should clarify that any answer to a why-question that satisfies a questioner's need for understanding will count as a folk psychological explanation, though it might not count as a scientific explanation. While the goal of scientific investigation is to get things right, the folk aim for coherence. This is not to say that there are no accurate folk psychological explanations of human behavior. Rather, it is a descriptive claim that when people offer explanations of behavior, they are recognized by the folk as explanations when they satisfy the coherence and understanding condition, rather than an accuracy or correspondence condition.

I develop and defend these points in chapter 7. For now, we can begin to look at the similarities between symmetry in science and folk psychology with this simplified definition.

The Symmetry Thesis

The assumption of symmetry in folk psychology can be traced back to the deductive-nomological (D-N) account of explanation offered by Carl Hempel and Paul Oppenheim (1948) and by the attempts of identity theorists and functionalists to explicate mental states in terms of observables. In the spirit of the logical empiricism of their day, Hempel and Oppenheim described the nature of explanation as a valid deductive argument that consists of a general covering law and initial conditions (jointly known as the explanans), which deductively entails the phenomenon to be explained (known as the explanandum). The scheme of the argument is presented as follows:

$$\frac{C_1, C_2, \ldots, C_k}{L_1, L_2, \ldots, L_r}$$
$$E$$

where the Cs represent the initial conditions or facts implicated, the Ls represent the relevant general laws, and E is the explanandum. Because the relationship between the explanans and the explanandum is deductive, the explanans can also be used to predict the explanandum. Thus, according to the D-N model, prediction and explanation are symmetrical.

Philosophers of mind who adopted this methodology attempted to give analyses of mental states in much the same way, as can be seen in David Lewis's 1972 account of psychophysical identifications. Lewis suggests that we should think of our folk psychology as a term-introducing theory that defines mental states functionally. The theory consists of all the commonsense platitudes that connect sensory stimuli, mental states, and behaviors, plus the platitudes that relate mental states to one another. We can predict behavior by appealing to the platitudes of folk psychology and the initial conditions (i.e., the facts of the agent's state of mind and her environment), and by virtue of having this information, we also have an explanation. Once folk psychology is understood as a theory in this sense, the corresponding claims of symmetry are a natural result.

As I have argued elsewhere, philosophers involved in the debate between simulation theory and theory theory assume the psychological symmetry thesis as well (Andrews 2003). Given the view that a theory's job is to predict and explain, the theory-theorists took their models to be capable of both predicting and explaining other people's behavior (e.g., Fodor 1987, 1989, 1991; Stich and Ravenscroft 1996). The inputs used to predict a behavior become the explanation of that behavior. Fodor takes the predictive structure of folk psychology to allow for the explanation of behavior, speaking of "explanation/prediction" (Fodor 1991, 19) and moving from a discussion of "predictive adequacy" to "explanation" in a way that presents them as two sides of the same coin (Fodor 1987).

The simulation theorists also accept the symmetry thesis. In response to Paul Churchland's worry that simulation theory does not account for our ability to explain behavior, both Alvin Goldman (1995a) and Robert Gordon (1995a) implicitly accept the requirement of symmetry by taking Churchland's remarks as a serious criticism and by offering simulation accounts of explanation.

Goldman, for example, writes: "Explanation can consist of telling a story that eliminates various alternative hypotheses about how the event in question came about, or could have come about. This is done by citing a specific set of goals and beliefs, which implicitly rules out the indefinitely many alternative desire-and-belief sets that might have led to the action" (A. Goldman 1995a, 89). That is, one generates a number of possible belief-desire sets that could have caused the action, and then tests these by using them as inputs in a simulation. When we arrive at a set of beliefs and desires that does produce the behavior in question, we take that set as a possible explanation of the behavior.

Gordon offers a similar account of explanation. He shows how model simulations can explain the behavior of what is being modeled because models are manipulable. If we have a model that can be manipulated until the object behavior is exhibited, we can determine which features interact to cause the behavior. Gordon observes that "in explaining one's own behavior, it would seem that one can—without invoking or using laws or theories—simulate *in imagination* various counterfactual conditions and test their influence by methods akin to Mill's. . . . And one can perform such thought experiments not just in one's own case but also within the context of a simulation of another" (1995a, 115). Gordon (2000) has argued that explanations of intentional behavior need not refer to a person's psychological state, but facts about a person's "epistemic horizon" can and do serve equally well as explanations. Thus even versions of simulation theory that take facts about a person's situation rather than her beliefs and desires as inputs to the simulation can provide satisfactory explanations. Both Gordon and Goldman take simulation theory, like theory theory, to be consistent with the view that explanation is merely backward prediction.

Criticisms of the Symmetry Thesis

An early challenge to the scientific symmetry thesis was given in the form of a counterexample: Consider a flagpole's shadow at 2 p.m. The length of a flagpole's shadow can be explained by reference to the height of the pole, the position of the sun, and the general law of rectilinear propagation of light. However, the height of the flagpole is not explained by these other facts, though we can derive it from the initial conditions of the length of the shadow along with the general law. Nonetheless this deduction does not offer an explanation even if it allows one to predict how tall the flagpole is (Bromberger 1966).

Or consider that early sailors understood that a constant conjunction holds between the phases of the moon and the tides, and they used this law to predict the tides. However, until Newton, no one knew why this constant conjunction existed, and no one was able to explain the movement of the tides.

In folk psychology, we can also find examples of asymmetries. We can predict behaviors that we do not have an explanation for. If Alfred wants to buy milk and believes there is milk at the store, and if people act to fulfill their desires given their beliefs, I can predict that Alfred will go to the store. For the person who wonders why Alfred is going to the store, reference to his desire to buy milk can serve as an explanation.

However, that answer need not provide an answer to the person's why-question. It wouldn't satisfy an explanation seeker who wanted to know why Alfred went to the store if the explanation seeker believed there was milk in the refrigerator. Is there something wrong with that milk? Or does Alfred need a large quantity of milk for some purpose? An answer to a why-question in terms of the particular beliefs and desires that were used to predict the behavior does not always resolve the explanation seeker's curiosity.

The problem with symmetry does not go only one way. We can also explain events that we cannot predict. Biographies often focus on explaining the actions of historical figures who took bold—and surprising—steps to change the course of society. Indeed, in our quotidian social relations, we are frequently concerned with explaining unexpected behaviors, behaviors that we could not have predicted. Why did Brenda leave her husband of twenty years? She discovered that he had had an affair, and she was unhappy that he had the affair. To put this explanation in terms of propositional attitudes, Brenda believed that her husband had had an affair, and she desired not to be married to someone who would cheat on her. These attitudes form a plausible explanation for the end of a marriage. However, these attitudes and conditions would not allow for a deductively sound argument entailing that a cuckquean would leave, or provide statistical information about how likely it is that Brenda will file for divorce. That is, while we can explain Brenda's behavior by referring to her mental states (or, as we will see in chapter 6, perhaps by referring to the details of the situation), knowing these same mental states of Brenda's does not allow us to accurately predict her behavior. Suppose you have coffee with Brenda soon after she discovers the affair. She tells you that she has solid evidence that her husband had an affair, and she doesn't want to be married to a cheater. You might not be surprised if she later files for a divorce. But at the same time, you would be well advised to refrain from telling Brenda how irritating you find her husband, given the possibility that they might work things out. Many a friendship has been strained by making too hasty a prediction about the demise of a relationship. While one should not predict that a marriage ends given knowledge of an infidelity, reference to the wronged party's belief that an infidelity occurred can serve as an explanation of a divorce after the fact. Thus we also see that the information provided by something that satisfies as an explanation may not be robust enough to form a good prediction.

A double disassociation exists between the prediction and explanation of people's behavior. We can predict what people are going to do without having an explanation, and we can explain behaviors that we could never have predicted. This disassociation leads to a wholesale rejection of the psychological symmetry thesis. Although the thesis seems implausible as soon as it is directly examined, its hold on philosophy of mind and psychology is strong. Given its influence in the literature, perhaps we all must guard against an implicit commitment to the symmetry thesis.

An Asymmetric Folk Psychology

Once we reject symmetry, we should also reject the claim that only one set of mechanisms accounts for our ability both to predict and to explain intentional behavior. Instead, as we will see in chapter 8, people use a variety of explanatory methods to answer why-questions about actions. In different circumstances and for different individuals, one offers different kinds of explanations. The same goes for methods of prediction. Given these situational influences on how a particular prediction or explanation is generated, we cannot map cleanly from explanation to prediction; no isomorphism holds between all cases of prediction and explanation.

This means that any theory that purports to offer a single mechanism that subsumes our folk psychological practices will be incomplete. It also means that we cannot make generalizations about explanation *simpliciter* based on characteristics of one particular example of explanation. The same is true for prediction. To fully understand the ability to generate explanations and predictions, we must first recognize that there are different varieties of prediction and explanation, and a variety of mechanisms at work.

With the rejection of the psychological symmetry thesis, the privileged position of psychological prediction goes too. We cannot simply examine how people predict behavior and from that build a theory that includes an account of folk psychological explanation. This means that knowing when a child can pass the false-belief task cannot on its own tell us anything about the child's ability to offer explanations. To build a theory of folk psychology, we need to investigate predictions and explanations, as well as other folk psychological practices, and we also need to examine the varieties of predictions that we make and the variety of explanations that we offer. Rather than asking how people explain behavior generally, we might ask how people explain familiar versus unfamiliar behavior, acceptable versus unacceptable behavior, behavior of friends and family versus behavior of strangers, and so on. It is time to ask different kinds of questions. This is true in the research on children, and, as I argue in chapter 12, it is essential if we are to move ahead on answering Premack and Woodruff's question about whether chimpanzees have a theory of mind.

In the next six chapters, I turn to an examination of prediction and explanation to defend my claim that an empirically adequate theory of folk psychology ought to be pluralistic with regard to mechanism. This point will be made via theoretical arguments and through a review of the psychological literature. I conclude that the mechanisms differ not merely *between* different folk psychological practices but also *within* a single practice.

II Prediction

4 How Do You Know What I'm Going to Do? You Know My Beliefs

Someone I don't know phones me at my office in New York from—as it might be—Arizona. "Would you like to lecture here next Tuesday?" are the words that he utters. "Yes, thank you. I'll be at your airport on the 3 p.m. flight" are the words that I reply. That's all that happens, but it's more than enough; the rest of the burden of predicting behavior—of bridging the gap between utterances and actions—is routinely taken up by theory. And the theory works so well that several days later . . . and several thousand miles away, there I am at the airport, and there he is to meet me. . . . The point—to repeat—is that the theory from which we get this extraordinary predictive power is just good old commonsense belief/desire psychology.
—Jerry Fodor

Prediction and the Propositional Attitudes

In the previous chapters, we saw that a tension exists between the accounts of folk psychology that accept both the claim that folk psychology consists primarily of mindreading, and the claim that folk psychologists are successful behavior predictors and explainers. I suggested that we resolve this tension by rejecting the central role of belief attribution for folk psychology and accepting that we have a plurality of methods for engaging in folk psychological practices. I also argued that we must examine the practices separately if we want to understand the cognitive structures that allow us to engage in the behaviors, because the presumption of symmetry should be discarded.

The argument against the centrality of belief attribution can be strengthened by looking at a particular folk psychological practice. In the next three chapters, I investigate the practice of predicting behavior, to uncover the cognitive mechanisms implicated in predicting intentional action. In chapter 2 we saw that infants anticipate action and thus predict behavior, though no evidence supports the claim that they attribute propositional attitudes. If infants are engaged in folk psychological prediction without attributing propositional attitudes, then attribution of belief is not necessary for predicting behavior. Adults, however, are the paradigmatic folk psychologists, so a stronger critique of the centrality of belief attribution could be made if we find evidence that adults do not attribute propositional attitudes when they predict behavior.

Of course, a simple discovery that humans sometimes predict behavior without appeal to propositional attitudes would not suffice to decide the issue. This is because, as all sides of the debate accept, the mature folk psychologist develops shortcut heuristics for predicting behavior after becoming a competent predictor of behavior. For example, Goldman recognizes that we can use the heuristic of induction to make predictions after having run successful simulations to predict behavior. He writes: "I am not saying, it should be emphasized, that simulation is the *only* method used for interpersonal mental ascriptions, or for the prediction of behavior. Clearly, there are regularities about behavior and individual differences that can be learned purely inductively" (A. Goldman 1995a, 83). Later he adds: "When a mature cognizer has constructed, by simulation, many similar instances of certain action-interpretation patterns, she may develop generalizations or other inductively formed representations (schemas, scripts, and so forth) that can trigger analogous interpretations by application of those 'knowledge structures' alone, *sans* simulation" (88).

So a true challenge to the centrality of belief attribution would come from folk psychologists who use methods for predicting intentional behavior that do not rely on prior applications of propositional attitude attribution. But this finding may not be sufficient either, since the claims of SFP have been tempered in some cases to talk about the *frequency* with which we use certain methods of prediction. In his more recent work, Goldman (2006) argues for a hybrid theory that emphasizes the role of simulation. Though this account draws on a combination of theory and simulation, Goldman continues to call it a version of simulation theory, in part because it stresses how often we need to simulate to predict behavior.

Thus, to undermine the central role of belief by looking at the act of prediction, I will need to show that other methods of prediction are frequently used by adult folk psychologists. Also, I must show that these methods do not rely on the prior ability to attribute propositional attitudes and should not be seen as shortcut heuristics. Finally, I will argue that we have no evidence that the attribution of propositional attitudes is the predominant or most frequent method for predicting intentional behavior. I will take on these tasks over the next three chapters.

In this chapter, I point to some theoretical worries about the current theories of folk psychological prediction. Chapter 5 presents empirical evidence on adult human methods of predicting behavior and offers a challenge to the view that attributing propositions is the predominant method for making predictions. I address the role of mental-state content in chapter 6 and argue that the evidence presented in the previous chapters should lead us to demote belief attribution to a minor folk psychological role.

Predicting Behavior

Humans are predictors extraordinaire, and we engage in predicting behavior on a daily basis. We predict others' behavior when planning a dinner party, considering how different individuals will get along with one another. We also predict our own behavior when we decide whether we can handle eight guests rather than four. Not all our predictions of behavior take such overt forms; most of the time when we are predicting behavior, we do so automatically, at the subpersonal level, and such predictions take the form of background expectations. I predict that people will keep their promises, that drivers will stay on the road, and that my students will show up to class. These are the sort of predictions that are only noticed when they are false.

Such background predictions are the ones stressed by Dennett (1991) when he says that the predictive power of folk psychology makes possible all our interpersonal projects and relations. If the people around us were wildly irregular in their movements, it would be extremely difficult to enter into any social relations, and the formation of cultural groups would be next to impossible. Acting in predictable ways allows us to see similarities among individuals, and people rely on these similarities when forming communities and distinguishing between in-group and out-group members.

Our ability to predict behavior accurately not only lets us get by in the world but is essential to the development of our social relationships. Without the ability to predict what our friends and family members will do in typical situations, we could not feel the close attachment to others that we do. The knowledge that your best friend will be willing to listen to you talk through your dark depression, or that your spouse will make dinner tonight, or that your mother will invite you to visit for the holidays serves to ground your social environment. The more our friends and family act against our expectations, the less comfortable those relationships become.

Since prediction is central to our ability to fulfill our basic daily needs—getting food, navigating from place to place, earning money, and so on—and central to our ability to form deep and satisfying relationships with others, it should not be surprising that the paradigmatic role of folk psychology has been taken to be prediction. Recall that many developmental and comparative psychologists use an individual's facility with prediction as the litmus tests for theory of mind.

Not only is prediction a central focus in the empirical literature on theory of mind, but it is also seen as the strength of folk psychology. Our ability to predict behavior is remarkable, says Churchland (1981), although the method we rely on to make these predictions is descriptively inadequate. We are quite good predictors, in many cases. In most of our daily interactions with people on the street, we are in a continual state of anticipating behavior. When walking down a city street, we are confronted with hundreds of people with whom we interact, however briefly. We must dodge people approaching us and move aside for those who want to pass. Our verbal and nonverbal interaction with other people is a constant dance choreographed by our society and our human impulse to anticipate similarity. If we were not skilled at predicting behavior, we would be paralyzed in the world, unable even to order a cup of coffee. Our predictions of behavior are ubiquitous, and to paraphrase Fodor (1989), predictions work so well they disappear.

While our success with prediction may be evident in the case of background expectations, it is less obviously true when looking at the predictions we make overtly. Will your new colleague bring a bottle of wine to the dinner party? If she were mugged on the way to the liquor store, how would she react? Would she run, or hand over the money, or try to talk her way out of it, or use a self-defense maneuver? What would you do in such a situation? We have difficulty predicting the behavior of people we don't know well, and of people we do know when they are in unfamiliar or anomalous situations; we even have difficulty predicting our own behavior. If I have never observed a person in a particular situation, such as being confronted by a mugger, I will not have a good idea of how that person might behave in those situations, just as I would have a hard time predicting how I might act in a strange or complex situation.

If our failures rest with unfamiliar actors and unfamiliar situations, where are our successes? We are most successful when predicting in familiar contexts. For example, suppose I need to get $100 from the bank. I can go inside the bank, fill out a withdrawal slip, and ask the teller for $100 from my account. Because I have done this many times before, and because

I was taught that this is normal behavior, I can predict that the teller will give me $100. I know what the teller is going to do because I know that tellers are supposed to honor withdrawal requests, so long as the customer has sufficient funds. I don't need to attribute beliefs to the teller to predict his behavior, and I don't need to imagine being him. I know that the teller will give me the money in the same way that I know that the automatic teller machine will give me the requested funds: they always (or at least usually) have in the past, and their function is to give me the money. I predict the person's behavior using the same reasoning as I use for the machine, by making generalizations from past experience and knowing the target's function.

We are good at making predictions based on familiar patterns of behavior, and not so good in complex or novel situations, because complex or novel situations cannot be directly mapped onto a scenario that had been previously learned. There are no familiar scripts, as in the bank scenario, to which we can appeal to know what will happen next in such unfamiliar conditions. Some behaviors are easier to predict than others. It is easier to predict the behavior of the teller in the context of his job at the bank than it is to predict what he would do when confronted with a moral dilemma. It is often easier to predict one's own behavior, or what one's family and friends will do, than to predict what strangers would do in the same situation. However, this isn't always so. If someone fits a stereotype or a social role, then, as we will see in the next chapter, we can use that stereotype to make predictions. For example, when I observe a lone firefighter in front of a burning building, I will expect him to attempt to rescue the people inside. But if I were placed in the same situation, with no one else around to rescue the victims, I have little faith in any self-prediction I would make. While I would like to think I would help if I could, I have no past experience with myself in such situations to help guide a prediction.

Accuracy of Predicting Behavior by Relying on the Attitudes

In the debate regarding the cognitive architecture that subsumes our ability to make predictions of behavior, the variants of theory theory and Goldman's versions of simulation theory, plus hybrid accounts, all rely on the attribution of propositional attitudes when predicting intentional acts. The main difference between simulation and theory theory in this regard is what we do with the propositions to make predictions. According to the story from theory theory, we use the propositional attitudes and environmental conditions as initial conditions, select the correct covering law that connects those propositional attitudes and relevant environmental conditions with behavior, and then infer that the target is likely to engage in the behavior. In the simulation theory account, we use the propositional attitudes as pretend beliefs and desires of our own, and adjusting for any relevant differences between ourselves and the target, we use our own practical reasoning system to determine what we would do as such a person in such a situation.

Given that the two primary models of standard folk psychology share this commitment that we (a) are excellent predictors of behavior and (b) predict behavior through attributing propositional attitudes, my first task is to defend the claim that knowing a target's beliefs and desires is neither necessary nor sufficient for accurately predicting her behavior. This leads to a number of problems for both theory theory and simulation theory and makes clear the need for a new account of folk psychology.

Propositional Attitude Attribution Is Not Sufficient for Accurate Predictions

When you really want to know what someone will do next, it may not be terribly helpful to know what her beliefs and desires are at a particular point in time. Recall one example of how propositional attitude prediction is supposed to work: you predict that Mary will not show up at the department meeting because she believes Fred will be there, and she doesn't want to see Fred. Notice that though these facts about Mary could help to explain why Mary didn't come to the meeting, you probably wouldn't feel comfortable relying on them to make a confident prediction about Mary's behavior, since these two pieces of information are consistent with Mary's attendance. After all, Mary might grudgingly attend the meeting if her desire to do her job well is stronger than her desire to avoid Fred. Other factors may be involved in Mary's decision to act. She may believe that she shouldn't let her feelings about Fred affect her work, for example. Or she may be on her best behavior, anticipating her tenure review. Unless Mary told you that she will not attend the meeting, in which case your prediction could rely on a "people generally do what they say" heuristic, or unless Mary has a history of never attending meetings when Fred is there, in which case your prediction would rest on simple induction, you have insufficient evidence to conclude that she will not show up.

If Mary's absence would guarantee that the vote would go my way, I would not rest easy after hearing this story about why Mary won't show up to the meeting. It isn't good enough information for making a real-world prediction. My response to hearing this story would be to ask, "Yes, but did she *tell* you that she won't come to the meeting?" A verbal promise to act is much more reliable than a just so story constructed out of a person's possible beliefs and desires (Gauker 2003).

For this belief-desire pair to serve as a good means of predicting Mary's behavior, I need to have more information about the relevant details of the situation. I need to know if Mary has other beliefs or desires that would defeat her belief that Fred will be there, or her desire to avoid Fred. I also need to know how rational Mary is in her behavior. And I need to know how strong her feelings are. Knowing only that Mary has the specified belief and desire doesn't disallow the possibility that she will say, "Oh, what the hell!" and allow a colleague to pressure her into attending the meeting, without much in the way of careful analysis of how best to fulfill her desires given her beliefs.

Or recall the example of Brenda, who learned that her husband had had an affair. I claimed that even knowing Brenda's beliefs and desires was not sufficient for predicting what Brenda would do next, because those beliefs and desires are consistent with both leaving her husband and staying with him.

Both are examples of people making decisions. Insofar as making a decision is an act that does not fit a familiar schema, successfully predicting the outcome of a person's deliberation is among the more difficult predictions to make. In this instance, it may be easy to predict Brenda's emotional response to the information: she will be sad about her husband's affair. But determining how Brenda will act given her emotional response is a different matter. Our behavior, after all, is underdetermined by our beliefs and desires. This indeterminacy may rest on the lack of specificity associated with our beliefs and desires, or on the lack of specificity associated with the beliefs and desires we are able to attribute to others.

For example, suppose Curt is trying to decide which flavor of ice cream to order. He looks at fifteen flavors and disqualifies five as undesirable. The remaining ten are possibilities. Curt says, "I like these ten flavors, and I desire a delicious ice cream cone." We know Curt's beliefs and desires, and Curt knows his beliefs and desires, but he has not made a decision, and knowing his beliefs and desires in this case cannot help us determine what his decision will be. In comparing the different flavors, he could compare them according to various different aspects—health (the sorbet versus the ice cream or nuts versus candies), past choice (the flavor he chose last time was good, but should he try something new or stay with the tried and true?), mood (light fruit flavors versus rich flavors), and so forth. This belief-desire pair can help us know what Curt *won't* do, but it doesn't let us make a specific prediction of what he will do. It only facilitates a less specific prediction. Some other method of prediction, such as predicting from Curt's past behavior, may in this case be more appropriate. If Curt orders pistachio 80 percent of the time, and there is no evidence that Curt is deciding against pistachio this time, then making a prediction based on Curt's past behavior may be all that is needed to draw a plausible conclusion about Curt's choice.

Propositional Attitude Attribution Is Not Necessary for Accurate Predictions

The folk psychology literature contains some classic examples of how we predict behavior by attributing beliefs and desires. However, many of these predictions could be made without reference to another's mental states. For example, to illustrate his intentional-stance version of belief-desire psychology, Daniel Dennett presents a case of what may seem to be a rather simple prediction. Mrs. Gardner's husband calls, telling her that he will be home for dinner within the hour and will be bringing the boss with him. Mrs. Gardner asks her husband to pick up a bottle of wine on the way home. Mrs. Gardner, of course, is able to predict that her husband will arrive home in one hour, with the boss and a bottle of wine. However, as Robert Nozick suggests, aliens of vastly superior intelligence who can predict behavior from the microphysical structure of the world could predict Mr. Gardner's behavior as well (and they would predict every motor activity that went along with the behavior, something no human can do). To these Laplacean aliens, however, Mrs. Gardner's prediction would "look like magic," since she was able to make the prediction without scrupulously calculating the placement of subatomic particles (Dennett 1987b, 27). How does she do it? According to Dennett, Mrs. Gardner, along with the rest of us, makes accurate predictions of this sort all the time, by attributing the appropriate beliefs and desires.

But do we *need* to attribute beliefs and desires to make this prediction? That is, are there other possible accounts of the reasoning that leads you to predict that your spouse will come home with a bottle of wine? Here's one: your husband usually keeps his promises, and he promised to pick up a bottle of wine on the way home from work, so you infer that your husband will keep his promise this time as well. Or perhaps you could have used an even more general law: people usually keep their easy-to-keep promises, your husband's promise to bring home a bottle of wine is an easy-to-keep promise, and thus you form the prediction.

To the aliens, our ability to generate such predictions may look amazing at first, but after conducting some anthropological research on humans, the aliens may well decide to stop calculating our behaviors with such precision. They may find that humans operate according to simple patterns, patterns that can be observed without having any knowledge of human beliefs and desires. What additional predictive accuracy would the aliens gain by attributing to your spouse the belief that he should keep his promise to bring home a bottle of wine, and the desire to keep his promises to you? The answer is simple: none.

The attribution of propositional attitudes is not required to make correct predictions in cases like this. Your success at predicting your spouse's behavior will be seen as less than amazing when the aliens discover that humans make many such predictions by following a simple inductive rule: people generally do what they say they are going to do. If we appeal to this rule, then no belief or desire attribution is required to make this prediction, and no simulation needs to be run. The people-do-what-they-say rule is quite reliable. Dennett has given us an example of a prediction that could be made by appeal to a simple, nonmentalistic heuristic, but the promise of folk psychology is to offer more than that.

Defenders of SFP suggest that we use the attribution of beliefs and desires when we make all sorts of predictions, from the prediction that someone will duck if you throw a brick at him (Dennett 1991) to the prediction that you will arrive on the 3 p.m. flight if you say you'll arrive on the 3 p.m. flight (Fodor 1989). But do we really need to attribute propositions to draw these conclusions? Take Dennett's brick example. If we just know that people duck when bricks are thrown at them, then ascribing beliefs and desires to a person in that situation is superfluous. We can make similar predictions about critters, since individuals of many species will duck in such a situation. But few would claim that an animal who anticipated his conspecific's behavior did so by attributing mental states, and it is unlikely that humans likewise ascribe such mental states when predicting the animal's action. Agents, whether human or nonhuman, generally try to avoid being hit by flying objects, and ducking is a good way of doing so.

Fodor's example is also easily explained without reference to mental states. I can predict that you arrive on the 3 p.m. flight by using the people-do-what-they-say rule. Neither Dennett's nor Fodor's example lends credence to the claim that we attribute beliefs and desires to predict behavior. Instead we see that behavioral generalizations can be used in both cases to make an accurate prediction.

It seems clear that we can make at least some predictions of intentional action without attributing beliefs and desires (though objections can be raised; I examine those in chapter 6). Given the ability of human infants to engage in predictions without the ability to attribute representational beliefs, the possibility that we start our folk psychological careers by attributing propositional attitudes, and only later begin to use shortcuts, inductive generalizations, behavioral rules, and so on, is unlikely.

Prediction in Theory Theory and Model Theory

As was discussed in the last chapter, the theory-theorists propose that we predict behavior through appeal to postulated beliefs and desires and environmental conditions plus some general covering law. In this account, we predict behavior automatically the same way we form grammatical sentences: by using a tacit set of principles that we do not have introspective access to.

In the debate between simulation theory and theory theory, the standard criticisms that have been leveled against theory theory have to do with its profligacy, the difficulty involved in specifying the theory, and the concern about ceteris paribus clauses. The worry about profligacy comes from an estimation of the vast cognitive resources that would be required to internalize a complete theory of behavior, compared with the much lower resource demands of the just-in-time processing posited by simulation theory. The second worry is based on the idea that if there is a theory, we should be able to say something about the principles of the theory. For example, the grammatical theory that we rely on to construct well-formed sentences is also tacit, and we do not have access to those rules through introspection. But it has been one of the successful projects of academic linguistics to uncover these rules for different languages by testing people's responses to different sentences, and to use these rules in formulating predictions about how sentences will be formed. A parallel project has been investigating folk psychological concepts (e.g., Jackendoff 2009), but the content of the folk psychological laws remains largely unexamined.

While these two criticisms have been much discussed in the literature, I think that a third criticism deserves further attention. It is of special concern that the laws of folk psychology, which are the key to making predictions and explanations of behavior, appear to be rather different from the laws of scientific theories. It does not take much investigation to see that folk psychological laws, such as "Thirsty people drink," either are false, strictly speaking, or must be qualified by a ceteris paribus clause. The worry is that this sort of qualification makes the laws empty. Given that this last criticism has led to a modified version of theory theory, let us examine the objection in some detail.

Even the most general laws of folk psychology, such as "People seek to fulfill their desires," do not allow for prediction of behavior given the target's desire. This is because we often have conflicting desires, and because we may not know how to fulfill our desires. Even more specific laws, such as "When you desire to drink a beer and believe there is a beer in the fridge, you will acquire a beer from the fridge," would be strictly speaking false, given possible exceptions to this law. Again, the competing desire to avoid becoming drunk or taking in too many empty calories may cause you not to acquire a beer, or you may be too lazy to get up. But you might also believe that the beer in the fridge is Miller Lite, and you hate Miller Lite, so you don't get the beer from the fridge and instead head to the cooler where you keep your favorite microbrew.

The general laws of folk psychology must be hedged in reasoning about human behavior, because human logic is nonmonotonic. The kinds of inferences humans make are ones in which defeaters may always show up and invalidate the inference. Humans do not draw deductive inferences about their world but make tentative ones that are revisable in light of new evidence. This goes for our reasoning about other people and the physical world. Thus, the folk psychological laws that we use must be of the form "$P_a \rightarrow Q_a$, ceteris paribus." For example, Kelly believes there is Zima in the fridge; she desires a Zima; ceteris paribus people act to fulfill their desires; thus Kelly will go to the fridge and get a Zima.

The main concern about ceteris paribus clauses is that generalizations using them do not allow for successful predictions, whether they are about social or other natural phenomena. The generalization "When you see cumulonimbus clouds, it will rain, ceteris paribus," can be read as "When you see cumulonimbus clouds, it will rain unless it doesn't rain." Unless you know what conditions are relevant defeaters of the generalization, you cannot use it to make predictions about the weather.

In response to criticisms about the emptiness of generalizations that use ceteris paribus clauses, Fodor (1991) argues that folk psychology is in no worse a position than natural sciences. He uses the partners-in-guilt strategy to avoid answering the worry more directly. In the natural sciences, laws with ceteris paribus clauses are nothing to fret about, so we ought not worry about them in folk psychology.

However, since the laws of folk psychology are thought to be internalized laws that describe the functioning of human cognition, and humans in fact use them to make predictions and explanations of behavior, there is a difference between scientific theories, which philosophers of science have agreed are idealized, and folk psychological theories, which are supposed to reflect the architecture of our cognitive processes. Though it is true that ceteris paribus clauses are used in the natural sciences, this fact doesn't help us understand how it is that we—or perhaps more accurately, our cognitive structures—actually apply laws when using them to make inferences about the physical world. A ceteris paribus clause says that there is nothing else of relevance that could limit the effect of the law. However, attempts to analyze the notion of relevance have been less than successful. As an idealization of knowledge structure, laws with ceteris paribus clauses can capture some of the relations that scientists have discovered. But as a description of human cognitive processing, this type of law leaves key features of cognition mysterious. Folk psychology is supposed to describe our understanding of other minds. Appealing to laws with ceteris paribus clauses as the currency of cognition leaves much unexplained.

Another response to the ceteris paribus criticism is to deny that theories are sets of propositions. By taking propositions out of theories, we remove the worry that these propositions are either false or empty. According to the received view, scientific theories introduce theoretical entities and find patterns between theoretical entities and observations that allow for prediction and explanation. The received view of scientific theories understands the pattern as an axiom system that could be used to define the theoretical terms and make the predictions and explanations through purely syntactic manipulations (Carnap 1956). This syntactic view describes theories as interpreted formal systems, where the axioms are statements that are true or false, at least some of which are universal generalizations (Suppe 1972).

The semantic view of scientific theory, on the other hand, takes theories to consist of models of the world rather than sets of propositions, and so it seems such views would sidestep the ceteris paribus criticism. The notion that the laws of folk psychology could be something other than propositions can be seen as a natural extension of Ron Giere's account of the structure of scientific theories and Paul Churchland's theory of cognition. Churchland (1989) and Giere (1996) both made this point during the heyday of the debate between simulation theory and theory theory. The model-based accounts of scientific theories reject the idea that statements or laws form the foundation of theories, because no evidence supports the existence of a single true law, when a law is understood narrowly without qualification by a ceteris paribus clause (Giere 1988). Some advocates of the model-based view of scientific theories suggest that what have been taken to be universal generalizations are instead part of a definition that is made true by some idealized model. The generalizations correspond to the idealized model, and the model can be manipulated to make predictions.

Churchland now accepts something like this account of scientific theory as a modification of his earlier account of the structure of folk psychology. While he still accepts that folk psychology is a theory, one that is akin to scientific theories, he has changed his views about what the correct account of scientific theory is. Churchland's account of theory is based on a connectionist model of knowledge representation where prototypes take the place of universal generalizations (Churchland 1991). A prototype of some concept P is a probabilistic structure that encompasses the properties of a P, such that an exemplar of P is something that has enough of the properties of the prototype. Variations of the idea that knowledge and cognitive processing operate on prototypes are widely found in cognitive psychology, as well as in developmental psychology (Rosch 1973), linguistics (Lakoff 1987), and AI research (Minsky 1981).

Churchland applies this notion of scientific theory to folk psychology and suggests that a "human's understanding of the springs of human action may reside not in a set of stored generalizations about the hidden elements of mind and how they conspire to produce behavior, but rather in one or more prototypes of the deliberative or purposeful processes" (1991, 64). Given this account of theory, some versions of simulation theory might count as theory, too. However, a distinction larger than the one between model-based and statement-based theories of theory may remain. Churchland also suggests that the prototypes will represent the traditional theoretical entities associated with the standard account of folk psychology. Beliefs, desires, intentions, and so on, and the relations between them will be represented by the prototypes, much in the same way that they were described in the platitudinal statements of traditional folk psychology. Thus, though Churchland suggests that we need not understand folk psychology as sets of propositions, we still need the concepts of beliefs and desires—the attitudes—to have a folk psychology that allows for predictions and explanations of behavior.

If our folk psychology is a theoretical model, then to predict behavior, we manipulate the model rather than make a deduction from principles. The model version of theory theory has not been fleshed out in great detail, though Maibom (2003) and Godfrey-Smith (2005) have done some work toward developing the suggestion that folk psychology can be theoretical while avoiding the problems of general laws. However, as in traditional accounts of theory theory, the models are thought to be used for both predicting and explaining behavior, and are thought to represent our knowledge of others' beliefs and desires. Thus, while avoiding the worries about ceteris paribus clauses, such accounts remain open to some other problems associated with the standard view, which I discuss in chapter 7. Still, for reasons I give in chapter 10, I think we have much to gain by understanding folk psychology in terms of model manipulation.

Prediction in Simulation Theory

The class of theories called simulation theory is even less homogeneous than the theory theories, but all versions have in common the negative claim that we do not use a folk psychological theory when predicting or explaining human behavior (Currie 1995; A. Goldman 1995a, 2006; Gordon 1995a, 1995b; Harris 1992; Heal 1995). According to the simulation theory, instead of using a tacit folk psychological theory, we use our own cognitive processes when predicting and explaining behavior; we appeal to the same mechanisms that we use when deciding what to do next ourselves.

The accounts of the inputs for the simulation differ according to the version of the theory. In some accounts, we use environmental factors and relevant differences between oneself and the subject of the simulation as the inputs (Gordon 1995b). Other accounts remain closer to standard folk psychology; these take the inputs to be beliefs and desires (A. Goldman 1995a). In this discussion, I focus on Goldman's view, because with Gordon's some unresolved difficulties persist in avoiding at least some attribution of belief and desire.[1]

In Goldman's account, the simulation gets started with an observation of the subject's environment, and from this information, "I infer that you have certain perceptual experiences or beliefs, the same ones I would have in your situation. I may also assume (pending information to the contrary) that you have the same basic likings that I have: for food, love, warmth, and so on" (A. Goldman 1995a, 82). This information is not gained by having a theory of folk psychology; it comes instead from an examination of the person's environment and situation. These hypothetical beliefs and desires are used as the input for the simulation. They are then manipulated by one's own practical reasoning mechanisms, the same cognitive processes used to determine one's own behavior. However, the output of the simulation is not behavior, as in the usual case, because the practical reasoning mechanisms have been taken off-line. Instead the output will be a prediction of behavior. According to this version of the simulation theory, the following methodology is used to predict behavior:

(a) Infer that the subject has beliefs B and desires D;
(b) Use B and D as initial conditions;
(c) Take your practical reasoning system off-line and input B and D;
(d) Note that if you had not taken your practical reasoning system off-line, you would have engaged in behavior H;
(e) Predict that the subject will most likely engage in H.

The critics of simulation theory have focused largely on three concerns: the origin of the initial inputs to the simulation, concerns about the collapse of simulation into theory, and the cognitive penetrability of our predictions. Theory theorists have suggested that step (a) in the mental simulation requires some theory, or at least a database of the kinds of beliefs and desires that a person would have in a particular situation. The worry about the origin of the inputs for the simulation blurs the distinction between the two theories, leading to a concern that simulation theory is just a variety of theory theory.

These first two worries may be overcome by some alternative account of the origin of the initial conditions. However, the cognitive penetrability criticism as developed by Shaun Nichols and colleagues (1996) is of more concern. Predictions appear to be cognitively penetrable insofar as gaining information about a situation or a general law can lead to a change in prediction. However, if simulation theory is true, a change in one's explicit knowledge should not lead to a change in one's prediction, because the prediction is a function of an implicit system, namely, one's own practical reasoning system. Any psychological phenomenon that affects one's own behavior would be activated during the simulation, and so it has been argued that the inability to predict the consequences of such phenomena is evidence against the simulation theory (Nichols et al. 1996; Stich and Nichols 1996).

Social psychology abounds with cases where individuals fail to predict the behavior that they would engage in. For example, a study by Ellen Langer (1975) focused on subjects' inability to make certain kinds of predictions. In this study, Langer organized a football pool among coworkers and sold tickets for $1 each. Some of the people were given a choice of teams, and others were offered only one. A few days later, Langer offered to buy back the tickets at a price set by the subjects. She found that the people who had a choice of tickets sold them back at an average of $8.67, whereas those who were not offered a choice set a significantly lower price, averaging $1.96.

The Langer study reveals a psychological effect that has been widely replicated. The general psychological lesson we might take from this study is that people feel that objects have more worth if they are freely chosen rather than randomly assigned. If someone unfamiliar with this study is asked to predict what sell-back price a person would set for a freely chosen ticket versus a randomly assigned ticket, will the estimated prices show the same statistical difference? That is, without being told of this study, can humans predict the Langer effect?

Shaun Nichols and colleagues (1996) used a modified version of Langer's experiment to answer this question. They tested thirty subjects who thought they were being tested on their ability to evaluate the grammar of sentences. Before the test, the subjects were told that a lottery was being arranged as a reward for participating. The prize was $30. Some of the subjects were given a lottery ticket; others were allowed to choose among three different tickets. The experimenter then read the fifteen sentences and had the subjects mark their answers on paper. After the test, which took about five minutes, the subjects were told that it might be necessary to run more subjects than planned, and to give everyone a fair chance at winning the lottery, the experimenter might be willing to buy back some of the lottery tickets. The subjects were then asked to indicate on the bottom of their answer sheet a price at which they would be willing to sell the ticket back to the researcher.

Langer's results were replicated in this study; those with no choice of ticket set an average price of $1.60, whereas those who selected a ticket set an average price of $6.29. Nichols and colleagues then tested observer-subjects on their ability to predict this phenomenon. They showed the observer-subjects one of two videos of a confederate performing the task described earlier. The only difference between the two scenarios occurred during the first two minutes, when the confederate was either given a lottery ticket or offered a choice of tickets. The observer-subjects were asked to predict how the subject on the tape would answer the questions on the grammar test. They were also asked to predict the price at which the confederate-subject would sell his ticket.

The observer-subjects were not able to predict the Langer effect in this study. The average predicted price for the choice of tickets was $4.62, in contrast to $3.47 for those who were not given a choice. Though the choice group did place a higher value on their tickets than did the no-choice group, the difference between the two prices is not statistically significant.

Why is it that adults cannot predict the Langer effect? Nichols et al. designed this test as a way to adjudicate between simulation theory and theory theory. Since the theory theory is cognitively penetrable, and information or lack of information about a domain can affect performance in that domain, the researchers hypothesized that the results of their study support the theory theory. A simulation is not cognitively penetrable, and thus we should not expect that lack of explicit knowledge regarding the Langer effect would cause failure in the predictive task. The theory theory's theory is only as good as the information one has regarding the domain at issue. If a person does not learn about the Langer effect, then it is not reasonable to expect that such a person could predict behavior based on that information. However, since the Langer effect does seem to be a part of our own practical reasoning system, and simulation theory accounts for our predictive abilities though the same practical reasoning system, according to the simulation account, we *should* be able to predict the effect.

In such situations, we need to learn something about human behavior to make an accurate prediction; having just read about the Langer effect, we are now in a better position to predict it. That is, we can use that knowledge to generate the beliefs and desires that serve as inputs to a mental simulation. But once we allow such information to play a role in the simulation, the account starts to look more like a hybrid between simulation and theory rather than pure simulation.

Leaving the Armchair

According to both theory theory and simulation theory, we predict behavior by first understanding the propositional attitudes of others. However, there is reason to think that attributing propositional attitudes is neither necessary nor sufficient for predicting behavior. While supporters of SFP would not deny that we can predict behavior without appeal to the propositional attitudes, they do believe that propositional attitude attribution is foundational to our ability to predict intentional action, and that other methods of prediction are derivative of our ability to see others as holders of beliefs and desires.

Any account of folk psychological prediction that aims to challenge SFP must be immune to at least some of the criticisms raised against the two standard theories. To avoid these criticisms, an accurate folk psychology will reject the claim that mindreading is foundational to all folk psychological acts, and this can only be done by moving beyond the armchair. We need to learn more about where we succeed and where we fail at making predictions, and develop an account of predicting behavior that reflects this information.

Studies from social psychology suggest a model of folk psychological prediction that is quite different from the standard view from philosophy of mind and action. Not only does the social psychological evidence offer a different view about the methods used to make predictions, but it also challenges the widespread philosophical view about the accuracy of our predictions. In the social psychological picture, humans make predictions of behaviors using a number of different methods, including appeal to stereotypes, trait and mood attributions, normative inferences about what people in such a situation ought to do, and other generalizations. In many cases, these heuristics do not result in predictions as successful as we might expect. But they do reflect our actual practice of predicting behavior, so we can turn to the social psychology literature to help develop a more complex, but more empirically adequate, account of folk psychology that captures how people understand people—rather than how minds understand minds.

5   How Do You Know What I'm Going to Do? You Know Me

The fundamental unpredictability of humans is "perhaps akin to unpredictability in physics."
—Lee Ross and Richard E. Nisbett

Mental Content and Intentionality

Though the philosophical tradition emphasizes the role of belief and desire attribution in the prediction of behavior, when we turn to look at the empirical research on behavior prediction from social and developmental psychology, a different picture emerges. Pluralism in the methods used to predict behavior appears to be an undeniable fact. In this chapter, I review the psychological literature to further undermine the idea that humans fundamentally consider propositional attitudes when predicting behavior. Some questions arise about the relationship between beliefs, desires, and the predictive methods discussed here, and I address those in chapter 6.

Around the same time that Wilfrid Sellars was developing his story about how minds understand other minds inferentially, a different approach to social knowledge was being developed by the social psychologist Fritz Heider. In 1958, Heider published his influential account of what he referred to as the "naïve analysis of action." Heider, like Sellars, was interested in how we know our own mental states and how we explain others' behavior. And, like Sellars, Heider can be seen as advocating a theory-theory account of folk psychology. Heider describes our knowledge of human behavior as "the unformulated or half-formulated knowledge of interpersonal relations as it is expressed in our everyday language and experience—this source will be referred to as common-sense or naïve psychology" (Heider 1958). For Heider, much of what we know about the mind stems from our natural, commonsense psychology, and this knowledge forms the foundation for research in scientific psychology. As Heider says, quoting Köhler, "The lack of great discoveries in psychology as compared with physics [is accounted for] by the fact that 'man was acquainted with practically all territories of mental life a long time before the founding of scientific psychology.'"

Heider's analysis differs from Sellars's given their different views of what is central to our understanding of other minds. Sellars's interest was in mental content, and he focused on the concepts of *belief* and *desire*; Heider was more interested in intentionality and correspondingly focused on the concepts *try* and *can*. In the psychological literature, Heider is portrayed as making a distinction between two dimensions of action analysis. The folk are said to see people as acting from their own nature, on the one hand, and acting due to environmental pressures, on the other. As Heider puts it, "In common-sense psychology (as in scientific psychology) the result of an action is felt to depend on two sets of conditions, namely factors within the person and factors within the environment" (Heider 1958, x). Heider applies this distinction to a number of different kinds of interpersonal relations, including moral ones. For example, his analysis of folk concepts led him to see oughts and values as dispositional, rather than necessarily motivating.

The internal factors implicated in action include the intentional concepts *can* (as in "p can cause x") and *try* (as in "p tries to cause x") (Heider 1958). Because these notions were analyzed according to power and exertion, they can come in degrees. Thus for Heider, we don't understand the behavior of others digitally—that is, as being fully caused by a belief and a desire, or deductively entailed by the propositional attitude plus general law. Rather, for Heider, there are degrees of intentional action, and our understanding of others' intentional action is likewise on a continuum.

The subsequent research in social psychology took Heider's insights as a given and focused on intentional action, ability, capability, and exertion, rather than on mental content in terms of beliefs and desires. Because social psychology had no tradition of perceiving social understanding in terms of beliefs and desires, social psychologists were free to understand the mind in fundamentally different ways from the philosophical tradition. Until recently, this research has been isolated from other branches of psychology and has not been part of the developmentalist's discussion of theory of mind. This, however, is changing as the findings of social psychology contribute to a growing understanding of the nature of folk psychology.

Methods of Prediction

To know how much of a role Heider's intentionality or Sellars's beliefs and desires actually play in our folk psychological predictive practices, we can first examine the extent to which we rely on the attribution of mental content when predicting behavior. In addition, since accurate prediction of behavior is touted as one of the benefits of belief-desire attribution, we might also examine whether SFP is more accurate than other methods of prediction. Of course, since humans are not optimally rational, merely finding that one method of prediction is most accurate cannot alone serve as evidence that the method is the one we in fact use. But since supporters of SFP assume that humans are behavior predictors extraordinaire, it will be useful to see whether attribution of propositional attitudes allows us to make better, or more, predictions of behavior than do the other methods.

As I have already discussed, predictions of behavior are ubiquitous for humans: we predict what the people walking down the street will do and not do, we predict that our students will show up for class, we predict that the waiter will bring the bill, we predict that the neighbor will say hello when she walks by. These predictions are automatic and go largely unnoticed. If the people on the street walk backward, if no students are in the classroom, if the waiter never brings the bill, or the neighbor walks by without a hello, we would be terribly concerned about what is going on in the world. Only when such quotidian predictions go wrong do we tend to notice that we made a prediction in the first place.

Supporters of SFP often point to these kinds of quotidian predictions as examples to support their case. However, the evidence shows that many of these sorts of predictions are generated automatically, without conscious effort and with very little information. For example, after meeting someone, within a few seconds we are able to make accurate predictions of behavior and attributions of personality traits or emotional states that can be used to predict behavior (see Ambady and Rosenthal 1992 for a meta-study). Social psychologists have likened this ability to the ethological concept of display behavior, which allows for the exchange of information automatically, on a non- or subconscious level (Goffman 1979). Like the female peacock who responds to the tail display of the male, or the chimpanzee who responds to the relaxed open mouth of a conspecific, humans respond to subtle cues expressed by gait, facial muscles, or vocal modulation. If peacocks and chimpanzees can make such automatic predictions, then we probably shouldn't expect that the attribution of beliefs and desires is part of the mechanism at work here.

Quotidian predictions should be distinguished from what we can call *prognosticating predictions*. Prognosticating predictions are not automatic and occur at a level of conscious awareness. For the social psychologists, quotidian predictions are not an amazing ability unique to humans but a continuation of abilities we see in other species. Consequently, social psychologists have been less interested in the mechanisms underlying our ability to make quotidian predictions than in the prognosticating predictions that shape our perceptions. Prognosticating predictions might be made of someone who has just been observed for the first time, for example, "She is going to make a good employee." We also prognosticate when we foretell the distant future: "He will marry his new boyfriend" or "She won't finish the marathon." Typically, we are aware of making prognosticating predictions, while quotidian predictions are those that occupy the background—the spontaneous judgments we make about everyday behavior: "The shopkeeper will say hello" or "My husband will make coffee when he wakes up."

While the heuristics and biases literature is familiar to many working in philosophy of psychology and mind, this research has important consequences that need to be more fully explored. In this chapter, I aim to show that entire classes of behavior can be predicted, and even prognosticated, without the attribution of beliefs and desires. Indeed, I aim to show that a number of different mechanisms are involved in making predictions of intentional behavior, and these mechanisms are extremely sensitive to factors including the context in which one is making the prediction; the kinds of knowledge available to the predictor; the predictor's own biases and past experiences, and the familiarity of the target; the mood of the predictor; and the target's status as in-group or out-group. I will discuss four methods of predicting behavior that arise from research in social psychology: predicting from the situation, predicting from self, predicting from trait attribution, and predicting from stereotype.

Though the general methods of predicting behavior are related to each other and to some less-studied methods of predicting behavior, such as making generalizations over an individual's past behavior or predicting based on a person's mood, I argue that these methods are not based on prior attributions of beliefs and desires. That is, individuals who are unable or unwilling to attribute content to an actor can use these methods of predicting behavior without having previously considered the actor's reasons for the behavior. Most importantly, I argue that these methods can be used to generate accurate predictions—at least as accurate as predictions made by the attribution of contentful mental states. Though these methods of predicting behavior have been uncovered by looking at biases in human reasoning, they have strong pragmatic value, as we will see.

All the methods of predicting behavior that I discuss here are kinds of generalizations. When you use yourself as a model for what another will do, you are generalizing from your past behavior, or your belief about what you would do in a particular situation, to another's behavior. When you use stereotypes, you are generalizing about how members of particular groups are supposed to act. Prediction by trait attribution appeals to a broader category than stereotype attribution. Even belief-desire psychology relies on generalizations, namely, the platitudes considered to make up the core of folk psychology (e.g., thirsty people will drink, ceteris paribus).

Given that all these methods are kinds of generalizations, it might seem as though drawing a distinction between them will not be useful in understanding how we predict behavior. Unfortunately the situation is even muddier than it might first appear. Not only are all these methods variations on generalizations, but they also overlap with each other. For example, we can understand stereotypes as generalizations about groups that refer in part to properties and traits that group members are seen as having. This definition of stereotype makes it clear that overlap occurs between trait attribution and stereotyping; both make predictions about how people will behave based on traits attributed to a target.

Despite the fuzzy edges, it makes sense to discuss the methods independently, because each method has its own necessary feature. Generalizing from self requires understanding oneself before making judgments about another. Stereotyping involves considering a constellation of personality traits and other properties when predicting behavior, and it can also activate in-group–out-group judgments.

However, there are limitations about what we will be able to conclude about these methods of predicting behavior. One might hope to construct a decision tree or a functional organizational chart of how an individual predicts behavior, but that would be a misguided goal. Over the years, attempts to determine when different methods are used have failed. For example, early in the study of stereotypes, researchers thought that we only use stereotypes to predict future behavior when we have no information about an individual's past behavior (Locksley et al. 1980). But stereotypes vary in strength, and studies found that some stereotypes, such as gender stereotypes, remain in the face of disconfirming behavioral evidence (Deaux and Lewis 1984; Jackson and Cash 1985; Swim 1993). Studies that simultaneously vary potential diagnostic features (e.g., stereotype and past behavior, or stereotype and trait) have found that in some cases an additive effect occurs, and in other cases behavior can override stereotype (Krueger and Rothbart 1988). Such findings suggest that the different methods of predicting are often used simultaneously when making predictions, and the final judgment will be the result of a combination of the various methods. Krueger and Rothbart point out that "in trying to predict the relative power of stereotypic categories and trait information, it may be necessary to examine more precisely the relation between categories and category attributions. Not all categories are the same, and it does not make sense to think that broad categories, such as gender . . . will be as predictive of people's attributes as more narrow categories" (193).

To predict what an unknown fellow female student would do in a particular situation, a male student might consider what he would do, what he thinks women in general would do, what people would generally do, what students generally do, and so on. He might also consider whether what he would do or what women would do is consistent with the stereotype about what students would do. All these considerations will interact when making the determination about how the unknown female student will act. And the final judgment will depend on the strength and consistency of these different possible behaviors, not to mention other factors, such as mood or affect. It quickly becomes apparent that the methods we use to predict behavior are related in complex and interesting ways. A satisfactory account of how the folk predict behavior will have to engage this complex dynamic.

Predicting from the Situation

Will the students show up for the final exam? Will the woman turn to face the door when she gets on the elevator? Will the audience applaud or boo at the end of the performance? Will your husband get up with the baby in the night?

Traditionally, social psychology has emphasized two different types of causes of human behavior: internal causes such as personality traits, moods, emotions, beliefs, intentions, and so on; and external causes related to the situation or a person's past experiences. One of the major findings from social psychology in the last fifty years is that people in the West tend to underestimate the effect the situation has on people's behavior when offering explanations about why someone acted as she did (L. Ross 1977). While we do not always recognize the extent to which the situation influences someone's behavior, we often predict people's behavior based on knowing what their situation is. Whether someone just finished a long bike ride or disembarked from a plane in a foreign country, it is easy to generate scenarios the individual might follow. The cyclist will probably drink some water and take a shower. The passenger might rush toward the customs line or use the restroom. If you needed to find the cyclist after he finished his ride, you would look in the kitchen and the bathroom. These predictions are based on likely scenarios and can be useful for finding a person when you have no other information about what she might be doing.

The social psychologist Kurt Lewin (1931) first suggested that people's behavior can largely be predicted from knowing the situation in which the behavior occurs, an insight that was followed up by both Gustav Ichheiser (1949) and Fritz Heider (1958). While the distinction between the person and the situation is widely attributed to Heider today, the psychologist Bertram Malle argues that Heider was more interested in the distinction between intentional and unintentional behavior and believed that people explain intentional behavior in terms of reasons, whereas they explain unintentional behavior in terms of causes (Malle 2004). Nonetheless it cannot be denied that the distinction between the person and the situation has played a huge role in the social psychological experiments conducted over the past fifty years. The person-situation focus solidified with the discovery that (at least in the West) people systematically underestimate the power of situations and thus make incorrect predictions about the behavior of others. In study after study, subjects were motivated by the situation to degrees that even the psychologists had not predicted, such as the subjects in Milgram's study who were willing to shock people at the suggestion of a person in a lab coat.

Once it was discovered that people underestimate the power of situations over behavior, understanding the mechanisms underlying this phenomenon became a central research project in social psychology. The tendency is called the "fundamental attribution error" or "correspondence bias," and it has variously been attributed to a lack of awareness, a faulty theory about how people in situations would or would not behave, poor categorization skills, or being cognitively busy with other tasks (Gilbert and Malone 1995).

What has not received as much attention is how much behavior is accurately predicted by appeal to situations. Successes in human reasoning are less interesting to social psychologists than are failures, so this emphasis should not be surprising. A variety of experiments show that people do refer to situations when explaining behavior (e.g., Gilbert et al. 1988; Heider 1958). We saw in the last chapter that making an inference from how we explain behavior to how we predict behavior is problematic, so we cannot rely on this evidence alone to show that predictions are made from the situation. As we know, studies suggest that people are often inaccurate when predicting behavior because they underestimate the relevance of the situation (L. Ross 1977; Dunning et al. 1990; Vallone et al. 1990). This result occurs even when predicting one's own future behavior (Vallone et al. 1990). A focus on the correspondence bias might lead one to think that while behavior is explained by situations, it is not predicted by appeal to situations. This, however, would also be a hasty conclusion. There are good reasons to think that we do predict behavior based on the target's situation.

For one, the conclusion of the famous situational studies is that the power of the situation is underestimated, not ignored. Psychologists were able to make predictions based on the power of the situation once they realized it to be a significant variable. The finding is not that we cannot use the situation to help us determine what someone will do but that in cases when multiple variables have to be simultaneously considered, the power of the situation is often discounted. The situational variables of the Princeton Seminary experiment (Darley and Batson 1973) were varied because the psychologists expected that people—even seminary students—who were running late would be less likely to stop and help a person in need. While the layperson finds this result surprising, the inability to make a correct prediction may have to do with the number of variables at play. The stereotype of a seminary student may have overridden the situational considerations in predicting the result. On the other hand, the folk would have little problem predicting that a random man who is not running late is more likely to stop and help a person with a flat tire than the man who is running late.

In addition, we can consider the kinds of predictions that subjects were asked to make in such studies. For example, while Vallone's research team found that people would be more likely to make accurate predictions of their own and others' future behavior by looking at the base rates for people in their situation, the kinds of predictions that subjects were asked to make were prophecies about the future (Vallone et al. 1990). For example, subjects were asked to predict whether they would end a romantic relationship, for example, or attend the big game later that year. The quotidian predictions that we make are perhaps more likely to be made through appeal to the situation than are prognosticating predictions. Appeal to the situation can easily answer the following questions about future behavior: What is Joe going to do when he walks into the bathroom? Is the driver in front of me going to drive off the road or suddenly reverse or stop? Will the student sit quietly in class? We often make predictions simply by considering what is done in certain situations. Students come to class, drivers stop at stop signs, and waiters bring our order. It is clear that we make these predictions, because we are puzzled (and sometimes irritated) when they don't come true. Why doesn't the waiter come with our food? Is it because he is too busy, or did he forget to place our order?

Such observations are consistent with a model of social prediction offered by Kahneman and Tversky (1982), according to which people predict behavior by setting up the situation and then running a simulation. The situation, while not the only diagnostic category for one's future behavior, is a significant variable. When considering the situation as well as one's own counterfactual behavior, however, one risks making a false self-centered or self-serving prediction, because the simulation may be based on an implicit assumption that others are like oneself; I discuss this point further in the next section. Note that not all predictions will require both setting up the situation and running a simulation. Consider situations that the predictor has never been in and could not foresee herself in, such as being awarded the Nobel Prize. We know what such a situation calls for (e.g., giving an acceptance speech) without having to consider what we would do in the situation. Instead this prediction can be generated by simple association. In the past, people who have been publicly awarded this prize have given grateful speeches, and the future cases of being awarded a Nobel Prize are relevantly similar to the current case, so the target is likely to behave as the past recipients did.

Experimental evidence also suggests that some kinds of predictions do take the situation to be diagnostic. We know that actors tend to take situational constraints into account when considering their own behavior, even while neglecting situational factors when predicting the behavior of another (Darley and Batson 1973; Griffin et al. 1990; Moore 2005; Pietromonaco and Nisbett 1982; Safer 1980). While perhaps more familiar in the case of explanation (Nisbett et al. 1973), the asymmetry between self and other holds for predicting behavior, as well. In one study, subjects were given a hypothetical bargaining scenario and were asked to predict the final sale price under two conditions. One condition imposed a final deadline for the bargaining; the other had no deadline. Participants were asked to predict the values their bargaining partner would assign to the two situations (Moore 2005). Subjects concluded that a deadline would hurt them more than their bargaining partner, regardless of whether the subject was a buyer or a seller. Across several studies, Moore found that actors predicted that a situational factor would constrain their own behavior more than it would constrain another's action.

Despite this finding, we should not conclude that predictors never take the situation into account when predicting others' behavior. As I suggested earlier, quotidian predictions are likely made through appeal to the situation. Experimental data also confirm the hypothesis that appreciation of the situation, coupled with knowledge of a person's past behavior in that situation, allows for fairly good predictive accuracy of the individual's future behavior (Lorei 1967; Mischel 1972). In one study that explicitly examined the kind of information a subject preferred to have before offering a prediction, information about past behavior in a similar situation was preferred to information about behavior in a dissimilar situation and to information about the target's personality traits. For example, subjects were presented the following question:

Paul is a junior biology major who is a member of his college track team. Paul's track team has weekly meets with teams from other schools.

How many hours will Paul spend training for next week's track meet? (Your answer should be in numerical form.)

Information that you may choose amongst (Check one choice)

___ the number of hours that Paul spent training for last week's track meet, according to an observer.

___ an estimate of how hardworking Paul is, according to his best friend. (Mischel et al. 1974, 235)

Subjects were significantly more likely to indicate the number of hours that Paul had previously spent training for the track meet. Perhaps because this finding is unsurprising, little research has been done on how much quotidian behavior is predicted via situational inferences. Research on prophecies tends to be more interesting and more likely to result in surprising discoveries. Confirmations of banal platitudes are less likely to appear in the journals, but this should not raise much suspicion that people predict future behavior by generalizing from past behavior in similar situations. It's how we predict much physical movement, and for reliable behaviors, we need not rely on a sophisticated manipulation of all the variables at play. Instead, if you want to know whether someone will take her coat before she heads out to work on a cold winter's day, you need only know that people wear coats during northern winters.

One conclusion from this social psychology research is that Westerners could be more accurate in their prognosticating predictions if they were better able to take into account the actor's social and physical environment. Nonetheless appeal to the situation is one of the tools all humans use to predict behavior.

Predicting from Self

If you needed to predict whether an advertising campaign would be successful, you might consider whether you would be motivated by it. And if you were asked who would be more upset, a person who missed his plane by five minutes or one who missed it by a half hour, you might also appeal to your own response in that situation. In that case, you would be predicting by appealing to yourself.

Since the 1930s, psychologists have found that the kinds of predictions we make are affected by our own past behaviors. The earliest work on this question found that students who had previously cheated on an exam were more likely to predict that other students would cheat, too (Katz and Allport 1931). In the subsequent eighty years, this result has been found to be robust: smokers think that more people will smoke, conservatives think that more people are conservative, and sushi lovers think that sushi is more popular. We think others are more like us than they really are, and we expect others will engage in similar behaviors and have similar traits and beliefs (Krueger 1998; Marks and Miller 1987; Mullen et al. 1985).

Children appear to use this method early on and predict that others will have the sorts of emotional reactions that they themselves would have in similar conditions. For example, when told a story about an actor who wants another child to be hit by a ball, subjects younger than five years are unable to suppress their own sentiments and will say that the actor is sad when the child is hit by the ball (Yuill 1984; Yuill et al. 1996).

Though at first glance simulating from self might appear to be the same as the method of predicting behavior promoted by simulation theorists, some important differences distinguish the two methods. First, not all generalizations from self occur at the subpersonal level. In some cases, we make an overt prediction from self when we ask ourselves, "What would I do if I were him?" But more interestingly, predicting from self is a simpler process than mental simulation, and it does not require the same subpersonal mechanisms. An essential aspect of constructing a successful mental simulation involves making the relevant shifts from self to other that allow for the discrepant beliefs that the target might have. The predictions from self we make often fail to make such adjustments. Predictions from self might lead a mother to expect that her sister would be happier once she had a child, for example (or unhappier, depending on the predictor's own experiences).

During the battles between simulation theory and theory theory, a study by Kahneman and Tversky (1982) was widely cited as evidence in favor of simulation theory. The study has been interpreted as evidence that we generalize from self when making some predictions of others' behavior. Specifically, in this study, subjects appeared to first determine how they would feel in the counterfactual situation, and then attribute that emotion to the target to make predictions about their behavior. Subjects were given the following vignette:

> Mr. Crane and Mr. Tees were scheduled to leave the airport on different flights, at the same time. They traveled from town in the same limousine, were caught in a traffic jam, and arrived at the airport 30 minutes after the scheduled departure time of their flights.
> Mr. Crane is told that his flight left on time.
> Mr. Tees is told his was delayed, and left five minutes ago.
> Who is more upset? (Kahneman and Tversky 1982, 203)

Almost all the subjects reported that Mr. Tees would be more upset. Kahneman and Tversky interpret this result as evidence that people predict behavior by setting up a situation, determining what they themselves would do in that situation, and then generalizing that response to the target. Some simulation theorists interpreted the study as evidence that people use mental simulation to predict behaviors (A. Goldman 1995b). Before accepting that interpretation, note what subjects *don't* have to do to make the prediction. Subjects are not forced to attribute discrepant beliefs to Mr. Tees and Mr. Crane, because a subject has no information about what beliefs they might have that differ from the subject's. So a natural response to this question is "I would be more irritated if I missed the flight by five minutes." It is a simple projection of one's own response onto another and does not require the cognitive shifts that are part of the machinery of mental simulation.

These differences between simulating and generalizing from self suggest that generalization from self may be more likely to lead to false predictions. Predicting from self gives us an egocentric bias and can cause us to focus more on our own actions and traits than on the actions of others (M. Ross and Sicoly 1979). We also have a tendency to anchor our judgments of others on behavior, traits, or attitudes that appear salient in the situation, so our own perception of the situation will lead us to emphasize features that matter to us, even though they may not matter to the actor (Quattrone 1982). Taken together, these two tendencies may lead us to expect that other people will behave in the same way that we will, and to think that other people are more like us than they are.

Because anchoring from an egocentric position does not involve discrepant belief attributions, it may lead us to make incorrect predictions and incorrect judgments. Egocentric judgments can cause great problems in cross-cultural contexts, where the differences between self and other may be much stronger than usual. For example, while a Western visitor to a rural town in a developing country may feel sorry for the local people's lack of access to an education, the local people may feel sorry for the Western visitor, whose family must not care about her to let her travel alone so far from home.

If predicting from self leads to such problematic judgments about other people, perhaps we ought to avoid it. Psychologists have long suggested that it is irrational to project onto others in this fashion. In a well-known study, Lee Ross, Greene, and House (1977) suggested that this method of prediction is an irrational bias, and dubbed it the false-consensus effect. They argued that generalizing from self is irrational because it is an inductive inference made from a reference set of one. If other information is available that could be used to make the prediction, Ross and colleagues suggest it is more rational to use that information because it would likely lead to a more accurate prediction.

But it seems that though people often do assume consensus when using themselves as models for others' behavior, the claim that this is an error in reasoning may be unwarranted. To make this point, let us examine another study by Ross and colleagues in which Stanford University students were asked to walk around campus wearing a sandwich board that read "Repent!" (L. Ross et al. 1977). After the students decided whether or not to comply with the request, they were asked to estimate the percentage of other students who would agree to wear the board. The students who had agreed to wear the board estimated that more than half of people would also comply, whereas the students who did not agree to wear the board estimated that less than a quarter of people would comply. From these results, the authors concluded that since the consensus estimates vary with the subject's own decision, the estimates must be, overall, incorrect.

There are several things to note about this study. For one, the subjects are asked to make an overall estimate about a population rather than to predict the behavior of a single individual. The only information that the subjects have about the targets is that they are fellow students. So in this situation, no other information is available that the subjects could use in making the prediction. There are no *individuals* whose behaviors the subjects need to predict.

A second thing to note is that the subjects are asked to make a judgment about a group of which they are members. Recent research suggests that estimates made by generalizing from self to members of an in-group result in relatively accurate predictions. This is because groups tend to be homogeneous in certain respects. For example, generalizing from self about other adolescents in one's peer group is an accurate strategy, given the strength of the group in fixing beliefs, traits, and behaviors (Prinstein and Wang 2005).

Given these facts, how should subjects come up with their estimates? Dawes and Mulford (1996) have suggested that subjects might perform a Bayesian analysis with a uniform prior distribution of belief. They suggest that we should expect results like those Ross found if subjects are first told about the behavior of one member of the group before being asked to make the decision about wearing the board. With no other information to go on, knowledge about the behavior of one member of the group, be it oneself or another, should rationally affect the frequency estimates. Further, they suggest that because members of groups often share characteristics, the consensus effect can lead to accurate predictions of behavior. Depressed adults do not show the same pattern of generalizing from self (Cross et al. 2002). Given that depressed adults may see themselves as outside all groups, this finding is consistent with the explanation for the consensus effect under conditions of low knowledge. When depressed, people tend to think that they are unique, and alone.

The conclusion is that if you know nothing about the target, or if you only know that you and the target are members of the same group, then generalizing from self can be an effective method. As the psychologist Robyn Dawes argued, generalizing from self is the primary method we use to predict others' behavior when we have no other relevant information (Dawes 1989).

However, we have reason to think that our methods of predicting behavior change with even a small amount of concrete information about an individual. For example, students who were asked to make judgments about most other students in the United States overestimated the population's tendency to take risks, but when asked to make a judgment about an unknown student sitting nearby, the subjects would significantly lower their judgment. Predicting the behavior of concrete strangers apparently activated different strategies than did predicting the general behavior of a population (Hsee and Weber 1997). And when asked to predict the behavior of a person outside their own group, people appear not to predict from self (Krueger and Zeiger 1993). Thus, if you have some information about another person, even if it is only a physical description, you then have the opportunity to activate other methods, such as predicting via stereotype.

Without additional information, it is difficult for most people to avoid predicting from self, if forced to make a prediction. Even when people are told that a false-consensus bias exists, and that to generalize from one's self when predicting behavior is an error in reasoning, people continue to demonstrate the consensus effect (Krueger and Clement 1994). This suggests that generalizing from self may be automatic and not under intentional control.

Children are perhaps principally predictors from self; it is with good reason that Piaget suggested children younger than seven years are cognitively egocentric. Children's egocentrism is offered as one explanation of the three-year-old's performance in the false-belief task. Recall that these children are unable to set aside their own privileged information about the location of a chocolate bar when they predict where Maxi will go to look for it. However, while the false-belief literature suggests that at age four children overcome this deficit, even after children pass the false-belief task, they continue to engage in false-consensus behavior. For example, four- and five-year-olds will fail to realize that information that was just learned (such as the fact that cats use their whiskers to determine whether they can fit into tight places) is not known by their peers (M. Taylor et al. 1994). Five- and six-year-olds have difficulty realizing that others cannot recognize the subject of a line drawing that is partially obscured, when they themselves are familiar with the picture (Chandler and Helm 1984). Note too that such studies offer corroborating evidence that children's understanding of representational belief continues to develop after they pass the false-belief task.

Children tend to generalize from self about emotional as well as information states. For example, like the adults in Kahneman and Tversky's study, we saw that children predict that others will have the sorts of emotional reactions that they themselves would have in similar conditions (Yuill 1984; Yuill et al. 1996). If both children and adults predict from self, but adults fail to make many of the mistakes that children make, what accounts for the difference? A couple of suggestions have been offered. Birch and Bloom (2004) suggest that the general problem with children's mind-reading ability can be attributed to the egocentrism that results from the so-called curse of knowledge. Knowledge is cursed when one has too much of it, and irrelevant information affects one's judgments. The children's knowledge that the chocolate bar has been moved when Maxi was out of the room is cursed, because it is difficult for the three-year-old to disregard that information when predicting Maxi's behavior. Though Birch and Bloom suggest that older children and adults pass mind-reading tasks because the strength of the bias diminishes with age, we have seen that adults also have problems with overgeneralizing from self.

Another suggestion for the increase in accuracy of older children and adults comes from Epley and colleagues, who suggest that adults have developed ways of correcting for their initial faulty egocentric judgments (Epley et al. 2004a). In a study comparing egocentrism in perspective taking between children and adults, the researchers found that when requested to move an object by a confederate who had a different visual perspective, both children and adults were as likely to initially look at the object that fit the confederate's description from their own perspective, rather than the object that fit the description from the confederate's perspective. Despite this initial similarity, adults were less likely to manipulate that object and made fewer egocentric errors than did the children. Thus adults must develop some method for overcoming their initial egocentric response, since they clearly have not outgrown it.

While both children and adults engage in generalizing from the self to predict others' behavior or to determine their judgments or emotions, the mechanisms used are unclear. Epley and colleagues suggest that assumptions of consensus are an example of the anchoring and adjustment heuristic, according to which people's estimates come from an implicitly suggested anchor and adjust up or down according to how representative they take the anchor to be (Epley et al. 2004b). When one predicts another person's response to some behavior, such as their willingness to wear a board reading "Repent!," one may use one's own response as the anchor and then, depending on how representative one thinks one is, make adjustments from there.

Explanations for egocentric consensus vary depending on whether the authors think that it is a useful heuristic for predicting behavior and judgments, or a bias that results in incorrect judgments. So, for example, Dawes and Mulford (1996) appeal to inductive Bayesian reasoning as a useful heuristic, whereas Ross and colleagues' original explanation for the consensus effect appealed to selective exposure and cognitive availability. They suggest that since one's own behaviors are the most salient and most readily called to mind, one's own behaviors are the most available (L. Ross et al. 1977). (For a review of the theoretical perspectives on the consensus effect, see Marks and Miller 1987.)

Regardless of the mechanisms involved, the tendency of both children and adults to base their predictions of other people's behavior on what they themselves would do appears to be widespread. However, adults do not use this method in all cases of prediction, nor do they use it with all targets. Though some researchers take generalizing from self to be a bias that leads to irrational thinking, in the cases where it is most widely used, with members of an in-group who are not otherwise described, or with complete strangers, it is a fairly efficient strategy. That is, in some cases, generalizing from self may be the best available approach for predicting someone's behavior. In naturalistic conditions, if one is forced to predict the behavior of an individual in proximity to the predictor, it may well work given the relative similarity of people in situations, peer groups, or other in-group conditions. When one has additional information, other methods of prediction come into play. We turn next to stereotypes.

Predicting from Stereotypes

On the first day of class, you see that the university's football star is in your seminar. How do you think he will do in the class? Different techniques are used to teach freshmen, graduate students, and nontraditional students, because we have different stereotypes associated with these three groups. We use stereotypes when we expect our Asian student will succeed, the freshman will be nervous, and the football player will be dim.

Stereotypes are sets of properties that are associated with a particular group or kind of person. We have stereotypes about any number of social groups, not just those that are defined by race and gender but also groups based on geographic location, age, vocation, avocation, and so on. We have stereotypes for vegetarians as well as obese people, professors, and plumbers. One and the same person is going to be subject to multiple stereotypes, and in different situations one stereotype may be most salient. For example, a white police officer and mother may be seen primarily as a mother at the funeral of her young child, but primarily as a police officer as she walks down the street in uniform. The stereotype that is used may be the one that is most useful for the attributor (Stangor et al. 1992), or the choice of stereotype may be affected by the degree of accountability that the attributor feels (Pendry and Macrae 1996). That is, if you are not worried that you might get called on your stereotype, you may be a bit sloppy in your categorization and use a broader category rather than a finer one.

Children begin using gender stereotypes—one of the strongest stereotypes—at a very early age. Some researchers suggest that at two years, children are already shaping their gender identity and developing an own-sex schema that they use to categorize activities as appropriate or not (Martin 2000). Children's early stereotypes of sex roles lead them to expect that boys won't skip rope and that girls won't play with trucks.

The properties associated with a stereotype can include personality traits, behaviors, beliefs, descriptions of physical appearance, goals, and so on, and these properties are thought to be structured—related to one another in some way. Given the view that stereotypes are knowledge structures that are an example of basic cognitive functioning, some regard stereotypes as schemas, which include a priori knowledge of how the different properties are related to one another (Hamilton 1981; S. Taylor 1981; S. Taylor and Crocker 1981; Schneider 2004). Much debate continues about the structure of schemas, how they are applied, whether they are hypotheses, and so on; and while I cannot begin to address these issues here, suffice it to say that the use of stereotypes is a more sophisticated and specific attribution than one based on past behavior, situation, or self. Stereotypes are also generalizations, but when we use stereotypes to predict an individual's behavior, we are making generalizations from a group of people to an individual. Predicting from stereotype attribution requires negotiation between the categories a person belongs to, determining the degree to which an individual fits in each category, the relevance of the category for the prediction, the strength of the stereotype, and the traits, beliefs, goals, and so on, associated with the stereotype.

We most often hear about stereotypes in the context of bigotry and prejudice, given that generalizations based on a person's race, sex, sexual orientation, ethnicity, religion, and so on, have historically been used, and unfortunately continue to be used, to justify everything from atrocities to daily irritations. But not all stereotypes involve prejudice or discrimination, and not all stereotypes are misleading. Some generalizations we make about groups are consistent with the comparative probabilities of having the properties between the group and the general population. For example, the stereotype that Asian American students are good students may be consistent with data on the relative percentage of Asian American students who go on to college after high school. However, like negative stereotypes, positive stereotypes can also cause problems for an individual; consider the Asian American student who doesn't fit the stereotype because she does poorly in school or desires to learn a trade. While some stereotypes exaggerate a trait associated with a group (Campbell 1967), other stereotypes systematically underestimate group differences (McCauley 1995). One worry, then, is that predictions of behavior based on stereotypic judgment will tend to be false. I return to this worry shortly.

Despite concerns about stereotypes and prejudice, stereotypes are an essential part of cognition. Like our other associative acts, relying on stereotypes allows us to make inferences without starting from scratch each time we need to predict someone's behavior. Stereotypes give us a starting position, without which judgments would be extremely difficult to make.

Stereotype attribution allows people to make rapid predictions of behavior, and some evidence shows that predictions made from stereotype attribution are faster and more efficient than predictions made from trait attribution (Andersen et al. 1990). Stereotypes appear to be richer categorizations than traits. Studies in which subjects were asked to ascribe features to a number of different stereotypes and traits have demonstrated that stereotypes tend to have more associations than traits and also use more visual elements than do traits (Andersen and Klatzky 1987). In addition, since traits are often strongly associated with stereotypes, and stereotypes are less frequently described as having core attributes that are associated with the related traits, some psychologists have argued that stereotypes are more distinctive and memorable than traits (Andersen and Klatzky 1987). Given the richness of the stereotype category, it is expected that people use stereotypes to make extensive inferences about individuals, both about what individuals will do in the future and why they act as they do.

Stereotypes do appear to facilitate predictions more quickly than does trait attribution, and this result is explained by suggesting that traits get their predictive power from the associated stereotypes, whereas stereotypes are more directly linked to likely actions (Andersen et al. 2000). In a set of studies, subjects were given a stereotype term or trait term and a description of an action and were asked to decide whether the type of person described by the stereotype or trait was likely to engage in the behavior. The sentences that associated a stereotype with a behavior were judged significantly more quickly than the sentences that associated a trait with a behavior.

The claim that activating a stereotype primes predictions that are consistent with the stereotype is widely accepted as part of commonsense psychology. For example, social groups and the popular media view stereotype activation as the cause of tragedies such as the shooting of Amadou Diallo, the unarmed young black man who was shot forty-one times by four police officers who mistook Diallo's wallet for a gun. The police officers predicted that Diallo was going to shoot them, because they had activated a stereotype about black youth.

Studies suggest that this interpretation of the Diallo tragedy is probably at least partially correct. Shortly after Diallo's death, the social psychologist Keith Payne studied some of the effects of the African American stereotype. Payne studied nonblack participants' ability to correctly identify a photograph of a tool or a gun after being primed with a photograph of a white or a black face. He found that subjects who are shown a black face are quicker at correctly identifying a gun than when they are primed with a white face, and when under time pressure they are significantly more likely to misidentify the object as a gun after seeing a black face (Payne 2001).

The predictive power of stereotype activation has been examined explicitly in another study of the negative effects of stereotypes. Class stereotypes were examined in a study of judgments about poor and wealthy children's academic abilities (Darley and Gross 1983). Subjects were shown a videotape of a child at school and playing in the neighborhood. Half the subjects saw video of a nine-year-old white girl named Hannah in an inner-city setting, and the other half saw video of Hannah playing and going to school in suburbia. Subjects in the inner-city condition were also told that the girl's parents had only a high-school education and had working-class jobs, whereas subjects in the suburban condition were told that the parents were college graduates with white-collar jobs.

Half the subjects in each group were asked to make predictions about the girl's academic ability after watching the videos, and the authors found no evidence of stereotype activation; subjects based their predictions on Hannah's age or year in school.[1]

The other half of the subjects were shown a lengthy videotape of the girl answering the test questions. The videotape was designed to provide no evidence about the girl's academic ability, and an independent measure confirmed this. These subjects did make stereotypical predictions based on class. The subjects who saw the girl in the inner-city environment had formed expectancies about how she would perform, and they subsequently interpreted the ambiguous performance on the test in a way that conformed to their expectations. On the other hand, subjects who saw the girl in a suburban environment had an implicit prediction that she would do well on the test, and this expectancy shaped their interpretation of her behavior.

These studies demonstrate that we do sometimes use stereotype activation when predicting behavior. However, these studies also raise the question of accuracy in stereotype prediction. Before we look at that issue, we should examine under what conditions we use stereotypes to make predictions. Judgments about the usefulness of a heuristic can only be made if we know what sort of information is available to the person using the heuristic.

One suggestion is that stereotypes are used to make inferences about people only when no other behavioral information is available. If we know only that the individual is a woman, we activate the woman stereotype to predict what the typical woman would do in a given situation. However, a host of studies suggests that this is not the case. There are studies galore on the force of gender stereotypes in judgments about job suitability and work evaluations, showing that gender remains a predictor even when subjects possess relevant information about the individual (Deaux and Lewis 1984; Jackson and Cash 1985; Swim 1993).

These studies suggest that relevant behavioral evidence might not always undermine stereotypic judgments; when the stereotype is strong, a predictor might disregard apparently contradictory behavioral evidence to avoid a dissonance with the prior stereotyped category. Gender stereotypes are among some of the stronger stereotypes there are, and it is relatively difficult to revise judgments that stem from them. Stereotypes about professional groups may be much weaker and easier to overlook in the face of disconfirming evidence. Theories about the interaction of stereotypes, traits, and behavior abound, along with views on the extent to which stereotypes are automatic or under one's control. Despite the disagreements about how stereotypes interact with other means of interpreting and predicting social behavior, there is good reason to think that stereotypes play a large role in our predictions of behavior.

Assuming that we do use stereotypes when making predictions, is this a matter of concern? The connection between stereotype and prejudice, the frequency of false gender stereotypes in the workplace, and so forth suggest stereotypic thinking cannot be an accurate method of predicting how a female job candidate will perform or whether a black youth is holding a gun. The generalizations we make from group membership to individual may be problematic in three regards. First, we may overestimate the prevalence of the property in the target group. That is, we may think that criminality is more prevalent among black male youths in America than it actually is. We may also overgeneralize from the group to the individual and attribute a relatively peripheral property of the group to an individual who is identified as a member of that group. Finally, we might think that a person is a member of a group that she does not actually belong to.

When we stereotype others, we form expectations about people's behaviors and their beliefs based on their group membership. These judgments are generalizations, and like our ability to generalize in other domains, our reliance on stereotypes to make inferences about an individual is only as good as the generalization is accurate.

It is true that stereotyping can lead to false conclusions about an individual. For example, one common error in using a stereotype to make a judgment is ignoring the frequency of the property or the behavior in the group. For example, one might predict that an American Catholic woman will not get an abortion if she has an unwanted pregnancy, because the Catholic Church forbids abortion. However, this would be a hasty conclusion, since it fails to consider the percentage of American Catholic women with an unwanted pregnancy who have abortions. Some studies suggest that rates of abortions among Catholics are higher than among Protestants, and the group Catholics for a Free Choice claims that a majority of American Catholics support legalizing abortion. This error is generalizable; we tend to attribute beliefs to individual members of a group that correspond to the group policies. This is so even when the policies are determined by a vote, and the policy passes only by a small margin (Allison and Messick 1985).

Overgeneralizations also occur when the predictor is encouraged to make a thoughtful decision (McHoskey and Miller 1994), when the predictor agrees with the belief or action (Mackie et al. 2001), and even when the predictor only has some stake in the issue, on either side (Allison et al. 1990; Worth et al. 1987). Overgeneralizations, however, are not unique to stereotype attribution but are a feature of associations more generally.

Despite the serious problem with attributing negative properties to individuals based on a prejudicial stereotype, a good deal of evidence suggests that our stereotypes are largely accurate and have pragmatic worth (Lee et al. 1995). Our stereotypes about gender (Diekman et al. 2002), nationality (Triandis and Vassiliou 1967), race (Ryan 1996), and other groups often turn out to be somewhat accurate when judged against relevant data or self-descriptions of the group by a member of the group. For example, in a study of stereotypes about men's and women's attitudes about political positions, Diekman and her colleagues (2002) found that people are fairly accurate in estimating the percentage of men and women who agree with policies that are either stereotypically female or male. Subjects were asked to estimate the percentage of men or women who support policies deemed to be female stereotypic (such as paid parental leave, affordable or public housing, and child care tax credits) and male stereotypic (such as government regulation of business, the man as the primary wage earner, the high rate of federal income tax). They found that while all subjects were generally accurate in estimating people's attitudes about such issues, they were slightly less accurate in estimating men's attitudes than women's attitudes.

In another study of stereotypic accuracy, researchers interested in the accuracy of ethnic stereotypes in Toronto asked subjects to estimate the academic performance of nine ethnic groups (Aboriginal, British, Canadian-born black, Caribbean-born black, Chinese, East Indian–Pakistani, Jewish, Portuguese, and Vietnamese) (Ashton and Esses 1999). Subjects were accurate in their judgments of the relative academic performance between the different groups, given data published by the Toronto Board of Education. That is, subjects were able to correctly rank the ethnic groups according to their academic performance. However, some estimates of average grade differed significantly from the actual average grade for three ethnic groups. This study suggests that though some accurate information can be had from stereotypes, specific claims about a group are more likely to be false compared to relative claims about groups.

One view about the accuracy of stereotypes is that most stereotypic attributions contain a kernel of truth (Campbell 1967). That is, our stereotypes are an exaggeration of the frequency of a property in a group, but the traits are accurately applied to some members. However, this cannot be a general truth about stereotypes, because many stereotypes *underestimate* group differences (McCauley 1995).

Given the association between stereotypes and prejudice, the accuracy of stereotypes has been more of a vexed issue than is accuracy in the other methods of prediction. As a result, there has been much debate on what is meant by accuracy in stereotype use. For the purpose of predicting behavior, the accuracy standard is clear. If stereotypes allow us to make accurate predictions of behavior, that will suffice.

Decades of social psychology suggest that human reasoning is rife with bias that leads to irrational thinking, but some have wondered whether these gloomy findings reflect a laboratory artifact. After all, if we were so terrible at making judgments, we should notice it at least some of the time. And we might think that the species would be in some danger. But that doesn't appear to be the case. William Swann (1984) has argued that we ought not judge accuracy about person perception in the same way we judge accuracy about the physical world. Rather, Swann suggests that personality is a negotiation between individuals in a social context, and perceiving is in some sense creating. Given this understanding of persons not as fixed entities but as malleable and context dependent, we can identify success in person perception as the promotion of shared goals. Swann's pragmatic-accuracy view takes as a goal circumscribed accuracy, or accuracy in particular situations, rather than global accuracy across situations.

Stereotypes are a necessary simplification that allows us to make inferences about others, and they interact with other information we have about people when predicting behavior. They enrich our understanding of others by allowing us to place individuals into a rich network of traits, goals, and behaviors. Seeing someone in such networks may be only a starting point, an implicit acceptance of a hypothesis that can be modified as we gain more information about people. But some stereotypic judgments are stronger than others and require more information to overturn. So while stereotypes are a useful means of predicting behavior and can provide accurate information, when it comes to false stereotypes related to groups that are the object of discrimination, judgments need to be revised.

A final word on stereotype attribution. While we have been focusing on the predictive force of stereotypes, some stereotypes also have normative force. The waiter who doesn't take our order is not just acting against the waiter stereotype; he also is not doing what he ought to be doing. Girls may be criticized for not acting feminine enough, and inner-city youths who talk with a newscaster's accent may be criticized for not being black enough. Gender stereotypes are a good example of prescriptive stereotypes, and evidence suggests that people are more inclined to think that females should be more nurturing than males and that blacks should be more athletic than whites (Burgess and Bordiga 1999; Eagly 1987; Fiske and Stevens 1993). At least some stereotypes not only are descriptions but include normative platitudes about what people ought to do.

Predicting from Traits

Who is going to give the best wedding gift, the stingy aunt or the generous colleague? The trait terms that we use in our descriptions of people suggest a stable disposition that person has; paradigmatically, trait terms refer to established personality dispositions. For example, when we say that Fred is rude, we mean that something in Fred's personality makes him accurately described as a rude person. In contrast, we can also use trait terms to describe a particular behavior (e.g., "That was rude"), to describe a person at a particular time ("Why were you so rude to him?"), to describe habitual behaviors ("He always acts rudely to this waitress"), or to describe a person over time ("He has been rude") (Newman and Uleman 1993).

Personality traits are some of the most studied aspects of social psychology. The dispositions and internal attributes that are studied in social psychology are usually related back to personality traits. This is with good reason; we learned early on that traits are widely used by North Americans. We describe people primarily using trait terms (Fiske and Cox 1979; Hampson 1983; Park 1986), and we explain behaviors, especially other people's behavior, by referring to their personality traits (Budesheim and Bonnelle 1998). Lee Ross and Richard Nisbett (1991) concur, claiming that we explain behavior in terms of traits by relying on a folk theory dubbed "lay dispositionalism." Though reliance on trait attribution is common among the Americans studied, it is less common among some American subpopulations such as Mexican Americans (Zárate et al. 2001) and among Asians (Cousins 1989; J. Miller 1984; Morris et al. 2001; Nisbett 2003). It has been suggested that collectivist cultures are less likely to use traits to describe or explain behavior than are individualist cultures, where personal action is emphasized (Nisbett 2003; Schneider 2004). However, when predicting behavior in cases where the situation is not salient, Koreans and Americans show no difference, both relying on internal traits (Norenzayan et al. 2002).

We can learn about an individual's traits by observing behavior and appearance, through stereotype categorization, and through personal communication with either the target or a third party. When traits are inferred from behavior, we can make inferences from extremely small amounts of behavioral evidence (Ambady et al. 2000). This result is accentuated when inferring negative personality traits (such as being selfish or rude). However, before attributing a positive personality trait, people require additional evidence (Rothbart and Park 1986). Inference from information about behavior to trait is seen as spontaneous—requiring attention but no conscious control (Uleman et al. 1996).

Regardless of how the information about one's trait is acquired, it is only indirectly perceived. That is, insofar as they are objective causal features of an individual, traits, like other mental states, are not directly observed. Traits, like beliefs and desires, are theoretical entities. In addition, insofar as traits are dispositions, traits are thought to be causally efficacious. That is, just as solubility can be seen to cause the sugar cube to dissolve in a glass of water, being rude is seen as the cause of rude behavior. Traits as causal properties are used to predict that an individual will perform some particular behavior in the kind of circumstances that activate the trait (Wright and Mischel 1987). Thus the relationship between traits and behaviors is like the relationship between beliefs and behaviors; in each case, the theoretical entity is thought to enter into a causal chain leading to the behavior.

Unlike beliefs, traits are taken to be stable properties of an individual. While I change my beliefs frequently, my personality traits are much more constant and can be changed with effort, training, or brain injury. Because traits are seen as stable and causally efficacious, we expect people to be consistent over time and across domains, and because of this, trait attribution is closely related to behavior prediction and leads us to make generalizations about related behaviors in other situations. Our inference from observing past behavior to a character trait (for example, from observing a colleague offering to chair a committee to inferring that the colleague is helpful) leads us to make predictions about that person's helpful behavior in other circumstances, as well (e.g., offering to take on extra household chores).

While traits make up some of the content of stereotypes, we saw in the last section that stereotypes are more specific than traits, and trait attributions are less rich and connected with fewer other properties. That is, while stereotype attributions allow us to make rather specific predictions about behavior, trait attributions may only allow for more general predictions.

Evidence suggests that predictions derive primarily from the traits that we attribute to others. When told that the target is introverted or extroverted, subjects tend to predict that the target will behave in the corresponding manner, regardless of the situation (Nisbett 1987). Once a target is seen as having a trait, people in the West expect that individuals will behave according to that trait, across situations (Nisbett 1987). We saw earlier that people tend to underestimate the effect of the situation on behavior. That bias is combined with what is thought to be an overreliance on personality traits as both causally efficacious and diagnostic of future behavior (Nisbett 1987; Nisbett and Ross 1980). When they are cognitively busy, people are especially likely to rely on trait attribution to such an extent that they ignore relevant situational factors (Newman 1996). Such studies suggest that people's prediction of behavior relies on a simple heuristic: they predict that a target will behave consistently with a trait attribution previously used to explain the target's behavior.

Prediction via trait attribution, and indeed the recognition of people as having traits that affect behavior, does not develop until middle childhood (Kalish 2002; P. Miller and Aloise 1989; Rholes et al. 1990; Wellman 1990; Yuill and Pearson 1998). Though predicting behavior based on exposure to a small set of exemplars about personal preferences and traits (e.g., preferring a yellow flower to a blue one, or being open to sharing) does not develop until after age five, younger children will use inductive generalizations to predict people's behavior when it appears not to be based on individual differences (Kalish 2002). For example, young children are good at making inductive generalizations about biological or physical properties of humans and other objects (Carey 1985; Gelman 1988), and at an early age they are able to accurately predict behaviors based on idiosyncratic physical attributes such as hearing acuity (Kalish 2002). But even once young children are able to use trait terms to describe an individual, they still fail to appeal to that trait descriptor when predicting that actor's future behavior (Rholes and Ruble 1984). By age ten, children are making inferences about the future based on past observations and will judge that a character who performed a nice action on one occasion is likely to behave nicely in a new situation (Cain et al. 1997; Heller and Berndt 1981; Heyman and Gelman 1999; Yuill and Pearson 1998).

Some psychologists see our reliance on traits to predict behavior as problematic, in the same way as prediction via stereotype. They worry that our reliance on traits is also an overestimation, but in this case, it is an overestimation of the causal efficacy of traits over the causal efficacy of the situation. Social psychologists have largely accepted that the environment plays a significant role in our action, as was famously demonstrated by Milgram's obedience experiments, where subjects were ordered to shock people at ever-increasing levels of voltage (Milgram 1963), and the Princeton Seminary experiment, which found that theology students' willingness to help someone in need was inversely correlated with how rushed they were (Darley and Batson 1973). These and other studies showed that small pressures in the environment could affect people's behaviors in ways they could not anticipate.

Though the situation has great influence on our behavior, this fact is often underappreciated by the folk when making predictions of behavior. Since Ichheiser's work in the 1940s, psychologists have noted that we commonly fail to adjust our predictions to take into account environmental constraints (Ichheiser 1949). Attributing traits to people causes us to be overly optimistic about people's consistency across situations and over time (L. Ross and Nisbett 1991). That is, once we have pegged someone with a particular trait, we use that information when making predictions about that person's behavior. However, cross-situational consistency of behavior is low. For example, an outgoing lecturer who eagerly engages with an audience of hundreds may be shy and awkward in a more intimate setting. And those who perform well in a job interview may be terrible at the front of a lecture hall, because behaviors are not consistent across situations (L. Ross 1977; L. Ross and Nisbett 1991).

Despite low cross-situational consistency of behavior and questions about the reality of personality traits, it seems that Westerners cannot help but attribute them. Predictions by trait attribution appear to be under little conscious control; even psychologists, who are well informed about the bias, fall prey to the fundamental attribution error in predicting behavior.

Trait attributions have been soundly criticized as a means of accurately predicting behavior across different kinds of situations. However, this does not mean we should deem prediction via trait attribution an unreliable method. As we saw with the other methods, overgeneralizations may occur, and relevant information may be ignored. Yet despite the recent focus in social psychology on the problems associated with trait attribution, no one is clamoring for us to stop using traits in this fashion. Even among those who have directed attention to the fundamental attribution error, it is argued that trait attribution is a useful heuristic. For example, if we use a trait to make a prediction in the same situation in which the trait was discovered, our prediction is likely to be fairly accurate. Traits don't turn out to work globally, across situations, but they do work for making predictions within a particular situation.

Though we can predict with some accuracy what others will do in a situation after having observed their behavior in that same situation, we have more difficulty predicting with any accuracy what people will do in other situations, given these sorts of errors in reasoning. Why, then, do we think that we are such good predictors of behavior?

Social psychologists have an answer to this question, as well. An expectation can cause us to interpret behavior so that it is consistent with that very expectation. Hence we think we are more accurate than we really are (Olson et al. 1996). In addition, we tend to notice things that correspond to our beliefs and expectations, and especially to remember successful predictions (Kunda 2002). Thus, although we may be poor predictors of behavior in some situations, it is possible that we will not notice this, because either we interpret the situation so that it corresponds to our expectation, or we forget about making the faulty prediction.

Another explanation comes from Ross and Nisbett (1991), who argue that our predictions are largely accurate because most of our predictions are made in the same situation, broadly construed. For example, if you form a trait description of Sue in the workplace, and you interact with Sue only in the workplace, your prediction is likely to be largely accurate. This is because traits are stable within situations. It is only when you attempt to generalize to another situation, such as how Sue would be as a road-trip companion, that your prediction is likely to fail you. Ross and Nisbett note, however, that the predictor is often part of the situation she predicts, and what may appear to be stability across situations may in fact only be the stability of the person's behavior in your presence. For these reasons, many of our predictions of behavior are correct.

Other Factors Involved in Predicting Behavior

So far I have briefly reviewed four different methods that social psychologists think are implicated in our behavior predictions. These are not the only variables that play a role in the predictions we generate. One of the simplest ways we predict a person's future behavior is to generalize from that person's past behavior in a similar situation. We can easily predict idiosyncratic behavior if we know that an individual habitually engages in the idiosyncratic act. Inductive generalization based on an individual's past behavior may be overt, like the waiter's prediction that a regular customer will order a tall soy latte. Or it may be less overt, such as the ability to recognize when someone is being deceptive. While we are not very good at determining whether a stranger is deceiving us, as we get to know a person, our ability to recognize deception increases; we are much more accurate in judging the honesty of a close friend's behavior than we are a stranger's. It is thought that the reason for this effect is that people, like some poker players, often have a telltale behavior that indicates they are being deceptive. Through exposure we come to associate the distinctive behavior with an act of deception, and then we can use that behavior to predict future acts of deception (Anderson et al. 2002). If you have evidence about a person's past behavior in a similar situation, simply inferring that the person will do the same thing again is an extremely reliable method (Krueger and Clement 1996). Perhaps for this reason, we are much better at judging the frequency of attitudes and traits of people we know than those of people we do not (Judd et al. 1991), and better at predicting familiar people and people from familiar groups than we are in predicting people who are not familiar to us (Kunda 2002).

This technique may be among the most cognitively simple strategies used to predict behavior. Indeed, some take this position when they argue that a theory of behavior is simpler than a theory of mind. As we will see in chapter 12, some ape researchers claim that experiments attempting to show that chimpanzees have a theory of mind can be explained equally as well by the simpler theory that apes have a theory of behavior (e.g., Povinelli and Vonk 2004).

We do know that human infants are great statisticians and are able to make generalizations from an early age. Even eight-month-old infants can make generalizations about a member of a population after being exposed to the population, and conversely can make inferences about a population from exposure to a sample of that population (Xu and Garcia 2008). It is not too far of a reach to suppose that they use this ability to make predictions within the social realm as well as the physical. By three years, children possess script-based knowledge and can make predictions based on what they know happens in situations such as a birthday party (Hudson et al. 1995).

We also predict that people will follow certain societal norms. For example, people walk facing forward, those who call meetings tend to show up, and people do what they say they are going to do. I can use the "people do what they say they will do" heuristic to predict that you will arrive today on the 3 o'clock flight, because you said you would arrive on the 3 o'clock flight.

Such methods of prediction, whether they are generalizations about an individual, a group, a theory of behavior, or a theory of appropriate behavior, are all rather uninformative when it comes to the cause of behavior. No theoretical entities with causal efficacy are postulated to make predictions given these methods; nothing is inferred that could later be used to explain the behavior. Such predictions are like our lay predictions of occurrences in the physical world. I predict that my car will start when I turn the key, not because I understand the mechanical structure of the car but because my car has always started when I turn the key.

Interactions between all the methods mentioned in this chapter, and between these methods and affective states, will also affect the predictions that we generate. Just as mood affects our behaviors in ways we do not expect (like making us more likely to help a stranger in need), so mood also affects the predictions that we make. For example, when people are in a good mood, they are more likely to categorize a person as a member of some group, even if that person is on the borderline for group membership (Isen and Daubman 1984; Isen et al. 1992), and hence would be more likely to make a prediction that draws from the group stereotype. We tend to predict behavior consistent with the affective state we are in at the time of prediction, so that we often make incorrect predictions when in a hot affective state and predicting the behavior of a person who is not in such a state, or when we are cold and trying to predict what we or others would do in a hot state (Loewenstein 1996). Errors like this often lead us to have false expectations about our future hedonic states and cause us to make bad decisions about the paths that will make us happiest (T. Wilson and Gilbert 2005).

Given the number of factors that are involved in predicting behavior, the various relationships between these factors, and the threat of confounding variables, any detailed model of how humans predict behavior would be impossibly complex. It would have to take into account how well the predictor knew the target, whether the target was an in-group or out-group member, the stereotypes the target fit into, the situation the target was in, and so forth. The processes involved in making predictions are dynamically interrelated, and while work in social psychology is able to illuminate some of the salient features involved in making predictions, and has offered general theories about how we make predictions, no general working model for behavior prediction has been offered. The same is true of philosophers working from within the debate between theory theory and simulation theory. None of the mindreading models on the table even approach the degree of complexity we see involved in the folk psychological practice of prediction.

If we are to learn more about the ways that humans predict behaviors, we first need to accept that we may use different methods for different instances of prediction. Psychological research can tell us where we succeed at making predictions, and where we fail. It can also enlighten us as to how we go about making different kinds of predictions. Plausibly, I do not use belief-desire psychology when I predict that the waiter will bring the coffee I ordered, and plausibly I do use it when I am trying to figure out where my foe will strike next in a complex game of cat and mouse. Just as plausibly, my predictions of the waiter's behavior will be more accurate than my predictions of the foe's. Whereas the waiter is following a familiar script, the foe is doing his best to avoid predictability, which will lead to complex and perhaps recursive lines of thought in an attempt to predict his behavior.

It is also likely that we use a number of methods to predict behavior in a single case, as is demonstrated in the following dialogue from William Goldman's novel *The Princess Bride*. Vizzini has accepted a challenge to partake in a game of wits. He is to determine which glass of wine contains the poison iocane, the glass in front of him or the one in front of his foe. Vizzini begins by saying:

"It's all so simple . . . All I have to do is deduce, from what I know of you, the way your mind works. Are you the kind of man who would put the poison into his own glass, or into the glass of his enemy? . . . Now a great fool would place the poison in his own goblet, because he would know that only another great fool would reach first for what he was given. I am clearly not a great fool, so I will clearly not reach for your wine."

"That's your final choice?"

"No. Because you knew I was not a great fool, so you would know that I would never fall for such a trick. You would count on it. So I will clearly not reach for mine either. . . . We have now decided the poisoned cup is most likely in front of you. But the poison is powder made from iocane and iocane comes from Australia and Australia, as everyone knows, is peopled with criminals and criminals are used to having people not trust them, as I don't trust you, which means I can clearly not choose the wine in front of you. . . . But, again, you must have suspected I knew the origins of iocane, so you would have known I knew about the criminals and criminal behavior, and therefore I can clearly not choose the wine in front of me. . . ."

"Truly you have a dizzying intellect," whispered the man in black.

"You have beaten my Turk, which means you are exceptionally strong, and exceptionally strong men are convinced they are too powerful ever to die, too powerful even for iocane poison, so you could have put it in your cup, trusting on your strength to save you; thus I can clearly not choose the wine in front of you." (W. Goldman 2007, 176–178)

First note that though Vizzini clearly uses folk psychology, he is not clearly engaged in an act of prediction. He is trying to figure something out, but he is not seeking an explanation. We might say that he is retrodicting—making a prediction about something that happened in the past—which demonstrates another role for folk psychology. Whatever we want to call it, we can analyze the passage as a piece of folk psychological reasoning. Despite Vizzini's use of belief attribution (B knows V is not a great fool), trait attribution (B is used to not being trusted, B is clever, B is strong), information about the situation (B acquired the poison from Australia, Australia is full of criminals), stereotypes (criminals are used to not being trusted, strong people think they will never die), and inductive generalization (B bested the Turk, so he will come out ahead in other tests of strength), Vizzini guesses wrongly and falls to the ground dead.

To avoid an analogous fate, philosophers who hope to build theories on top of descriptive claims regarding how humans predict behavior are well advised to recognize the complexity of behavior prediction. Social psychology has given us a start in cataloging the different methods we use to predict behavior. In constructing our models of folk psychological mechanisms, philosophers need to take seriously what is already known. Vague as that knowledge may be, it suggests a radically different perspective from the one taught in philosophy classes today.

6 The Role of Propositional Attitudes in Behavior Prediction

Prediction is very difficult, especially if it's about the future.
—Niels Bohr

Predicting Behavior and Mental Content

I invite you to dinner, and you tell me that you will bring a bottle of wine. Later, when I am doing my wine shopping, I take into account the fact that you will bring a bottle of wine. I have made a prediction that you will bring a bottle of wine, a quotidian prediction that you will do what you said you would do. I may even be able to predict to some extent what kind of wine you will bring. If I told you that I am preparing steak for dinner, I might without reflection expect that you will bring a bottle of red wine.

How do I make this prediction? The standard folk psychology answer is that I mindread; I implicitly attribute beliefs and desires to you, activate some mechanism, and output the prediction. But if I did engage in such an operation, I would also have access to a theory about your reasons for acting—your reason explanation. That is, not only would I predict what you would do, but I would have some knowledge of why you did it.

In chapter 3 I argued that we cannot explain all the behaviors we can predict. The research from social psychology discussed in the previous chapter bolsters that conclusion. To predict that you will bring a bottle of red wine to dinner, I could be relying on my knowledge of your habits, and I need not know anything about your wine beliefs. If I know that you are a traditional wine drinker, who chooses red for beef and white for fish, then this prediction is easy to make. Maybe the correct explanation for your behavior is that you believe drinking red wine with beef is socially required, or perhaps you believe that the fruit and tannins of a robust red accentuate the taste of the meat. Perhaps you want to have a fine aesthetic experience, so you buy the Borolo, or maybe instead you buy it with the desire to impress me with your good taste and financial success. I can predict what you will do, if I know your habits, but I may not have a good understanding of why you buy a certain bottle of wine. I could generate any number of possible explanations for your behavior, even if I were able to predict that behavior with great success.

Sometimes we predict behavior by considering the beliefs and desires of a target. But sometimes we do not. The advocates of SFP claim that our wide-ranging success in predicting behavior is based on our ability to attribute beliefs and desires. Given the availability of multiple methods for predicting behavior, should we finally reject this claim? Before drawing that conclusion, let us consider two rejoinders that SFP supporters could give in the face of evidence that we routinely rely on methods other than belief-desire attribution for predicting behavior.

The first criticism of the claim that we can predict someone's behavior without attributing beliefs or desires is based on the idea that the methods of prediction identified in the previous chapter all require having some knowledge of mental content. For example, personality traits might be associated not only with behaviors but also with intentions, beliefs, desires, and other internal contentful states. This is a view that some psychologists advocate (Schneider 2004). If this view were right, then a trait attribution would be shorthand for the attribution of some set of beliefs, desires, and so forth; and if that were true, then anyone who was able to predict in terms of trait attributions would also have facility with belief attribution. If trait attribution is simply shorthand for belief or desire attribution, then our ability to predict behavior by attributing personality traits relies on a prior ability to attribute beliefs and desires. Once again, the attribution of propositional attitudes would play a foundational role.

Another worry about the view I am defending is that prediction via the attribution of beliefs and desires may be more accurate than prediction using other methods. The response might begin thus: Of course we use different methods to predict behavior, and some heuristics work well enough. But once humans began making predictions through the attribution of mental states, predictions became more accurate, and those who were able to make such predictions were better able to manipulate and control others. The development of a theory of mind started an evolutionary arms race that forced most humans also to develop a theory of mind to become viable competitors. Thus, while we have other methods for making rather inaccurate predictions of behavior, humans are amazing in their ability to accurately predict what others are going to do, and such successes in predicting can only be accounted for by mindreading. The critic may worry that the alternative methods of prediction I presented are not true alternatives, because they do not permit successful predictions in the way attributing mental content does.

Does Trait Attribution Require Attribution of Mental Content?

Of all the methods of prediction discussed in the previous chapter, prediction based on trait attribution appears the most likely to be based on the attribution of mental states. Indeed, one might expect that a trait attribution is merely shorthand for mental content. If so, then belief-desire psychology can be made consistent with the social psychological story, such that when I appeal to Sue's generous nature to predict that she will contribute to hunger relief, I simply mean that Sue wants to help others and believes that she can fulfill that desire by contributing to hunger relief. Understanding traits in this fashion reconciles at least part of the social psychological picture with the traditional philosophical one, and thus the evidence from social psychology about trait attribution would not undermine the claim that we predict behavior through the attribution of beliefs and desires. The apparent conflict may be seen as arising from the different terminology used in the different disciplines.

However, we have good reason to think that trait attribution is a practice distinct from the attribution of beliefs and desires. People can categorize an individual as personifying a trait and use that categorization to treat the individual differently, even when they have an impaired ability to attribute beliefs and desires.

For example, children on the autistic spectrum who are unable to attribute mental states can come to learn how to predict behavior by attributing personality traits. Social Stories Therapy is an intervention method designed to teach social skills to children with autism (Gray 2000). Therapists teach children how to recognize a salient behavior, apply a character trait or mood term to it, and then associate other behaviors with that label. After successful therapy, the child is able to make predictions using the trait identifier, but she does not gain a theory of mind or an understanding of beliefs and desires as parts of a folk theory of behavior. For example, a person with autism might be taught to associate a smile with the term *happy*, and the term *happy* with a number of specific behaviors (e.g., hugging, laughing, etc.). The child with autism can be taught to describe a smiling person as happy and, given that trait, can predict that the person will engage in happy behaviors. Although one might be inclined to describe the autistic child's new knowledge as a theory, it is a theory of behavior, not a theory of mental states.

Not only do some children with autism use traits to predict behavior, but some animals may use this method, as well. Growing evidence shows that animals, like humans, have personalities. Individual differences that take the form of personality traits have been identified in a number of different species, including orangutans, chimpanzees, cats, dogs, even octopuses and guppies (Gosling and John 1999). Animal behavior researchers who study personality, temperament, or behavioral style look for individual differences in behavior that persevere across time and through a variety of situations. Individuals are assessed either by measuring their responses to sets of stimuli designed to elicit exploratory or avoidance behavior (Wilson et al. 1993; Verbeek et al. 1994) or by the ratings of researchers or caregivers who have worked with the animals over time and have observed or interacted with the individuals in social settings (Gosling and John 1999; Capitanio 2004; Weinstein et al. 2008).

While humans can use these personality trait assessments to make predictions of an individual's future behavior, we do not know whether animals use trait categorization to anticipate what others will do. Future research will have to address that question. However, we have suggestive evidence that they might; we know that acquisition of certain traits affects the quality of relationships in other species. For example, rhesus monkeys tend to form friendships with others who share the same temperament (Weinstein and Capitanio 2008).

If we can investigate the possibility that nonhuman animals who lack a theory of mind use personality ascriptions to make predictions, then we have already admitted a conceptual distinction between understanding beliefs and desires, on the one hand, and understanding personality traits, on the other. The conceptual distinction alone shows that without evidence to the contrary, one should not expect that trait attribution is somehow derivative of belief-desire attribution.

Just as nonhuman animals and some people who lack a theory of mind may use traits to form expectations of behavior, so typical adults can, as well. Rather than referring to mental states, a trait attribution could refer to a class of behaviors, which would allow a person with autism to predict behavior without appealing to mental states. Though the average adult human understands that others have mental states, and these mental states may explain a person's behavior, typical adults could also use trait attribution to predict action without appeal to the attitudes. If there is a normal folk theory of behavior, it involves connecting specific traits with other traits and with behaviors. Some evidence supports this view, since the data suggest that humans understand which sets of traits are consistent, and which are not, and such models are used when we predict what someone with certain traits will do (see Ross and Nisbett 1991 for a review). I take these considerations as reason to think that without good evidence to the contrary, we should not consider trait attribution to be shorthand for attribution of belief in any nondispositional account of belief.

However, one might object that predicting behavior requires seeing the movement of an individual as behavior, and this requires understanding another's beliefs, desires, and intentions. That is, to understand others involves attributing mental contents. This is part of the Gricean picture of communication, certainly, and is also part of Davidson's account of interpretation (Grice 1969; Davidson 1973). The idea goes like this: For me to understand what another is saying, I must attribute propositions to the speaker, because true communication requires that the audience recognize that the utterer has a particular mental state. To predict from my student's utterance that he will make up the exam at 3 p.m., I have to decode the meaning of the acoustic blasts emanating from the student, and I must believe that my student believes that he will be in my office at 3 p.m., ready to take the exam. Thus one cannot use a simple heuristic like "people generally do what they say they are going to do" without attributing a belief to the utterer.

While it may be true that communication between two people involves the recognition that the other is an intentional agent, it does not follow that for each particular utterance made, the audience must consider the mental content associated with that particular utterance. Here again we can turn to the example of young children. Before they are three years old, children do not use false-belief contrastives in conversation (Bartsch and Wellman 1995), nor are they passing the false-belief task (Wellman et al. 2001) or demonstrating understanding of the opacity of propositional attitudes (Apperly and Robinson 2003; Hulme et al. 2003). These young children do not understand much about representational belief. Yet children do appear to understand very well what others mean by their utterances at this age, and are able to treat others as intentional agents. All the data reviewed in chapter 2 suggest that even very young children recognize that others are minded, intentional agents, but this knowledge is not dependent on the ability to attribute representational belief.

Without explicitly acknowledging that another has beliefs with specified content, a child can use the "people generally do what they say they are going to do" heuristic to predict that father will chase her when he says, "I'm going to chase you!" The child need only know that she can usefully apply the heuristic to the utterer. To make largely accurate predictions, the child must realize that her father, unlike the tape recorder that emits the same sounds, is an intentional agent. However, in this model, the child doesn't need to attribute to him a particular belief associated with his utterance. She doesn't do that because she can't, not until she gains a more robust understanding of belief. Yet she is still able to make the prediction.

Predicting behavior comes in many varieties, but not all methods of prediction require attributing mental content. Very young children, even infants, form expectations of behavior, as do nonhuman animals, and they use these expectations in their relations with others. Long before humans are able to attribute a personality trait, we predict behavior based on the "primary intersubjectivity" we see in infants when they imitate, engage in joint attention and triadic interactions, respond emotionally to facial expressions and speech prosody, and so on (Trevarthen 1979). We share this method of predicting behavior with other apes such as chimpanzees, insofar as both human and chimpanzee infants follow the same pattern of social development in the first few months of life. For example, neonatal smiling and imitation occur during the first two months of life in both chimpanzee and human infants. These behaviors disappear around the same time in both species, to be replaced with social smiling and mutual gaze at three months (Matsuzawa 2006).

As young children, we can also make predictions through the attribution of mental states that are nonpropositional, such as emotions, intentions, and perceptions. Young children and chimpanzees are also sensitive to these mental states at an early age. For example, a study by Felix Warneken and Michael Tomasello (2006) established that chimpanzees engage in helping behaviors in response to a human caregiver's nonverbal request for an out-of-reach object, as do eighteen-month-old children. Though the children demonstrated a greater degree of helping behavior across task types than did the chimpanzees, the chimpanzees did seem to recognize the caregiver's goal in some of the situations. Without a full-blown understanding of representational belief, both children and chimpanzees were able to predict that the caregiver would be satisfied once he received the requested object.

Like children, nonhuman animals are skilled at predicting behaviors of their conspecifics, predators, and prey, though it is doubtful that most other species understand representational belief. Given that young children and nonhuman animals are able to predict behaviors without considering the content of another's belief, it follows that being capable of attributing both a belief and a desire is not necessary for predicting some behavior.

How Accurate Is Standard Folk Psychology?

We are most likely to make accurate predictions of behavior when making general predictions in familiar situations or when making more specific predictions of people with whom we are familiar. I can predict that my husband will open a beer when he gets home from work today, but I hesitate to predict whether any of his colleagues will. If I have to guess, my predictions might rest on stereotypes (gender, age, nationality), reliance on base rates (the percentage of philosophy professors who engage in daily beer drinking), or generalizing from self (how likely am I to crack open a beer at the end of the day?). Or I might make the prediction by mindreading—attributing to the colleague the belief that beer is a good way to relax after a long day of teaching, the belief that he or she did a lot of teaching today, the desire to relax, and so on. The question we have to consider here is which of these methods would lead to better predictions. Or since it is difficult to individuate the methods, we can rephrase the question: is a prediction that takes into account an actor's beliefs and desires more or less likely to be accurate than one that does not take mental content into account?

Let me point out some difficulties with giving a general answer to this question. For one, it assumes that all predictions are the same, whether I am predicting my husband's behavior or that of his colleagues. And we know that different levels of accuracy are associated with predicting different people, depending on how well we know them, how well they fit into a stereotype, how consistent their behavior is, and so forth. Despite this worry, we can make a few general observations about the accuracy of these methods.

Traditional folk psychology is praised for making accurate predictions of behavior: the predictive skills humans have are thought to be amazing, we are generally correct in our predictions, and so on. On the other hand, social psychologists are gloomy in their portrayal of human predictive abilities. We operate under biases that lead to all manner of incorrect predictions, from expecting others to act like us to misidentifying an object in a black man's hand. Perhaps the attitudes of the philosophers reflect the relatively high accuracy of the folk psychological method, compared to the methods that come out of the social psychology research. Perhaps we should conclude that predicting through trait attribution is a less accurate method than predicting through appeal to beliefs and desires. However, given other findings in social psychology, this conclusion would be hasty.

Predicting from trait attribution is not as problematic as the foregoing discussion suggests. We have a number of reasons to think that the discoveries of social psychology do not have much of an impact on actual social reasoning. For example, when making predictions about an individual based on a trait we have learned to associate with that person, chances are we are making the prediction in the same situation in which the trait was generated to begin with. Since the worry about trait attribution as a means for predicting behavior is that traits are not stable across situations, when predicting in the same situation, we avoid the concern altogether. For example, if you form a trait description of Purwo in the workplace, and you interact with Purwo only in the workplace, your prediction will likely be largely accurate, since traits are stable within situations. Only when you attempt to generalize to another situation, such as how Purwo would be as a road-trip companion, is your prediction likely to fail. In their discussion of the fundamental attribution error, Ross and Nisbett (1991) point out that the bias does not cause a wholesale failure in our predictive abilities, since we make most of our predictions in the same situation, broadly construed. They also suggest that the predictor is often part of the situation she predicts, and what may appear to be stability across situations may in fact only be the stability of the person's behavior in the predictor's presence. For these reasons, many of our predictions of behavior are correct.

In addition, we have reason to challenge the prima facie claim that prediction via the attribution of beliefs and desires is more accurate than other methods given the biases that are activated in making such predictions. In describing the intentional-stance account of prediction, Dennett observes that the intentional stance "is notoriously unable to predict the exact purchase and sell decisions of stock traders, for instance, or the exact sequence of words a politician will utter when making a scheduled speech, but one's confidence can be very high indeed about slightly less specific predictions: that the particular trader *will not buy utilities today*, or that the politician *will side with the unions against his party*, for example" (Dennett 1987b, 24). Another way of understanding this limitation is to see that the beliefs and desires associated with an action are underdetermined. The prediction that the stockbroker will not buy utilities today is consistent with any number of reasons that the stockbroker might have had: don't buy utilities when they are trading above a certain amount, don't buy utilities from today's seller, don't buy utilities when bonds are low, and so on. And because the actor's reason is often opaque to us, we cannot make the more specific predictions that Dennett refers to.

Given the underdetermination of the reasons by behavior, when making a prediction, we would ideally generate all the plausible reasons the actor might have for acting, determine which among them are most plausible, and generate the prediction from that set. However, the need to generate belief-desire hypotheses raises a problem for predicting behavior via mindreading. When considering a person's beliefs and desires, we sometimes actually decrease the accuracy of our predictions, because prediction via belief-desire attribution involves considering the reasons our target has for behaving in a certain way, and studies suggest that by considering someone's reasons for action, we come to see the action as more likely (T. Wilson and LaFleur 1995). For example, when college students were asked to predict whether they would act in a friendly or unfriendly way toward another student, Wilson and LaFleur found that participants who were asked to consider their reasons for acting subsequently judged their prediction as more likely than did a control group who were not asked to consider their reasons. Wilson and LaFleur also measured the participants' actual behavior and found that the experimental group made less accurate predictions.

This effect is explained as an example of a confirmation bias. In general, when we examine whether a theory is correct, we use a positive test strategy and attend to the information that makes the hypothesis seem more likely. Thus, in developing a theory, we are likely to accept the first plausible explanation and act on that.

When predicting behavior based on a belief-desire set that is consistent with the situation, we should be expected to make the same error. Because many different belief-desire sets are consistent with any one situation, and belief-desire sets are paradigmatic reasons for others' behavior, these findings suggest that we would likely fixate on the *first* belief-desire set we generate, rather than the *best* belief-desire set available. Any subsequent predictions we make will then be biased because of this.

In addition, cognitive biases may also cause fans of folk psychology to overestimate the extent to which people make accurate predictions. While it might seem as though our powers of prediction are amazing, this seeming might not be accurate. Other research in social psychology has shown that human reasoning is flawed when it comes to making these kinds of judgments. For example, after forming an expectation about how a target will behave, the subsequent behavior is then interpreted to conform to the expectation. This is one possible reason that humans think they are more accurate predictors than they really are (Olson et al. 1996). In addition, since humans suffer from a confirmation bias such that we tend to notice things that correspond to our beliefs and expectations, and we have selective memories, it is more likely that humans will notice and remember instances of successful predictions rather than failures. Thus, although we may be poor predictors of behavior in some situations, it is possible that we don't recognize the failure either because we interpret the situation so that it corresponds to our expectation or because we forget about making the faulty prediction. These concerns challenge the prima facie evidence that belief attribution is a successful method of predicting behavior.

Social psychologists do not typically distinguish between trait attribution and belief or desire attribution; the distinction they have found most salient has been the distinction between the person and the situation. Thus when Heider discusses predicting in terms of internal dispositions, he includes traits, emotions and moods, and beliefs and desires among the internal features. For Heider, all these methods of prediction involve a kind of naive factor analysis (Heider 1958). Appealing to theoretical entities, whether dispositional or contentful, is a heuristic that simplifies the data processing, taking a huge number of behaviors and categorizing them into fewer groups.

Evidence suggests that internal attributions are biased, whether they are attributions from traits or from beliefs and desires. Both methods are subject to the fundamental attribution error. Even if our predictions using these methods often result in false predictions, perhaps this is not a real object of concern. Accuracy might not be the central goal for predicting behavior.

Gilbert and Malone (1995) offer three reasons why people might make dispositional inferences although the mental attributions are not accurate. First, such attributions are quick and easy heuristics that are sometimes accurate. Second, even when they are false, they sometimes generate correct predictions, as when the situation that causes the behavior is an effect of the person's internal states. Third, mental-state attributions give observers a sense of control over the actor and the situation as a whole, and while this sense of control may be illusory, it might have greater psychological benefits than a more realistic feeling of powerlessness.

What Place Is There for Traditional Folk Psychological Prediction?

While mental-state attribution might not be generally more accurate than other methods of predicting behavior, it may be that some predictions can be made only by using this method. Can a detective use the Sherlock Holmes method without getting into the mind of the criminal? Can you be a really successful used-car salesman without understanding what your clients want and believe? Can you be a good teacher? Probably not. Traditional folk psychological prediction certainly has a place in our world. That place just may be rather smaller than the place it has traditionally been given in philosophy (and it may be smaller than the place given it by detectives, salespeople, and teachers who may mindread more often than others). Before ending the discussion of prediction, I want to run a thought experiment with you.

Consider a world full of our Rylean ancestors, who have not yet gained from the insight of Sellars's Jones. Recall that this is a world where no one thinks about other people's mental content. The question I want to pose is: what predictive advantage do we gain by coming to see others as being moved by their beliefs and desires?

Two of the benefits of attributing beliefs and desires are said to be engaging in deceptive behaviors and predicting people's actions when they have a false belief. However, both could have developed without an understanding of the notions of belief or desire, so long as the individual was a skilled observer of patterns of behavior. Our ancestors could have engaged in the very behaviors that have been touted as evolutionarily advantageous, such as hiding food or having forbidden sex, without attributing mental states to one another. For example, an ancestor may have come to notice that every time he found food, he made a certain sound, and when he made that sound, everyone else came and took away some of the food. He may have wondered what made everyone come running when he found food, and perhaps he experimented with different aspects of his food-finding behavior. One variable he tested was the food-discovery cry. Once he noticed that people came when he uttered the cry, he learned not to utter the cry when he wanted to keep the food for himself. We describe this behavior as deceptive, and coming up with this trick would surely have been an advantage for our ancestor, as it represents a cognitive step toward scientific reasoning and would offer him a benefit when living in a large social group. However, it does not require the attribution, or even the concepts, of belief or desire. Note the similarity between the analysis of behavior here and the killjoy explanations of animal behavior. The similarity is intentional; the methods that are used to explain away nonhuman animal psychological reasoning can be used to explain away much human psychological reasoning, as well. But just as the existence of killjoy explanations for animal behavior does not argue against the possibility that animals attribute beliefs in some contexts, so we should not take my example as arguing that we never need to attribute beliefs. Of course, we will need to appeal to mental states in situations that are about mental states to begin with (e.g., when one wants to determine how to stop another from feeling angry about some injustice), but those situations would not have arisen among our prementalistic ancestors.

False-belief predictions, on the other hand, can be made through a more straightforward inductive generalization about past behavior. Take the child's prediction in the false-belief task. While the child may think about the puppet's belief that the chocolate is in the cupboard, she could also predict that the puppet will go to the cupboard to find her chocolate because people seek out objects in the same place they left them. Our pre-folk-psychological ancestors could make these kinds of predictions, even without the folk psychological concept of belief. Our ancestors might have known that when people say "chocolate," they walk over to where they left their chocolate, even if the chocolate has been moved while they were away. It does not require an extremely clever observer to make a prediction like this, even without the concept of belief, so long as she has been exposed to similar behaviors in the past and does not have any cognitive deficits that would keep her from noticing, recalling, or generalizing from the behaviors. So long as she has some prior experience with behavioral invariants that she can use to make predictions regarding future behavior, appeal to mental states is not necessary.

When, then, must we use the attribution of beliefs and desires to make a prediction of behavior? Rather than deceptive or false-belief cases per se, the primary condition under which our Rylean ancestors would need the ability to see others' mental states to predict behavior is in an anomalous situation. A situation in which one has no past experience, or in which a person's behavior was unexpected or unusual, will not be open to generalizations from self, stereotypes, past behavior, or relevant traits. This sort of situation would not even be understood by the predictor, so he could not even ask himself what he would do in such a situation. To take advantage of the new information that we get when someone engages in anomalous behavior, our ancestor would first seek to understand the behavior. To do that, she may have had to consider the target's beliefs and desires.

To predict behavior in an anomalous situation, we must seek to understand the situation. That is, we must develop a construal of the situation, which means that we need to explain the behavior. While observers more often explain behavior by appealing to the causal history of the individual, and actors more often explain their own behavior by appeal to beliefs and desires, in some conditions observers do explain others' behavior through belief-desire attribution (Malle 2004; Malle et al. 2007). Malle has found that observers will attribute beliefs and desires to actors when they are motivated to portray the behavior in a positive light. I suggest that when a group member acts in an anomalous manner, others in that group will be motivated to portray that behavior in a positive light, and hence the sorts of explanations that will be generated will tend to be reason explanations in terms of propositional attitudes.

However, given the underdetermination of propositional attitudes by behavior, these explanations may not be accurate. But to understand the state of affairs involves asking for an explanation of what led up to the current situation, and this leads us to generate the beliefs and desires that the actor might have. After having developed a plausible explanation that cites an actor's beliefs and desires, we can use that attribution to make a prediction. In an anomalous situation, a prediction of future action will only come after an explanation for the agent's past behavior. Thus predicting behavior based on the attribution of beliefs and desires relies on a prior ability to explain—or at least construe—behavior as being caused by beliefs and desires. This suggests that before our ancestors began explaining behavior, they had no ability to attribute propositional attitudes. Developmental evidence supports this contention; children tend to begin asking why-questions around thirty-five months, which is six to twelve months before they pass the false-belief task (L. Bloom et al. 1982). Rationalizations are paradigmatic uses of the propositional attitudes. I develop this point in chapter 11, where I present an alternative evolutionary account of the development of our ability to attribute propositional attitudes.

Predicting Behavior without Attributing Propositional Attitudes

We saw that the accurate prediction of intentional action does not typically require the attribution of beliefs and desires, and the traditional emphasis that philosophers have placed on the necessity of understanding mental content for predicting behavior does not hold up. Thus, as far as prediction is concerned, we have reason to reject the SFP claim that folk psychology is the attribution of propositional attitudes.

Further, we saw that predicting behavior through the attribution of mental states derives from explaining behavior. This means that to understand the attribution of propositional attitudes, we must examine the role that beliefs and desires play in the explanation of behavior.

In the next three chapters, I turn to examining the role of propositional attitude attributions in terms of explaining behavior. While philosophers of mind have emphasized the role of propositional attitude ascription in prediction, I show that it is more important to our explanations of behavior. Belief and desire attribution does take a central place when it comes to our practice of explaining behavior.

III Explanation

7 What Is Folk Psychological Explanation?

I may have said the same thing before . . . but my explanation, I am sure, will always be different.
—Oscar Wilde

A Preliminary Account of Folk Psychological Explanation

At this point, we have seen many reasons to reject the claim that folk psychology should be understood as the attribution of the propositional attitudes, because we do have robust success in predicting behavior without having to attribute beliefs. Though in some cases we do need to appeal to propositional attitudes, I argue that we do so largely when making prognosticating or deliberate predictions rather than in our typical and largely automatic quotidian predictions.

Turning now to folk psychological explanation, we will see that attributing propositional attitudes is a common way of explaining behavior, but it is by no means the only method we use. In turn, explanatory pluralism raises a challenge against the view that the folk take propositional attitudes to be the cause of all intentional behavior. Before defending these points, I must first make clear what we are doing when we offer folk explanations of behavior.

So far we have been working with a preliminary account of folk psychological explanation (or *FP explanation* for short) as something that fulfills a person's drive to understand another person or as an answer to a folk psychological why-question. This working definition of FP explanation is unsatisfying for a number of reasons. For one, it is rather vague. For another, it might appear to be subjective. In this chapter, I intend to address these issues and develop a fuller account of FP explanation that is descriptively accurate, rather than normative. As in the discussion of predicting behavior, what I am interested in here is how we in fact explain behavior, rather than in developing a prescriptive theory about how we should be explaining behavior. The account I develop will be compared with the descriptive accounts derived from theory theory and simulation models, and I argue that my account is more empirically adequate than the others.

To illuminate what is at stake in FP explanation, it may be useful to compare it with scientific explanation. Compared to FP explanation, an enormous amount of philosophical work has been done on the notion of scientific explanation. To a certain extent, I think a theory of scientific explanation has simply been imported into the standard account of FP explanation, to the detriment of our understanding of FP explanation. I hope to show how the goals of FP explanation are different from the goals of scientific explanation, to set the stage for developing an empirically adequate model of FP explanation that is distinct from models of scientific explanation.

Scientific explanation has as its object of understanding the actual physical world, and it purports to offer something more than a description of the world. The standard way of drawing the distinction between a description and an explanation is to say that descriptions are accounts of singular events, whereas explanations refer to underlying principles to offer a general account of why things happen as they do. In science, an explanation is part of a larger theoretical model, and one goal of science is to find true theories that cite the laws of nature. One purpose of science is to uncover the truth, so evaluating explanations in science demands a strong veristic criterion.

On the other hand, we have the kinds of explanations people offer when engaged in nonscientific inquiry about others and their actions. While science has truth as its goal, FP explanation does not share this single-minded focus. Empirical evidence demonstrates that people offer explanations of their own and others' behavior to fulfill a number of pragmatic goals; we explain behavior to impress other people, to condemn other people, and even to reduce the discomfort associated with having seemingly inconsistent beliefs about a person. These goals are more central to typical behavior explanation than is the goal of truth, and while our FP explanations tend to be consistent with the other things we know, we have no veristic requirement for whether something counts as an FP explanation or not. Psychologists who study our explanatory behavior do not analyze explanations in terms of justification or truth. As Heider puts it, regardless of whether a person's explanations are true, they are that person's explanations and "must be taken into account in explaining certain of his or her expectations and actions" (Heider 1958, 5).

Thus, while one might be prima facie concerned with the preliminary account of FP explanation insofar as it implies that explanations do not need to be true, this concern is based on a misunderstanding of the differences between scientific explanation and FP explanation. Scientific explanation has truth as its aim, and epistemic criteria dictate how best to construct scientific explanations. FP explanation is a folk practice and has as its goals whatever the goals of the explainers are. The goal may be truth, but we have reason to think that truth would be only one among many other goals of FP explanation. Our examination of FP explanation is a study of a natural practice, so our account of FP explanation will be a descriptive one; it is an answer to the question "How do people actually go about explaining behavior?" The preliminary answer to that question has been that an FP explanation is any answer to a why-question that fulfills the explainer's drive to understand.

We are interested in the kinds of explanations people actually give for intentional action, and the structures of those explanations. And while we may be interested in the pragmatic usefulness of these explanations, insofar as they help humans with their social practices, it is a violation of this descriptive task to insist that our account of folk psychological explanations be limited to explanations that are truthful or justified; they are explanations as long as they fulfill the subjective requirement for the individual seeking the explanation. I should also point out that we should not see the philosophical work in action theory as a method for understanding FP explanation. The action theorist, like the scientific psychologist, is interested in the actual causal explanation for behavior, but the folk psychology theorist is concerned with what the folk *think* serves as an explanation for behavior. That is, we are doing folk action theory in our conversations and gossip, and folk psychology or folk action theory may or may not relate to the mechanisms that really do serve as a basis for our actions.

While the epistemic goals of scientific and FP explanation can lead to different explanations of the same event, both types of explanation share the pragmatic goal of increasing understanding of the explanandum. The various models of explanation in the philosophy of science all hold that understanding is a central feature of explanation, but they differ on how understanding is generated. Hempel and the logical empiricists suggested that we gain understanding when we know the general laws and initial conditions that deductively or inductively entail the explanandum—when we have a covering-law explanation. But as Wesley Salmon pointed out, having this information is not sufficient for understanding all explananda, because covering-law explanations can be causally irrelevant. Consider the following explanation:

(L) All males who take birth control pills regularly fail to get pregnant.
(K) John Jones is a male who has been taking birth control pills regularly.
(E) John Jones fails to get pregnant. (Salmon 1971, 34)

While the law and the initial conditions do deductively entail the explanandum, they do not satisfy our desire to understand why John Jones didn't get pregnant. The budding physiologist who wonders why John Jones doesn't get pregnant presumably knows that males don't get pregnant, regardless of whether they take birth control pills regularly. Salmon's analysis of this example is that it fails to explain because no causal relationship holds between the covering law and the explanandum. Salmon argued that we must replace the covering-law model of explanation with one that accounts for the causal nature of explanations. Discussion of causal models of scientific explanation continues today (see, e.g., Cartwright 1979; Glennan 2002; Salmon 1971, 1984, 1994; Spirtes et al. 1993; J. Woodward 2003).

However, another way to understand Salmon's example is to say that it does not help to unify our understanding, or that it does not dispel the wondering that led to the question in the first place. One might say that the problem with covering-law explanations doesn't have to do with causality but rather is due to failures in terms of unification (e.g., Kitcher 1989), or the resolution of a wondering-why (van Fraassen 1980). A causal explanation may be the best way to unify our knowledge or to psychologically fulfill our need to understand in some cases, but it won't always suffice.

All models of scientific explanation are first judged on their correspondence to our commonsense understanding of what explanations are supposed to do. This criterion is perhaps clearest in the pragmatic account of scientific explanation offered by van Fraassen, who argues, "An explanation is not the same as a proposition, or an argument, or list of propositions; it is an *answer*" (1980, 137). More specifically, an explanation is a contrastive answer to a why-question: a why *this*, rather than *that*, answer. In this model, even answers that might appear to lack explanatory power can count as an explanation in the right situation. For example, van Fraassen gives a story that undermines Bromberger's purported counterexample of the D-N model of scientific explanation. Recall that Bromberger pointed out that while the height of a flagpole can be deduced by reference to the length of the flagpole's shadow, the position of the sun, and the general law of rectilinear propagation of light, the height of the flagpole is not itself explained by these other facts. But this example is compelling only in the absence of a context that makes sense of the explanation. Van Fraassen suggests that if there were a mad chevalier who wanted to build a tower to commemorate an ill-fated relationship he had with his maid, such that the tower's base is at the spot where he killed her, and the shadow covers the place where he first declared his love to her, Bromberger's argument *would* be explanatory. Given this story, we can explain the height of the tower by referring to the (in this case necessary) length of the shadow (van Fraassen 1980). Thus explanations are not context independent, but the correctness of the explanation depends on the conditions under which the question is being asked.

Such pragmatic features of scientific explanation are shared with FP explanation. Our explanations for people's behavior arise from wondering why they did this rather than that, and an explanatory response to the wondering-why will be dependent on the information we already have. If you wonder why Anne didn't come to work, and someone answers that she called in sick, this does not explain Anne's absence if you already knew that she had made the phone call. This is because it does not resolve the affective state that led you to wonder why in the first place; you are still wondering why Anne isn't around—if she is *really* sick, or if she wanted to watch the soccer match.

Wondering-why should not be seen as limited to linguistic why-questions. If it were, explaining would be limited to those who are adequate users of a natural language. Anglophone children do not begin to ask why-questions until three years (Brown 1968; Ervin-Tripp 1970; Labov and Labov 1977; M. Lewis 1938), and they do not begin offering explanations in their spontaneous speech until about a year later (Sabbagh and Callanan 1998). However, it is thought that children engage in explanatory practices as two-year-olds (Hood and Bloom 1979) or even earlier (Chouinard 2007). If verbal behavior is required for engaging in explanatory practices, children younger than three years would not count as explainers, though a host of evidence shows that children both seek and offer explanations before they gain mastery of the why-question syntax. A linguistic requirement would also exclude the possibility that humans with language deficits, including some children with autism and nonhuman animals, might engage in explanatory practices.

So rather than taking the practice of explaining to consist of asking and answering why-questions, I will be talking about explanation as involving seeking and generating explanatory information. The practice of FP explanation begins most basically with an affective state that will drive a person to engage in some explanation-seeking behavior, be it the linguistic behavior of asking "Why?" or nonlinguistic behavior that seeks knowledge from another person, one's own cognitive resources, or the environment.

Though scientific explanation and FP explanation share the feature of fulfilling a wondering-why, the differences between the two types of explanation are great. Scientific explanation is largely propositional, social, and discursively learnable. While scientific explanations are intended to be disseminated and used to develop a body of information that can be communicated to others, FP explanations are not generated to construct a textbook of human behavior or a database of general principles that parents can give to their children. We don't learn about human behavior from textbooks, the way we learn a lot of science. And often we both seek and develop explanations without communicating our actions to anyone. For example, if you observe that someone walking down the street toward you is acting strangely, you might wonder why the person is acting that way to determine whether the individual will be a threat or not. If you see a beer in his hand, you explain the behavior as drunkenness. If you see a cell phone bud in his ear, you explain the behavior as animation due to a conversation he is having. In this case, you want to explain for your own benefit, and the explanations you develop are not communicated to anyone else. Furthermore, you may be satisfied with the explanation that the man is drunk, even if that isn't true.

What is central to FP explanation is one person's drive to understand another's behavior. Instead of an answer to a why-question, we can conceive of an FP explanation as a response to explanation seeking, or wondering why, about a person or her behavior. Given these considerations, we can describe the three features of satisfactory FP explanations as follows:

1. FP explanations are constructed by individuals as a response to an affective tension, such as a state of curiosity, puzzlement, fear, disbelief, and so on, about a person or behavior. This affective tension drives explanation-seeking behavior.

2. FP explanations reduce cognitive dissonance and resolve the tension that drives the explanation-seeking behavior; generating an explanation promotes a feeling of satisfaction.

3. FP explanations are believed by the explanation seeker and are not believed to be incoherent given the individual's other beliefs, regardless of whether the belief is true or consistent with those beliefs.

These three features also describe the three stages involved in FP explanation. The first stage comes from being in the affective psychological state that leads a person to seek an explanation. The second is the explanation-seeking behavior, and the third comes about when an explanation is generated such that it resolves the tension that started the process in the first place.

The claim that explanation-seeking behavior is associated with an affective state of curiosity, befuddlement, confusion, and so on (for convenience I will refer to such states as "curiosity states"), follows in a long psychological and philosophical tradition that recognizes that an affective discomfort can be associated with epistemically challenged states. David Hume talks about the pain associated with not knowing something one wants to know, and suggests that curiosity, as the passion that drives us to seek truth, is a response to the uneasiness caused by lack of knowledge. It is the desire to clear up "doubt or difficulty" about a topic of interest (Hume 1978, 453). Charles Peirce describes doubt as an irritation that drives us to form beliefs through inquiry; doubt is like the irritation of a nerve that causes a reflex action toward inquiry, and inquiry ceases once we reach the "calm and satisfactory" state of belief (Peirce 1877, 5). Thomas Hobbes is more vehement when he expresses a similar sentiment: "There is a lust of the mind, that, by a perseverance of delight in the continual and indefatigable generation of knowledge, exceedeth the short vehemence of carnal pleasure" (quoted in Gopnik 2000, 299).

This idea has been pursued more recently, as well. Eric Schwitzgebel (1999) argues that the phenomenology associated with our explanatory practices is a biological drive, stating that the phenomenological aspect of explanation is a crucial feature of explanations generally, and the drive to seek explanations will lead us to develop theories that we take to be good, regardless of whether they are in fact true. Others have argued that though a feeling of understanding may be neither necessary nor sufficient for explanatory behavior, humans evolved to experience satisfaction with the development of explanations. Alison Gopnik agrees with Schwitzgebel that explanation seeking and generating are closely associated with affective states, but she denies that the relationship is a necessary one (Gopnik 2000). Gopnik suggests that Hobbes, and the rest of us, receive such a great satisfaction from generating explanations for the same reason we receive such a great satisfaction from having sex: it is nature's way of encouraging us to engage in that behavior. According to Gopnik, the sense of understanding is not an epistemic marker but rather a phenomenological marker for the operation of our theory construction system, and it is usually working when we offer explanations. However, the more explanation seeking and generating we do, the more likely we are to gain knowledge about the world, so the goal of the phenomenological marker is the generation of accurate theories. But just as not all acts of sex lead to reproduction, not all acts of explanation seeking lead to additional knowledge about the world.

A similar view emerges from David Velleman's (2003) account of narrative explanation. While Velleman's interest is in what makes something a story rather than an unintelligible series of events, and whether providing information in narrative form offers greater explanatory success than the same information provided in nonnarrative form, his central claim about narrative is also true of FP explanation. He argues that stories enjoy an explanatory power that leads us to experience a greater understanding of the events by both initiating and resolving an emotional cadence.

Psychologists are identifying the same phenomenon when they talk about cognitive dissonance. In some cases when people lack information about an area of interest, or when their information conflicts with other beliefs they hold, they feel a physical discomfort that leads them to take action to resolve the state. When in this affective state, adults will ask questions to resolve their cognitive disequilibrium (Graesser and McMahen 1993). In the face of this unease, people seek the kind of information needed to resolve the discomfort, says Hume, as surely as the hunter seeks the game or the gambler seeks the win.

The tendency to feel uncomfortable while in certain epistemically challenged states appears to be a universal property of humans. Cross-cultural studies of cognitive dissonance find that East Asians are also subject to cognitive dissonance effects, though the situations that create cognitive dissonance may differ between cultures (Hoshino-Browne et al. 2005), and East Asians may be less concerned about internal contradictions about the self (Spencer-Rodgers et al. 2009). Consider, for example, the phenomenon of choice justification, such that when people are given a choice between two objects, they quickly upgrade the desirability of the chosen object and downgrade the desirability of the rejected one. Cross-cultural studies have found this phenomenon across cultures, and ongoing research programs are examining the similarity and differences in the conditions that trigger it. One set of studies on cross-cultural choice justification found that

Japanese and Americans respond differently to "social eyes"—Japanese justify their choices more when in the presence of an observer or even when alone and merely exposed to a schematic face. Caucasian Americans, on the other hand, justify their choices less often in the presence of social eyes (except when the social eyes are perceived as powerless), perhaps because they feel their choice is constrained in such situations and thus is less representative of the self (Imada and Kitayama 2010). While both Americans and Japanese are subject to choice justification, there appear to be differences in the conditions that trigger the affective response that creates the effect.

These affective states are associated with epistemic states, since the affective state is caused by a lack of information or a conflict between pieces of information one has. In the choice justification cases, this lack of information may lead the individual to wonder things like "Does the observer think I made a strange choice? Does she now have a different opinion of me? What can I do to give her a good opinion of me?" As such, this affective state depends on the existence of a complex cognitive state in which the individual is responsive to the fact that she lacks information. This is not to say that the cognitive state must be metacognitive, in that the individual is considering her epistemic state. It may be, but it could also be an automatic process that requires no metacognitive knowledge. In either case, the affective curiosity state is a marker that the individual's epistemic state is in disarray, and a new piece of information is needed to resolve that tension. But note that what counts as epistemic disarray can vary between cultures and even between individuals.

The second stage of explanatory behavior is the explanation seeking, which can include manipulation of the physical world (such as exploratory behavior), verbal behavior (such as thinking out loud), or contemplation. Developmental psychologists have long been interested in children's exploratory behavior, and since the seminal work on exploratory play by Berlyne (1954) and Piaget (1936/1952), psychologists have identified a number of behaviors associated with exploration and seeking explanations, including the following:

- Touching objects
- Manipulating objects
- Observing attentively
- Visual awareness of the environment
- Detailed observation
- Aural awareness of the environment
- Listening attentively

- Asking questions
- Searching for answers
- Using different methods to search for answers (Chak 2007)

As we will see in the next chapter, even infants can engage in some of these exploratory behaviors.

In complete FP explanation, the explanation-seeking behaviors will lead to the final stage of explanation generating and accepting. Explanation accepting involves considering the possible explanations that have been generated, though one might accept the first explanation generated, so it is not as if explanation accepting requires testing alternative hypotheses. Rather, we have reason to think that in our lay reasoning, we tend to accept the first explanation that we generate (Wason 1968). The human tendency toward a confirmation bias leads us to look for reasons why a hypothesis is true, rather than for reasons why it might be false, which often leads us to accept the first plausible explanation that we generate.

Once we generate an explanation that meets the limited rationality constraints just described—namely, the belief that the explanation is true and doesn't conflict with any of one's other beliefs—the affective state that caused the seeking behavior is replaced with a different affective state of satisfaction, such as relief or happiness.

Each of these three aspects of the folk psychological practice of explanation—the arising of a curiosity state, the explanation seeking, and the explanation generating—can be experienced without going on to the next step. One might experience curiosity and have a drive to seek an explanation but have other reasons for avoiding a search. For example, your curiosity may be culturally prohibited, so that, given the standards of your community, you refrain from asking all the questions you'd like. In other cases, one can have a curiosity response and engage in seeking behavior without ever finding a satisfactory explanation. An explanation seeker may become bored or distracted and never generate an explanation. Or an explanation seeker may not have the cognitive capacity to come up with an explanation for the particular behavior, and thus stop seeking in frustration.

One might object to this account of FP explanation by pointing toward examples of individuals who take information to be an explanation although they were not initially in a curiosity state. After all, it seems that we can be given explanations for phenomena we are not at all interested in. While not all explanations need to include the phenomenological aspect, without it we do have a real question about whether the answer should count as an explanation. In such cases, we might want to say that the person is engaged in quasi-explanatory behavior; she is in the domain of the explanatory. Because I do not pretend to offer necessary and sufficient conditions for FP explanations but instead aim to make clear the paradigm of FP explanation, it should come as no surprise that questions will arise about borderline instances of explanation.

Another initial objection to this account may be that the pluralism about explanation that is entailed leads to a problematic relativism about explanation. While it is true that explanations are relative to the explanation seeker, and what satisfies as an explanation for one person might not satisfy for another (given different epistemic backgrounds or different degrees of tolerance for different kinds of epistemic disarray), this kind of relativism does not permit just anything to count as an explanation; it must fit the right functional role. Also, the relativism does not lead us to a world of inconsistent idiosyncratic explanations, such that each individual feels satisfied with her explanation of someone's behavior, but the account fails to satisfy anyone else. Because the healthy, rational person is open to revising her explanation in light of evidence against it, and we presume that the majority of humans fall into this category, the process of discussing explanations will lead individuals away from idiosyncratic explanations and toward societally shared ones.

The three features of FP explanation presented here make up the paradigmatic case of FP explanation as it plays out in an individual. Given the decades of research on the nature of explanation, and the lack of consensus about even the most basic elements of explanation, it is likely that the term refers to a family of behaviors that share a resemblance relation. I take these three features to describe the standard cases of FP explanation offered in the literature, and not as a set of necessary or sufficient conditions.

These features remain independent from claims about the structure of folk psychological explanation. They are consistent with an account of explanation in terms of a theory, subsumption over general laws, or models. They do not presume a quasi-linguistic element to explanations as answers to why-questions. They are also consistent with the possibility that folk psychological explanations are given in terms of the propositional attitudes that are taken to be the causes of the behavior to be explained, so I am not begging the question. They offer a framework that is compatible with the differences we see in explanatory styles between individuals, and the differences we see across cultures. What this account emphasizes is that FP explanation is something we do; it is a practice that humans engage in, rather than an abstraction or a set of principles.

In addition, this account of FP explanation is a subtype of folk explanation more generally. It is meant to describe how individuals explain behavior, and thus there is no such thing as an unqualified FP explanation. An FP explanation is satisfactory or not relative to the explanation seeker; people can disagree about whether a behavior has been well explained or not. If an explanation seeker denies the truth of some proposition offered as an explanation for behavior, she will not accept that explanation, since she would not gain a feeling of satisfaction from the purported explanation.

Another important feature of this account of explanation is that it separates the practice of explanation seeking from that of explanation offering. A young child may be able to seek an explanation, insofar as she is striving to resolve a tension between her beliefs, yet she might be cognitively incapable of resolving the tension by postulating hypotheses because of her cognitive limitations. For example, if an explanation in terms of the actor's belief is needed, and the child is unable to engage in reasoning about beliefs, she will fail to satisfy her need. However, if an explanation in terms of the individual's emotional state would suffice to resolve the tension, then the same child might be successful in offering an explanation, since an understanding of emotional states develops before a child is proficient at attributing propositional attitudes. While I speak of offering an explanation, remember that this does not require any verbal behavior. A child may offer an explanation to herself simply by understanding an individual as having an emotional response. As we will see in the next chapter, children are sensitive to such emotional features from a very early age.

Explanation and Prediction

We saw in chapter 3 that folk psychological explanation is often taken to be nothing more than backward prediction, and researchers in philosophy and developmental psychology have widely assumed that if we have a good account of how we predict others' behavior, we will also have a good account of how we explain others' behavior. However, we saw that not all methods used to predict behavior will also offer explanations of behavior. Now it is easier to see why: if a purported explanation in terms of past behavior or stereotype does not serve to reduce affective tension to an acceptable level, such a statement will not be accepted by the explanation seeker. Or if the statements are accepted (e.g., one might say, "Yes, I know that she's female and females often φ, but I still don't understand why she φed!"), they might not resolve the tension between the explanation

What Is Folk Psychological Explanation?

seeker's beliefs, because they do not identify where the tension between beliefs rests, or they do not fill the gaps between the right beliefs.

In addition, a difference between prediction and explanation comes from understanding better that explanation is a multistage process. The wondering stage of explaining behavior is largely automatic and not under conscious control. That is, a curiosity state can arise in an individual without being the result of a conscious thought process. Of course, we can also consciously decide to wonder why a state of affairs occurs, as we do in the practice of science and much academic research, where we actively seek out things to explain. However, FP explanation does not usually result from a purposeful search for some behavior to explain. Rather, we become curious about behaviors as they occur, or as we hear about them. Our world has no shortage of interesting people whose behavior activates our curiosity.

The next stages of explanation—the searching for explanations, generating potential explanations, and perhaps adjudicating between potential explanations—involve more controlled cognitive processes. The curiosity state leads to an intentional response to the curiosity, which typically results in an investigation into the behavior. Thus explaining behaviors in most cases will include both automatic and intentional cognitive processes.

On the other hand, predicting behavior, as a ubiquitous part of human social interaction, is largely automatic and can be done without our even realizing it. As with explanation seeking, we can intentionally decide to make a prediction, as political pundits and celebrity gossip writers do. But the prediction that the driver in front of you will stop at the red light, or that Maxi will try to retrieve his chocolate from where he left it, do not require an intentional act of working things out. They are a part of our automatic cognitive processes and exist from a very early age, as is shown in the infant theory of mind studies.

If FP explanation is largely an intentional and controlled cognitive act and prediction is largely an automatic act, then we should expect a significant cognitive difference between predicting and explaining others' behavior, which gives us another reason for rejecting the presumption of cognitive symmetry between our practices of FP prediction and explanation. However, we must be careful about what the rejection of the symmetry of FP explanation and prediction entails. From the rejection of symmetry, it does not follow that there cannot be a connection between the cognitive processes subsuming explanations and predictions in some cases. The rejection of the symmetry thesis only leads us to reject the idea that explanation is backward prediction in all cases, but it does not cause us to reject the possibility that in some cases, the same method we use to make a prediction of behavior can be used to provide a resolution to someone's curiosity state.

For example, personality traits are one common way of explaining behavior, just as they are a common way of predicting behavior. Knowing that he is a pushover, I might predict that the professor will let the student into his overenrolled class. If someone asked for an explanation of the professor's generous act, I might respond by giving the same uncharitable answer and report that he is a pushover. But note that while there may be apparent symmetry here (the same psychological property I used to make a prediction is used to explain the behavior to someone else), there is an asymmetry in who the predictor and the explanation seeker are. If I wondered why the professor let the student in, it would not suffice to remind myself of the method I used to predict the behavior. I already have that information, and if there developed in me a wondering-why, or some curiosity about the behavior, it would be because I want some understanding at a different level of explanation. I might be wondering why he is so generous to students, and to answer that why-question, I need some additional information. The question might be answered by another trait attribution (e.g., he is friendly and helpful to everyone, and thus he is helpful to students) or by a causal story about his past experience (e.g., his professors never helped him when he was an undergrad, and he doesn't want to cause the pain that others caused him).

Four Questions about FP Explanation

This view of explanation invites many questions that I investigate in the following two chapters. The four key questions are:

Do all explanations of intentional behavior rely on attribution of mental content, either directly or indirectly?
Are all folk psychological explanations propositional?
Are folk psychological explanations part of a folk psychological theory?
Do folk psychological explanations purport to cite the causes of behavior?

Before giving my own answers to these questions, I want to talk about how they are answered by advocates of the simulation theory and the theory theory. Furthermore, I will examine an additional view of explanation that can be extracted from the model theory of folk psychology. While I have already introduced the theory-theory and simulation theory views regarding FP explanation in chapter 3, here I will examine them in the

What Is Folk Psychological Explanation?

present context and point out weaknesses with the accounts to the extent that they fail to satisfy the three features of FP explanation.

The mechanisms underlying our ability to explain behavior are extremely important to us, given that discussing people's behavior is one of the primary occupations of a human being. The psychologist Robin Dunbar (1996) suggests that we spend two-thirds of our conversational time talking about what people are doing and why they are doing it. As we will see in the next chapter, this trend is evident among humans at a very young age; children's conversations are overwhelmingly about people and actions, rather than physical events or states (Hood and Bloom 1979).

The folk psychology literature focuses mostly on the cognitive mechanisms involved in offering an explanation and gives almost no attention to the curiosity state or explanation seeking. A closer look at how theory theory, simulation theory, and the model view of folk psychology can account for the practice of FP explanation will bring to light weaknesses with each view. I now look at those accounts and show what is missing from the models and where the problems lie.

Explanation in Theory Theory

As we saw in chapter 3, the account of FP that we call theory theory adopted its structure from David Lewis's (1972) account of mental states in terms of psychophysical identifications. Those who developed a formulation of folk psychology as a theory, such as Paul Churchland (1981) and Jerry Fodor (1990), continued to accept Lewis's general framework, which itself is modeled after the D-N model of scientific explanation.

FP explanation takes the following form:

1. General covering law(s) relating mental content, sensory experience, and behavior.
2. The individual's relevant mental content or sensory experience.
3. Behavior to be explained.

Because (3) can be derived via the application of the general law(s) to the behavior to be explained, in this account FP explanation takes the form of an argument, just like D-N explanation in science. A standard example of FP explanation, given the standard FP model, goes like this:

1. People act to best fulfill their desires given their beliefs, ceteris paribus.
2. Joe believes that he is thirsty, that water quenches thirst, and that he can find water at the water cooler. Joe also desires to fulfill this thirst.
3. Joe walks to the water cooler.

This argument purports to explain Joe's behavior. It tells us that he walked to the water cooler to acquire water rather than the latest gossip. And it gives us that information by telling us what causes Joe's behavior, what his reasons are.

Because theory-theorists take FP explanation to be derivable from a causal theory of behavior that consists of a database of general principles about how propositional attitudes cause behavior and a description of an individual's beliefs and desires, constructing explanations appears to be a simple matter of finding the appropriate beliefs and desires. For the theory-theorist, the cognitive mechanisms involved in explaining intentional behavior are the same ones involved in constructing covering-law explanations of physical events and states of affairs, given that they require the ability to make inferences between laws and initial conditions and actions. It is in the theory theory account of explanation that we see most clearly how a theory of scientific explanation has been imported wholesale into the domain of folk psychology.

Theory theory has clear answers to our four questions. In this view, all explanations of intentional behavior rely on the attribution of mental content in propositional form. Without knowing an actor's beliefs and desires, we would not have an FP explanation. Explanations are part of an FP theory, and they provide a causal explanation for behavior. The theory-theorist answers all four questions with a yes.

As I argued in some detail in chapter 3, the covering-law model for FP explanation offered by supporters of the theory theory suffers from some serious problems. For one, theories of scientific explanation are not cognitive theories. Rather, they are normative theories of how scientific explanations should be structured. Theories of FP explanation, however, have as their object the practice of FP explanation among the folk; they are concerned with what people actually do. Determining the best account of scientific explanation is not a descriptive task, but description *is* the primary concern of those developing accounts of FP explanation. It would be quite a coincidence if the best description of FP explanation were identical in structure to a largely discredited theory of how we ought to formulate scientific explanations. The similarity between the two accounts is more plausibly attributed to the direct influence of logical empiricism on the development of functionalist theories of mind.

The theory-theorists' focus on the structure of FP explanation leads to the assumption that the cognitive processes must be reflected in the structure. Thus the theory-theorists' analysis of the cognitive mechanisms implicated in constructing explanations consists of having or acquiring a theory and having the correct inferential reasoning systems to allow the manipulation of that theory. But one might worry that inferential reasoning alone cannot account for how we choose the correct beliefs and desires from all the belief-desire sets that are consistent with the behavior. This worry arises given the underdetermination of reasons for action by behavior. If we want to know how we explain behavior, the missing part of this story is how we choose the mental states that are most consistent with the behavior to be explained, since any one behavior can be caused by a number of different mental states. For example, there are at least as many potential reasons for going to the grocery store as there are items one might expect to buy there. In addition, an actor may have had multiple reasons for acting, as Davidson (1963) pointed out. Jack may have eaten the cake both because it looked delicious and because he wanted to please the cake baker. At the least, an account of explanation in terms of covering laws leaves much of the cognition involved in our FP explanatory practices in the dark.

The major concern comes from the implication that FP explanation and prediction are symmetrical. While we may use a belief-desire set to make a prediction of behavior, it will not suffice as an explanation, given the pragmatic nature of explanation. While it is clear that we may use belief-desire psychology when providing psychological explanations of behavior, citing beliefs and desires is not always sufficient for the construction of a satisfactory explanation. Consider, for example, the following belief-desire explanation: "He believed that the towers would fall if they were hit by a plane, and he desired that the towers fall." As an explanation for a terrorist attack, this claim is probably useless, because a request for an explanation of a terrorist attack is a request for further information about why someone would engage in such behavior. The belief-desire attribution does not tell us why the terrorist would have that desire. To provide that explanation, one must go beyond belief-desire psychology and talk about traits (he's a monster) or social conditions (he was poor), biology (he was responding to a perceived attack), the situation (the United States has troops in Saudi Arabia), the terrorist's personal history (his sister was killed by an American gun; he was mentored by an inflammatory imam; he became friends with the wrong person), and so on.

While I take these arguments as sufficient for rejecting a D-N model of FP explanation, the theory-theorist may be able to develop an account of FP explanation that neither entails the symmetry of prediction and explanation nor denies the pragmatic aspect of FP explanation. For example, one might agree that FP is a theory but deny the propositional nature of theories and the account of explanation as argument. The semantic view of theories, according to which theories consist of models rather than propositions, entails a very different view of the nature of explanation, but one that shares some similarities with both theory theory and simulation theory. Before examining the model view of FP explanation, let us look at how the simulation theorists understand our ability to explain behavior.

Explanation in Simulation Theory

For the simulation theorists, generating an FP explanation requires a bit more in the way of imaginative work. In classic simulation, our understanding of others relies on our own cognitive processes. We predict behavior by using these processes to determine what behavior the target individual will engage in, or what decision the individual will make. But this method doesn't work backward. That is, we can't run our cognitive mechanisms from behavior to generate a cause.

Instead, recall that Alvin Goldman (1995a, 2006) suggests that a simulator can construct explanations for behavior by using a generate-and-test strategy, such that we generate hypotheses about possible causes of the behavior we want to explain, and then test the hypotheses by using a mental simulation. But how do we generate the hypotheses? What information do we use to decide which belief-desire sets to test?

While in his early views Goldman seemed to suggest that such hypotheses could be generated without appeal to theory, more recently he claims, "Theorizing seems necessary to generate hypotheses about states responsible for the observed effects" (2006, 45). This apparent need for theory to explain behavior is one reason Goldman gives for preferring a hybrid account of folk psychology that combines elements from theory theory with simulation theory. Here Goldman opens himself up to the same questions we have for explanation under the theory theory account: how do we choose inputs given the overdetermination of behavior by mental states, and how do we deal with the possibility that the actor has multiple reasons for one behavior?

This move removes one of the standard virtues of simulation theory. An argument often given for simulation theory over theory theory has to do with their relative parsimony. Theory theory claims that each of us carries an enormous information store that we rely on to engage in FP practices, while simulation theory removes the need for such a database of FP platitudes. By using our own cognitive mechanisms to simulate, we do not need to develop and rely on a full-blown holistic theory of human behavior. If we need theory to explain behavior, this appeal to parsimony seems to be lost, but it might be preserved if we can generate hypotheses without the full-blown theory needed for the theory theory. To generate inputs for simulation, must we appeal to a holistic theory that connects sets of propositional attitudes with behaviors?

Take the following example of how we explain behavior given Goldman's neosimulation view. Suppose you want to know why Kurt killed himself. The first step is to use theory to generate possible rationalizations for Kurt's behavior; you consider the beliefs and desires that Kurt could have had before he pulled the trigger. After selecting the most plausible belief-desire sets, you next input each belief-desire set into your own practical reasoning system—you imagine being Kurt with those beliefs and desires—and you continue inputting belief and desire sets until you come up with the set that would lead to Kurt's suicidal behavior.

As a description of how humans actually explain behavior, this scenario offers several reasons for skepticism. For one, humans have a difficult time engaging in such a powerful identification; we go to great lengths to avoid imagining being in such states of despair, from ignoring the homeless on the street to changing the channel when the Oxfam advertisements come on. But we are consummate explainers of tragedies, and the public spends millions of dollars to hear possible explanations about the exploits of celebrities. Do we really need to imagine being the tragic figure to offer an explanation of his behavior? When teenagers say that Britney Spears treats her children so poorly because her parents mistreated her, are they coming up with this explanation by imagining how they would feel and act if they were Britney? Do gossip magazine writers come up with their accounts via a simulation of their targets? It seems unlikely.

In addition, the kinds of explanations we read about in the celebrity gossip magazines, and the kinds of explanations we offer for our own tragedies, don't often refer to the full propositional attitude set that leads to the behavior. While one might claim that our explanations are simple truncated belief-desire sets, and that conversational practices have us leave out the easily inferred member of the set, this cannot answer the problem in all cases. Some of our explanations fail to refer to content at all. Why did Kurt Cobain kill himself? People have blamed his wife, his hatred of fame (an emotion directed at a state of affairs, not a propositional attitude), his drug addiction, his brain chemistry. While these sorts of explanations may require some kind of theory, such as theory about the biological basis of depression or drug addiction, they do not require a theory of mental content—they do not require that the explainer is following SFP.

Perhaps most troubling is the question of how we go about determining which of the mental-state sets is the best explanation, given the overdetermination of propositional attitude sets for any particular behavior. Goldman suggests that we can limit the possible sets of mental states to test via appeal to theory, plus perhaps information recalled about prior simulations. Once we have a limited number of sets to test, we likely use mental simulation to decide between them. Goldman's view of explanation via simulation turns out to be very much like the view of explanation we have from theory theory, so it suffers from some of the same problems. This is evident given the weakness of his commitment to a pure simulation account of FP explanation; Goldman suggests that the hypotheses we generate through appeal to theory are *plausibly* tested *sometimes* using simulation—though he admits that no strong evidence supports the claim.

The claim that theory can be used to limit the search space when generating propositional attitudes to test may well be correct, but the worry is that theory—especially a theory of standard folk psychology—will not be able to limit the search space enough to allow for an effective search. While the theory might allow me to conclude that an individual's beliefs about space travel are irrelevant when determining why she is going to the grocery store, the theory does not allow me to decide what she wants to buy. A general theory of human mental states and behaviors cannot explain individual differences, and it is individual differences that we are so often interested in when seeking explanations. How do I explain why my sister went to the store this morning? Rather than looking for universals about human behavior, I might consider my sister's idiosyncrasies. If I know she eats yogurt every day, and I see there is no yogurt in the house, I can infer that she went to the store to buy yogurt. While this could be construed as theoretical knowledge, it need not refer to her beliefs, but only to her habits.

While Goldman hopes for a merging of the simulation and theory theory accounts of how we go about engaging in our folk psychological practices, he may give up too much by accepting the standard view of theory theory. He answers our four questions in a way that is quite similar to the theory-theorist. In his account of how we explain, Goldman focuses on explanations in terms of mental content, though I think his view is more consistent with the idea that we can explain in terms of emotions and moods as well as beliefs and desires. In his recent view, there are two levels of FP: low-level simulational mind reading, which is independent from theory and allows us to understand others' emotions and moods; and high-level simulational mind reading, which allows us to understand others' decisions and behaviors and explain behavior, and may rely on theoretical knowledge of propositional attitudes (A. Goldman 2006). If we can simulate what people are going to do using a low-level simulation of another's mood or emotion, and if an appeal to the actor's mood or emotion would resolve someone's wondering why a person acted as she did, it seems reasonable also to accept that we can make explanations without the attribution of mental content. While this is not something Goldman explicitly claims, it is consistent with his two-tiered account of our FP mechanisms.

Goldman is cagey about whether psychological explanations are propositional, but given the need to appeal to theory to generate FP explanations, his view is also consistent with a positive answer to our second question. His answer to the fourth question is unambivalent: FP explanations are causal explanations, since the simulation model is a causal model.

In characterizing the nature of FP explanation, Goldman's generally positive answer to our four questions aligns him with the theory-theorists. But other accounts differ on at least some of these dimensions. Within the realm of simulation theory, other ways of describing how we explain behavior do not rely on the heavy machinery of a folk theory of human beliefs and desires.

One of those alternatives is offered by Robert Gordon. Unlike Goldman, Gordon does not give in to the theory camp in his account of FP explanation. Gordon explicitly rejects the standard view, inherited from the logical empiricists, that explanations must be given in the context of a theory or some relevant causal law. He uses Davidson's causal view of reason explanation as his foil and argues that Davidson cannot accept at face value explanations such as "Sam's running was caused by its raining" or "Joan flew to Hawaii because there will be a solar eclipse there tomorrow" (Gordon 2000). Rather, Davidson would claim that such explanations need to be understood as statements about the reasons the individuals had for acting, since facts do not cause action, but attitudes toward facts do. Gordon challenges the view that explanations for behavior must cite the cause of behavior. Instead explanations can be facts that are considerations for acting in a certain way. This shift from causal features to considerations not only allows for the existence of mixed motives for action but also allows for a counterfactual analysis of explanation without the need for a counterfactual account of causation.

A simulator can determine his own reasons for having acted as he did, Gordon suggests, by generating a situation very similar to the one in which he acted and running a simulation to determine if, in the counterfactual scenario, he would have acted differently. If the outcome of the simulation is the same as the outcome in the actual case, then the altered factor does not explain the behavior. However, if the simulation of the counterfactual situation leads to a different outcome, then the fact that was altered does serve to explain the behavior. Gordon gives the following example: "Suppose that among the partners at Price Waterhouse who voted against the female candidate there was a particularly scrupulous individual who asked himself, Would I be making the same decision if the candidate had been a male with like credentials? To answer this question, he need only imagine the decision to concern a male candidate with like credentials" (Gordon 2000, 77).

Gordon points out that this method of explaining behavior involves a level of pretend play that is open to young children who do not yet have an understanding of representational belief. They can figure out that Sam is running because it is raining, because they can engage in a pretend situation in which it isn't raining, and by using simulation they can determine that Sam would not be running (all else remaining unchanged). Children's proclivity to engage in pretend play precedes their ability to pass false-belief tasks, and we will see that children are already experimenting with explanations at this point. As children develop cognitive sophistication, their ability to consider more complex counterfactual situations develops, as well.

While Gordon offers a pure simulation view of FP explanation, his view also has some limitations. For one, his appeal to "considerations" instead of causes is vague. His counterfactual analysis may be taken by some to be a causal analysis, and many of the examples he gives appear at least prima facie to cite causal factors, even if those factors are not psychological ones.

A second question arises regarding how one goes about deciding which features of a situation may be potential explanations. Since an infinite number of features exist for each situation, an explainer must have some method for determining which of the features of the situation should be modified when developing and testing a counterfactual model. In the sexist hiring case, the decision to run the simulation while varying the sex of the job candidate was based on a prior hypothesis that the decision may have been due to prejudice. Thus Gordon's simulation offers a way of testing explanations, but not of developing them. If you don't have a prima facie hypothesis, how does the counterfactual model account help one get started? And if some other method is needed to generate the hypotheses, and simulation is only used to test the hypotheses, we have reason to think that some information about the situation is required, and inferences about the situation could be made. Those inferences might be about information we have gathered about the individual, or about general principles of human psychology. Gordon does not provide a convincing argument that theory can be eliminated. What he does do is point out that not all explanations need be stated in terms of one's beliefs and desires. But this leaves open the possibility that theory or knowledge of beliefs and desires is needed to generate the plausible counterfactual situations.

Another problem is that simulations are not going to provide all the explanations that we are able to generate. To return to an earlier example, it seems unlikely that we would be able to determine whether or not the personality of Kurt's wife had anything to do with his suicide. In Gordon's view, we would be able to determine whether Kurt killed himself because of his horrible wife by running a mental simulation of Kurt in which Kurt's wife is charming. But given the number of different factors that could have played a role in Kurt's suicide, it is not possible to draw any conclusions from this modification. Maybe he would have, and maybe not.

Perhaps this is simply a limitation of the case owing to the lack of information we have about Kurt's life. But this limitation does not keep people from confidently asserting his wife's actions as an explanation for his suicide. Given the definition of explanation that I am assuming here, regardless of whether Kurt's rationalization involved thoughts about his wife, reference to his wife does explain his suicide, for some people. Again, at this point I am not concerned about how best we can determine a person's actual reasons for acting. Rather, the focus is on the cognitive mechanisms that lead us to generate explanations that fulfill the five features of a successful explanation.

Gordon's simulation account of explanation significantly diverges from the accounts we get from theory theory and from Goldman's hybrid simulation. Of our four questions about the nature of explanation, Gordon answers three negatively and remains neutral (so far as I know) on the question of whether all FP explanations are propositional in form. We need not attribute mental states to explain behavior; sometimes we explain by citing features of the situation. FP explanations are not causal in nature but cite factors that are considerations in acting. And FP explanations are not part of a folk psychological theory.

Despite these worries, Gordon's account has its merits. A theory of FP explanation must be empirically adequate, and I argue that Gordon's answer to at least one of the four questions about the nature of explanation is consistent with what we know about how people actually explain behavior. Insofar as Gordon deviates from the standard account of explanation as limited to causation, he is on the right track.

Explanation in Model Theory

The view that folk psychology can be understood as facilitation with a model, which has been advocated variously by Peter Godfrey-Smith (2005), Heidi Maibom (2003), and Ron Giere (1996), is not as developed as the traditional approach to the theory theory or the simulation theory, and little has been said about the nature of FP explanation according to the model view. However, I believe that model theory is a promising approach to understanding how people understand one another, and in this section I try to integrate the work that has been done on the semantic view of scientific explanation with the work Godfrey-Smith has done to develop an account of FP explanation as model facilitation.

Godfrey-Smith suggests that modeling is a strategy used in many domains of science, such as robotics, artificial intelligence, physics, and evolutionary biology, as well as in our lay understanding of the social world (Godfrey-Smith 2005, 2006). A model is a fictionalized and simplified version of some part of the world, which makes the world easier to work with. Such models permit a kind of understanding through engineering.

When practicing folk psychology, Godfrey-Smith suggests, a person will construct a psychological profile, or multiple profiles, of the target. A profile is built from elements including propositional attitudes, emotions, moods, and sensations, and these elements are connected by the appropriate logical relations (Godfrey-Smith 2005). The person then inputs the relevant initial conditions and runs the model to get a behavior prediction as output. The profile can also be used to explain a behavior in terms of its cause, presumably by running the model backward.

While initially this suggestion might sound much like simulation theory, it has three important distinctions. For one, Godfrey-Smith's model is a theoretical and artifactual one, unlike the physical model implemented in our practical reasoning system that the simulation theorists accept. It therefore avoids the problems that simulation theory has with explaining how we can run our cognitive mechanisms backward to explain behavior. A theoretical model can be used for both prediction and explanation.

Another way in which this type of modeling differs from simulation is that we may have personalized models for many different individuals. While we may also have some generic model of humanity, much of our predictive and explanatory work will appeal to more detailed models of specific people and perhaps types of people. Given this plethora of models, the model view does not enjoy the parsimony that many simulation views do.

Further, theoretical models are things we have to construct. Godfrey-Smith suggests that we may use both a top-down and a bottom-up strategy to develop a psychological model of an individual. The top-down strategy will involve using general principles we have developed about human behavior, in a way similar to theory theory. The bottom-up strategy could use mental simulations to fill out the details of the profile. We would hypothesize possible psychological properties and then use our own mental processes to examine how those properties would interact with the general principles.

While prediction is relatively straightforward in the model view, explanation requires a bit more work, given Godfrey-Smith's distinction between a model and its construal. While we can understand a model as pure structure, the construal of a model is its interpretation and can include commitments about the existence of theoretical elements or the realism of the model's causal patterns. When we use these models to predict behavior, we need not have any construal about the model; we can predict without taking a position on the realism-eliminativism-instrumentalism debate, or the nature of belief, and without having any commitment to the closeness of fit between the psychological profile and the target. But generating explanations requires a construal.

Godfrey-Smith illustrates the difference between prediction and explanation by pointing out that the same model (or variations of the same set of models) can be used to predict the behavior of a human, an organization such as a corporation, and a nonhuman animal. However, when we come to explain the behaviors of these different targets, we will probably construe the model differently—perhaps as a metaphor in the case of a corporation, as a useful anthropomorphism in the case of the animal, and perhaps as an accurate description of the causal mechanisms in the case of the human. The model cannot be used to provide explanations with definite truth conditions, because the models do not "say anything" about the target system (Godfrey-Smith 2005, 11). Rather, the explanatory work is done by the construal of the model.

Godfrey-Smith says little about the cognitive mechanisms underlying construal, but given his remarks, it is plausible that construal is constrained by consistency within the models at play and the other things we believe about the world. He also leaves open the kind of construal that would be involved in using a model to explain, given that a model can resemble a target in different ways, and he rejects isomorphism or any similar concept as ways to formalize the resemblance relationship between model and world. Since construal plays an essential role in explanation via model, we can examine the implications of different kinds of construal for the account.

Consider a realist construal first. One might worry that if the folk psychological explainer takes a more realist view about the relationship between the model and the target, the model is construed as a largely accurate causal map of the target system, and the problem of symmetry between prediction and explanation arises once again. A model that is used to predict, and then is used to explain once some realist construal of it is made, allows an explanation that refers to the same processes that permitted the prediction. But this worry could be avoided, since multiple models exist within a domain, and the explanation could involve picking among the models. This way, the model that explains may be different from the model used to predict, and no symmetry is required (though, as we would hope, it is possible).

Another implication of a realist construal is that all the explanations would be taken to be causal in nature. However, construing the models as real causal accounts of the target does not reflect all our FP explanatory practices, an idea that I elaborate in the next chapters. We do offer explanations of behavior that do not take the form of causal explanations.

Alternatively, we could understand the construal as metaphorical rather than realist, as in the use of folk psychology to talk about corporations. While metaphors may satisfy as an explanation in some cases of human behavior, it is unlikely that such a construal would have widespread success in resolving affective tension.

Another possible construal of the FP models could come from something like Nancy Cartwright's (1983) simulacrum account of explanation. Cartwright, like Godfrey-Smith, sees models as fictions and also accepts that, depending on the goal of the model, a realist model may not always be the preferred type. But unlike Godfrey-Smith, she takes a model to include an interpretation of the world; she presumes a formal resemblance relationship. A simulacrum explanation leaves out the details of the target and focuses on its form, but it doesn't say anything misleading about the target. Thus, while the model should not be construed in a realist sense, because the causal details are left out, it is more than a metaphor. The success of an explanation comes in degrees; the more information contained in an explanation, and the more precise the explanation, the better it is. Once you have a model that can be manipulated, any why-question about the model can be answered, and in this sense the model itself serves as an explanation.

To understand what a simulacrum explanation might look like, we can turn to Mehmet Elgin and Elliott Sober's development of Cartwright's account. They provide an example of how an optimality model in evolutionary biology, describing the evolutionary trajectory of an asexually reproducing population, can help to explain some states of affairs. They claim, to begin with, that we might derive the following conditional from the model:

(7) If organisms are fitter the closer they are to the optimal value α and if no forces other than selection are at work in the population, then the population will evolve to a state in which all organisms exhibit the trait value α.

They continue:

Suppose the optimality model correctly describes how selection acts on the trait of interest:

(8) Organisms are fitter the closer they are to the optimal value α.

Given this information, suppose we observe that

(9) The *n* organisms in the population have trait values $\beta_1, \beta_2, \ldots, \beta_n$ (where each β_i differs only negligibly from α). (Elgin and Sober 2002, 447)

Elgin and Sober suggest that (7) and (8) explain (9) without being an argument for (9) or making (9) more probable. The description of the model we get in (7), along with the description presented in (8), makes sense of the traits that individuals display in the population by saying something about a cause of the explanandum and by making a general claim about the model. Instead of the explanans entailing the explanandum or making it more probable, the explanans shows some of the causal forces involved, since the value described in (9) is close to the value predicted by (7).

Exporting these views to explanation in folk psychology, under a simulacrum construal a folk psychological explanation involves developing a model of the target that will provide what the explanation seeker takes to be at least a simplified version of the causal story, and that will answer the explanatory question. In this account, too, FP explanations are causal explanations, given the assumption of closeness of fit between model and world. Again, the worry arises that model FP explanations do not reflect the diversity in our FP explanatory practice, since not all our explanations take the form of causal explanations.

Despite the question about how the models can be construed, the model view possesses certain virtues. For one, the model view of FP explanations differs from the other accounts, since an explanation need not be a propositional attitude. Recall that Godfrey-Smith's FP model is a psychological profile, which includes the target's moods and emotions, as well as mental states. Given that the content of the model is not limited to mental content, the kinds of explanations that can come from the model are more diverse, reflecting more of our actual practice. However, to more fully capture the pluralism in our practice of explaining behavior, we need to know more about the various ways in which a model can be construed, so as to accommodate noncausal explanations, as well.

In the model view, the natural answers to the four questions are the following:

(1) Do all explanations of intentional behavior rely on attribution of mental content, either directly or indirectly? *No*
(2) Are all folk psychological explanations propositional? *No*
(3) Are folk psychological explanations part of a folk psychological theory? *Yes*
(4) Do folk psychological explanations purport to cite the causes of behavior? *Yes, in some construals.*

FP explanations are not propositional, though they can be stated as propositions. It is more accurate to say that they are properties of models. And because explanations are properties of theoretical models, they are part of a folk psychological theory.

Explanation according to the model view can account for some pragmatic aspects of FP explanation. However, it is not obvious that this view can accommodate explanations that are not true but believed to be true by the explanation seeker. Given the substantial work being done by construals in Godfrey-Smith's account, we need to know more about the variety of ways in which one can construe a model before determining whether this account is empirically adequate. If FP explanation assumes that the model is a realistic simplification of the human it models, then the result of model manipulation would be true causal explanations of human behavior. But FP explanations need not be true, and as we will see, they need not be causal. The worry about the model account as developed here is that it fails as a descriptive account of how people in fact do explain behavior. However, as we will see, aspects of this view nicely correspond to our practice of explaining behavior. The idea that we construct psychological profiles that we then use to predict and explain behavior is an insight I return to in chapter 10.

What Is Folk Psychological Explanation?

My Answers to the Four Questions

Given the constraints on explanation, all three accounts of how the folk explain behavior discussed in this chapter make claims that can be empirically examined. In chapter 8, I look at what we know about how the folk in fact explain behavior. By examining the real practice of explaining people and their actions, I will be able to defend my answers to the four questions that framed this chapter. We will see that people's explanation of behavior is not limited to attribution of mental content and cannot always be understood as propositional in form. While explanations may be a part of an FP theory, the answer to the third question depends on how one understands theory. But most important, what becomes clear is that people do not limit their FP explanations to causal explanations. Some explanations of intentional behavior are given in terms of noncausal dispositions, statistical generalizations, or enabling features. Thus it will be evident that the folk do not assume that all intentional behavior has a determinate psychological cause. These empirical findings form the basis for an account of folk psychology that begins with FP explanation, and according to which the key to being a folk psychologist is not reading minds but recognizing persons—fully fleshed individuals with pasts and futures, embedded in a web of relationships, and rich with moods and personalities.

8 The Science of Folk Psychological Explanation

Child: Mommy, I always ask why. Why do I always ask why?
Parent: Because you are curious about things.
Child: What is curious?
—Maureen Callanan and Lisa Oakes

Aspects of Explanation

In the last chapter, I suggested that theories of FP explanation are descriptive theories, unlike the normative theories of scientific explanation. I described paradigmatic FP explanation as consisting of three distinct elements: a curiosity state regarding a person or her behavior, the explanation seeking, and the generation of an acceptable explanation that resolves the affective tension that drove the explanation seeking in the first place. An FP explanation is information about the social domain that leads one to experience *aha*! (or at least leads to a decrease in the discomfort associated with cognitive dissonance).

In this chapter, I review the empirical research on explanatory behavior in children and adults to further undermine the claim that folk psychology requires the attribution of the propositional attitudes. We will see that in both children and adults, many explanations of intentional behavior make no reference to propositional attitudes. These data also undermine the idea that the folk think that propositional attitudes are the cause of all intentional behavior. We find that the folk think that some behaviors are caused by moods, emotions, traits, and other nonpropositional features. But we also find that some explanations do not cite causal features at all.

This discussion of what the folk actually do when they engage in explanatory behavior will help to form the account of FP explanation that is developed in the next chapter. With a greater understanding of what we in fact do when we explain behavior, we will be in a better position to answer the four questions regarding what a good theory of FP explanation must consist of.

We can begin by looking at the development of explanation seeking in children. As we will see, infants are already engaged in FP explanatory practices, and young verbal children begin to offer explanations of human behavior before they have much understanding of representational belief.

Explanation Seeking in Children

Infants

When do children begin to wonder why? In many accounts, infants are almost immediate wonderers. Long before they develop the ability to ask why-questions, infants engage in exploratory behaviors and make facial expressions such as pursed mouths and furrowed brows that some developmental psychologists interpret as expressing puzzlement and distress (Gopnik 2000). For Piaget (1936/1952), infants' early exploration of their environment and their interest in novelty stem from the child's need to make sense of the world in which she finds herself. The affective state of curiosity has motivational force (Berlyne 1960; Keller 1987) and drives exploratory behavior (Voss and Keller 1986). Infants' early exploratory behavior is a sign of a curiosity state, and I argue that exploratory behavior in the social domain is an early form of FP explanation seeking.

Prelinguistic infants engage in many exploratory behaviors from an early age. According to some accounts, children are already exploring the world as two-month-old infants, as demonstrated by their tendency to give tongue protrusions to both social and nonsocial stimuli, and at four to six months with their reaching behavior (Chen et al. 2006). At this age, they are also coordinating their behavior, emotional expressions, and communicative attempts with mothers (Trevarthen 1977). The infants focus attention on caregivers' vocalizations and facial expressions and attempt to elicit responses from caregivers, and such behaviors are a kind of social exploration.

While many developmental psychologists suggest that children are curious about people and their actions, one might worry that this does not demonstrate curiosity about people or their actions qua intentional agents. Perhaps children explore their social world and their physical world without wondering about people. However, evidence shows that infants distinguish between the social and the physical at an early age. For example, Trevarthen's observation that children respond differently to social and physical stimuli suggests that children see a difference in kind between agents and objects.

More recent experimental studies also suggest that infants have an early tendency to see some movements as agential and other movements as nonagential. Infants can distinguish between objects that are self-propelled and those that are not, where the self-propelled objects are interpreted as intentional agents acting according to their goals (Premack 1990). Infants also seem to see action as rational. Heider famously discovered that adults tend to describe the movements of geometrical shapes as actions performed by rational agents, and that people make up stories about these objects as if they were actors in a soap opera (Heider and Simmel 1944).

Infants also seem to perceive some kinds of abstract movement as rational (Gergely et al. 1995; Csibra and Gergely 1998). Using a violation of expectation paradigm, the researchers showed twelve-month-olds a video of a small circle moving over a rectangular barrier to a larger circle. Once the child habituates to this stimulus, she is shown one of two new videos. In both videos, the two circles remain, but the rectangular barrier has been removed from the scenario. Children shown the old-action video, in which the small ball continues to move over the now nonexistent barrier toward the larger ball, show renewed attention. Children shown the new-action video, in which the small ball now moves in a straight line to the large ball, fail to demonstrate any renewed interest. Gergely and colleagues interpret this result as indicating that the children see the old action as something novel, because they perceive the small ball as an actor with the goal of getting to the larger ball as directly as possible. The child shown the old-action video looks longer because the small ball is now behaving anomalously, given its goal. Gergely and colleagues suggest that this behavior indicates that infants have an innate cognitive system for identifying intentional agents from a pattern of rational behavior. The infants recognize the behavior type and use the information to determine that the object is in fact an agent (Király et al. 2003).

Continuing research is uncovering more about how the infant distinguishes between actors and nonactors. A series of studies by Woodward and colleagues examined the features of movement that lead infants to see movement as behavior (Woodward 1998). For example, in one study Woodward used a violation of expectation paradigm to examine whether different objects that were engaged in the same motions would be interpreted in the same way. Infants were habituated to a human reaching toward an object and then were shown one of two behaviors. The new object condition showed the human reaching in the same direction, but toward a different object. The new side event showed the human reaching in a different direction, but toward the same object. Infants as young as six months expected the hand to reach for the same object, rather than in the same direction, thus suggesting they perceived the movement as goal oriented. However, when Woodward repeated the experiment using inanimate objects rather than hands—things such as a mechanical claw or a rod—the researchers found that infants did not show the same result. They concluded that though infants appear to see human movement as action, they do not easily generalize the same motion to inanimate objects.

In follow-up studies, researchers examined whether the infants were attending to some feature of biological versus mechanical motion. Guajardo and Woodward (2004) investigated this question by testing infants' responses to disembodied hands. They found that infants' responses to the movement of an ungloved, disembodied hand are the same as their responses to a person's action, but the identical movement of a gloved hand is not interpreted as an action.

It remains an open question how exactly infants divide agents from the rest of the world, and what features of actors they take to be relevant in determining whether or not actors should be perceived as agential. Nonetheless these studies, along with the infant theory of mind studies discussed in chapter 2, provide compelling evidence that preverbal infants distinguish action from mere movement, and actors from mere objects. This suggests that the curiosity and the exploratory behavior that infants demonstrate toward other people represent curiosity about others as agents, rather than as inanimate objects in the environment. If this is so, then twelve-month-olds have the ability to see others as agents. Infants are engaged in exploratory behavior toward people, and since they see others as intentional agents, it is reasonable to suggest that they are already engaged in seeking FP explanations.

Verbal Children

One might object that preverbal children's behavior cannot provide enough evidence for explanation seeking, because extremely young children cannot ask questions. While some evidence suggests that preverbal infants make nonlinguistic requests for information in terms of a gesture, expression, or vocalization (Chouinard 2007), we can turn to look at the questions asked and answered by verbal children.

We know that, across cultures, children begin asking *wh*-questions in a determinate order. *What* and *where* (terms that refer to observables) emerge earliest, soon followed by *who*. Only later do *how*, *why*, and *when* (terms that refer to abstractions) emerge (Brown 1968; Clancy 1989; Ervin-Tripp 1970; Labov and Labov 1977; M. Lewis 1938). By the end of the third year, children are able to utter why-questions, which is six months or more later than their use of the early what-, where-, and who-questions (Clancy 1989).

Although children don't ask why-questions until they are nearly three, researchers generally accept that children understand the semantics of "why" as two-year-olds. For one, explanatory questions can be phrased in other terms, such as "how come?" In addition, evidence suggests that the order of acquisition of the *wh*-questions does not reflect the child's developing ability to understand the concepts, since during the process of learning a second language, the order of acquisition of why-questions remains the same (Felix 1976; Lightbown 1978).[1] Finally, we know that children use terms referring to temporality and causality in their declarative statements (e.g., they use terms such as *because, so, and then*, and *when*) at twenty-six months, all terms associated with explanations (A. Bloom et al. 1980). Such evidence is taken to indicate that children are offering causal explanations at two years. It may be that children ask for explanations even earlier; Chouinard (2007) argues that younger children ask syntactically incomplete explanation questions, such as "Daddy break?" in response to an observation of the father breaking an object. This question is interpreted as a request for an explanation, given the context of the utterance.

We know that two-year-olds will ask for explanations, but what are these explanations about? While the topics of children's questions vary, from the beginning children are much more likely to ask about an individual's behavior and motivation than anything else (Dunn 1988; Callanan and Oakes 1992). And though they are asking questions by eighteen months, they rarely ask questions about others' beliefs, desires, knowledge, other mental states or personality traits until they are two and a half to three years old (Chouinard 2007). At eighteen months, children wonder about the behavior of people and animals, and before they ask questions directly about mental states, children ask questions that fall within the domain of social cognition, such as "What is he doing?" or "Why is he sleeping?" (Chouinard 2007, 19, 64). While these questions differ from the questions that children ask a year later, the answers to these questions about people's behavior will often refer to mental content, emotions, and motivation.

While the content of children's requests for information is often taken to be a request for causal information, other plausible interpretations exist. In one study that looked at parents' answers to their children's why-questions, the authors stated that the answers overwhelmingly cited causal features such as a mechanism, a prior cause, a purpose or teleology, or some combination (Callanan and Oakes 1992). For example, Callanan and Oakes take as causal the child's question "Mommy, I always ask why. Why do I always ask why?" because they understand the mother's answer, "Because you are curious about things," as stating the cause of the child's behavior.

But it isn't clear that dispositions such as curiosity are indeed causal in nature rather than a mere description of the person. By calling the child "curious," the parent may mean only that he often asks questions, a description that at best provides statistical information about the child but certainly doesn't offer a causal explanation for the behavior. If the child then asks a question about the nature of curiosity, the answer will not help him understand any better the causes of his questioning behavior. However, this answer could give the child other kinds of information. The child might be told that children of his age usually ask those questions—an explanation consisting of more general information. Given that the child is presumably learning something new, that explanation may satisfy, though it does not take a causal form.

Another study gives us the example of a causal why-question, "Why [did the crawfish die]?," and the parent's answer, "Well, maybe he's old" (Chouinard 2007, 103). It isn't age that caused the crawfish to die; rather, age is associated with diseases and decay in organisms, and it was disease and decay that caused the death. So, again, this is not a causal answer but an example of an explanation that takes an inductive statistical form. Another example from this set of studies is "How come I cannot go outside?" (Chouinard 2007, 17). This is supposedly a causal explanatory question but can easily be interpreted as a request for information about a rule, reason, or description (e.g., "When it's dark, children are more likely to get lost outside"), rather than a cause (e.g., "Because the door is locked and we cannot open it").

While it is clear that children do engage in causal reasoning from an early age, what is less clear is the extent to which children are seeking causal information when they ask questions about human behavior. Instead perhaps children are simply seeking information, some of which will appropriately be causal, but some of which may be about whether the behavior is typical, acceptable, or connected with other behaviors. For example, when a parent tells a child that she should share toys because it is the nice thing to do, the parent is offering a normative reason to share and letting the child know that sharing is a virtuous action. Or when a toddler asks, "Why?" after a caregiver says, "Please don't kick the cat," the response might be, "Because only mean people hurt others, and you don't want to be a mean person, right?" Exchanges such as these give children information about the social world, about what is good and bad, liked and not liked, rather than citing an actor's personal reason for acting or psychological information about why humans don't like being attacked. Not all our FP explanations provide a causal story about the target behavior.

Explanation Generating in Children

Although explanation seeking may be something that humans do almost as soon as they are born, it is more difficult to determine when children begin generating explanations. Nonverbal behaviors that we might associate with explanation generation, such as a cessation of exploratory behavior, could also be due to boredom or a shift in attention due to a new stimulus. Given verbal behavior, though, we know that by two years, children are also offering explanations for a variety of things, and evidence from children's naturalistic language demonstrates that two- and three-year-olds are extremely interested in psychological explanations that focus on people, their behavior, and their mental experiences (Dunn and Brown 1993; Hickling and Wellman 2001; Hood and Bloom 1979; McCabe and Peterson 1988).

Turning to the contents of children's early FP explanations, it is clear that they do not begin to explain behavior in terms of the actor's propositional attitude. Rather, children's early explanations refer to other psychological features of an individual (such as their desires for objects or emotions), social-conventional features (such as rules), and physical or biological features (such as the weather or someone's age) (Hickling and Wellman 2001).

Let us look at three typical examples of children's intentional action explanation. Young children will answer a why-question by citing their own desire (Twenty-eight-month-old child: "Open it" Adult: "Why?" Child: "Because I want you to open it") (Hood and Bloom 1979, 7), or will cite an emotion, "I not gon go up . . . because I'm afraid of her" (Hickling and Wellman 2001, 671), or will describe the situation (Adult: "Why are you taking off your socks?" Thirty-one-month-old child: "Because it's not cold outside") (Hood and Bloom 1979, 6). Researchers categorized all three of these explanations as psychological. However, of these three examples, only the desire explanation is possibly interpreted as a propositional attitude attribution. We know that children appear to understand something about desire at eighteen months, and the early use of desire and other emotions in children's explanations reflects this understanding. The second example has a child attributing behavior to fear, which is an intentional emotion rather than an attitude with propositional content.

In the third example, the child is interpreted by Hood and Bloom as referring to her own belief, but it is more in keeping with what we have subsequently learned about the trajectory of children's developing belief concept that this explanation is a situational one. It reflects the child's understanding that socks are worn when it is cold; since it isn't cold, she doesn't need to wear socks. While adults can reinterpret the child's utterance as providing a reason explanation for her action, the child need not have conceptualized the state of affairs *as* her reason. That is, the child need not have metarepresentational knowledge of her own beliefs at this stage.

Indeed, children appear to lack an ability to offer explanations in terms of belief until they are four or older (Andrews and Verbeek, unpublished data; Moses and Flavell 1990; Wimmer and Mayringer 1998; Wimmer and Weichbold 1994; but see Bartsch and Wellman 1989 for evidence that children refer to false belief to explain at a younger age). Even when children are asked to explain their own behavior through reference to a prior false belief, three-year-olds have great difficulty. Atance and O'Neill (2004) tested children's ability to recognize their own intentions by giving them a modified unexpected-contents task. In one condition, children are shown a box of crayons and asked what is inside. After the child answers the question, the researcher says, "Look, there's some paper over there. Why don't you get it to draw on with the crayons?" The child retrieves the piece of paper, and then the experimenter opens the box, showing the child that candles, not crayons, are inside. The child is then asked what she previously thought was inside the box. If the child answers "candles," the experimenter immediately asks, "Why did you go get the paper then?" Fifty percent of the subjects failed the past-belief part of the test; of these, 81 percent were unable to explain their paper-retrieving behavior. However, in 35 percent of trials where children passed the false-belief test, they still failed to cite a plausible explanation for their behavior. This suggests that explaining behavior predicated on a false belief may be more difficult that predicting it.

The picture that emerges of children's developing ability to explain behavior is that at a very early age, children begin to seek explanations, and they are particularly interested in understanding the behavior of agents. Sometime during the second year, children are explaining behavior, but these explanations are not given in terms of propositional attitudes. Children do not explain behaviors in terms of belief until four years and do not understand beliefs as referentially opaque until even later. Children's lack of understanding of representational belief forces us to interpret their explanations not as truncated belief-desire explanations but as explanations that make reference to some other aspect of the person, such as an emotion, a goal, or a desire, or some aspect of the situation that makes sense of the behavior.

What becomes clear from a review of the developmental literature is that children engage in both explanation seeking and explanation offering long before they are able to attribute propositional attitudes in the way described by SFP, and these explanations need not be directed toward causes.

The Purposes of FP Explanation

We see that children seek and offer explanations at an early age. But what purposes are served by our drive for explanations? That is, what makes us explain some things and not others? That question has no simple answer, and the variety of reasons we have for offering explanations, combined with the nature of FP explanation as inherently context dependent and individually relativized, further undermines the view that we give FP explanations fundamentally in terms of propositional attitudes. In addition, if we look at the contents of adult explanations, it becomes clear that not all explanations of behavior are going to be causal.

At least four types of purposes can be given for FP explanation seeking: to acquire new knowledge, to reduce cognitive dissonance, to gain greater control, and to evaluate behavior. Though these purposes can be interrelated, I will examine each in turn.

When we seek explanations to gain information about a situation, it may be because we want to better understand the elements of the situation and how they fit together. For example, an executive who is touring the shipping department of his company may notice a man reading out numbers as he is putting boxes in a pile. Seeing no one responding to the packer's behavior, the executive might ask his tour guide, "Why is he reading off the shipping numbers?" If the guide points up to the catwalk, where a supervisor with a clipboard is checking off numbers, the executive promptly gains a better understanding of how the system works. He now knows that the packer is reading off the shipping numbers so that the supervisor can keep track of the packages. But this explanation may or not correspond to the packer's reasons for reading out the numbers; if he is cognitively disabled, he might be reading the numbers because he was told to, not because he has an understanding of how that action fits into the larger system of the shipping department.

Or consider the child who asks his father in the car, "Daddy, why don't you go?" When the father shows the child the stoplight and explains how it works, the child learns something about how to drive a car and the rules of the road in his society. In this case, when the father explains the function of the stoplight, presumably he is giving his reason for stepping on the brake.

These are examples of how an explanation of behavior can give us information about the norms at play in different social situations. Such explanations also give us greater control, insofar as they allow us to make predictions that we might not previously have been able to make. Once the executive realizes that this packer is reading out numbers to keep track of the packages, she can predict that other packers will read out numbers, as well. She has learned that this isn't just an idiosyncratic behavior of an individual packer, it is what packers should do. The same goes for the child who learns about stoplights. He can then expect that cars will stop at red lights, and can use this information to decide when to cross the street.

Sometimes we seek explanations primarily as a means to avoid affective tension, and we generate explanations without much concern for rational constraints such as evidence. This reason for asking why is associated with cognitive dissonance theory (Festinger and Carlsmith 1959; Frey 1982). Cognitive dissonance is an affective response that arises when an individual has beliefs that conflict with one another, which then leads people to resolve the tension by finding some way to reconcile the apparently conflicting beliefs. Cognitive dissonance theory has people resolving this tension in any way necessary, even going so far as to reject true or justified information simply because it is incompatible with their preexisting beliefs (Edwards and Smith 1996; Lord et al. 1979). This means that the kinds of explanations we look for are not always aimed at the truth but can instead be aimed at a pragmatic goal that is unconcerned with, or even opposed to, the truth.

Developing an explanation that reduces dissonance can also have the effect of giving the explainer greater control. For example, a person who sees another engage in an anomalous behavior can develop a tension between the observed behavior and the belief that led her to expect a different kind of behavior. Seeking an explanation for the anomalous behavior is also seeking an explanation for why her prediction was wrong. This explanation will give the explainer additional information about the actor or the situation and will allow the explainer to make better predictions in the future.

A third reason to explain behavior is to gain greater control (Heider 1958; Ichheiser 1949; Kelley 1971; Kelly 1955). With control over the situation, an individual can use the explanatory information to present herself in the best light, managing how an audience perceives her. Having an explanation can also give someone greater facility at working within the situation or making future predictions. From this research, we know that people are more likely to seek explanations about others when they expect to meet them in the future (Berscheid et al. 1976; Elliott 1979; D. Miller et al. 1978), and when they are already feeling a lack of control (Swann et al. 1981). When we expect to meet someone in the future, having an explanation for their behavior helps us understand how to interact with them and will help us to predict their behavior insofar as it may provide information about individual differences. If you learn that a person is reading classic novels in preparation for taking the GRE, when you meet her again, you will be in a position to talk about something she is concerned about, which might make her more kindly disposed toward you.

We also have evaluative reasons for offering explanations; the kinds of explanations we give for behaviors are related to our normative judgment of the behavior. People tend to give more explanations in terms of belief when they want to appear rational (Malle et al. 2000), and decrease their appeal to propositional attitudes when explaining behavior judged to be negatively valanced (Malle and Nelson 2003). This finding reflects the common observation that behaviors deemed immoral by society are rarely explained, and people who try to explain immoral behavior are often taken to be justifying the immoral act. For example, in response to an announcement that Alliance Atlantis was going to produce a miniseries about Hitler's early life, his upbringing, and early political career, many people were concerned that the documentary would serve to explain Hitler's genocidal acts. Protesters appeared to want Hitler's acts to remain unexplained; for example, Abraham Foxman, national director of the Anti-Defamation League, argued, "Why the need or the desire to make this monster human? The judgment of history is that he was evil. Why trivialize the judgment of history by focusing on his childhood and adolescence?"

The evaluative function of explanation is also reflected in the difference found between how people explain their own behavior and how they explain others' behavior. One of the classic findings of social psychology has to do with this difference, namely, the claim that we explain others' behavior in terms of personality traits or other personal characteristics, rather than in terms of the situation (Ross 1977). When people explain their own behavior, however, many researchers have noted that the types of explanations differ according to whether the behavior is seen as a success or a failure. One's own successes are explained in terms of personal characteristics such as traits, whereas one's failures are more often explained in terms of situational features (Ames et al. 1977; Jones and Nisbett 1972; Small and Peterson 1981; S. Taylor and Koivumaki 1976; Zuckerman 1979). This self-serving bias can be seen when, for example, a person explains that she forgot to keep a promise by citing her busy schedule rather than her absentmindedness, but fails to accept similar situational features as explanatory when her colleague forgets his promise.

While this general claim has come under fire (P. Lewis 1995; Malle 2006a), a host of evidence nonetheless demonstrates that people use different explanatory styles for evaluative or normative purposes, and styles of explanation differ by individual (Buchanan and Seligman 1995). Studies of explanations in written accounts suggest that people tend to explain more negative than positive events (Peterson et al. 1992; Peterson and Seligman 1984), and when putting a positive spin on a behavior, people tend to explain it in terms of mental states such as beliefs and desires (Malle et al. 2007). Depressed people are more likely to explain their own behavior as due to a stable personality trait (Peterson et al. 1992).

As empirical research on the purposes of explanation continues, we will probably find that factors about the explainer, such as explanatory style, cultural background, age, and emotional state, interact with the type of action being explained (be it positively or negatively valanced, a typical versus atypical behavior, performed by someone from an in-group versus an out-group, or self versus other) in a complex manner. Knowing how these and other variables work together will perhaps offer more information about why we explain behavior. Indeed, as we will see, such issues are probably just as important to ongoing work in how we explain behavior.

Explanation Types and Contents

In both developmental psychology and social psychology, the focus has largely been on causal explanations. As understood by social psychology, explanation, like prediction, can involve attributing mental states, but it also involves the external factors of the situation, the individual's perceived character traits and past behavior, and even the observer's response to the situation. Social psychology takes both our predictive and explanatory practices to be caused by a heterogeneous set of mechanisms. However, social psychologists (e.g., Kelley 1972) have largely shared with developmental psychologists (e.g., Gopnik et al. 2004) the view that explanations are primarily causal. The literature on attribution theory has largely focused on a view of folk psychology according to which we understand other behavior as being caused by the person, the situation, or a combination of the two. The emphasis on causal accounts of folk psychology is also evident in the explanatory-style literature, which focuses primarily on individual differences in kinds of explanations offered for one's own behavior (Buchanan and Seligman 1995).

Despite these emphases, once researchers began to look at the explanations people actually give for behavior, they discovered a variety of explanation types. Bertram Malle pioneered the investigation into the kinds of explanations that adults provide for intentional behavior by examining the linguistic behavior of adult participants in an experimental setting. He found that while people predominantly explain behavior in terms of reasons, we also cite nonreason causes, including causes given the actor's past history. In addition, we offer explanations that cite features of the individual or situation that made the behavior possible, even though these were not part of the event that caused the behavior (Malle 1999, 2004; Malle et al. 2000).

Malle thinks that folk psychological explanations of intentional behavior can be classified into three types: reason explanations, causal history explanations, and enabling factors explanations. While reason explanations are generally taken to be propositional attitude explanations, Malle's reason explanation category includes reasons not only in terms of belief and desire but also in terms of goals and valuings. Malle defines reason explanations as "those behavior explanations that cite agents' reasons for intending to act or for acting intentionally" where reasons are "agents' mental states whose content they considered and in light of which they formed an intention to act" (Malle 1999, 27). This definition of reason explanations mirrors the familiar account of rationalizations offered by Davidson (1963). A second kind of explanation for action is Malle's causal history explanation, which does not cite the actor's reason but instead refers to what Malle calls a "mere cause." A mere cause is any cause of a behavior that is not a reason, including the actor's mood, personality trait, emotional state, or some other fact about the person. Causal history reasons refer to "factors that lay in the background of the agent's reasons, such as in her upbringing, personality, culture, or in the immediate context" (Malle 2004, 91). Enabling factor explanations, on the other hand, are not seen as causal explanations. These explanations refer to a feature of the person or the situation that allowed a person's intention to result in a successful action, such as an individual's skill or the simplicity of the action.

Malle uses these categories to analyze explanations offered by his research subjects for behaviors described to them, such as yawning in class, inviting someone to dinner, refusing dessert, and so on. The subjects were asked to explain each behavior and to rate the extent to which the action was intentional. It was found that they tended to provide reason explanations, citing beliefs or desires, for actions they deemed intentional. If the action was not deemed to be intentional, people tended to explain the action in terms of some nonpropositional property of the agent or in terms of the situation (Malle 1999).

In his frequency analysis, Malle reports that people usually cite reasons, though these rarely take the form of an explicit propositional attitude attribution; in such cases, the coder infers that the speaker suppressed a mental-state marker. Thus when the question "Why did she refuse dessert?" is answered with "She's been gaining weight," this is presumed to be shorthand for "She thinks she's been gaining weight" (Malle 2004, 97). In explaining others' behaviors, subjects in the study explained 61 percent of behaviors by reasons alone, 16 percent by causal history of reasons, and 23 percent by a combination of the two kinds of explanation.

These studies demonstrate that people do not limit their explanations to causes. Rather, the evidence shows that when we look for diversity in the kinds of explanations people offer, we find it. Indeed, there may be even more variety in our explanation types than have been discovered so far. The causal history of reasons category, for instance, blurs the traditional distinction between explanations in terms of the actor's psychology and explanation in terms of the actor's situation. There is some reason to keep that distinction, given the evidence that these explanatory styles differ in frequency in East Asia and North America (J. Miller 1984; Morris and Peng 1994; Norenzayan et al. 2002; Nisbett 2003). For example, Chinese and U.S. newspapers were found to give very different kinds of explanations for an action that made news in both countries. Gang Lu, a Chinese physics student at the University of Iowa, opened fire in the physics department, killing his adviser and several other people before turning the gun on himself. An analysis of the newspaper reports in the two countries discovered that U.S. papers tended to explain Lu's actions by citing psychological characteristics, such as having a bad temper or believing that guns are a good way to solve problems. The Chinese papers, on the other hand, tended to explain Lu's action as being influenced by situational features, such as his isolation from Chinese society, the prevalence of guns in the United States, and his lack of relationships (Morris and Peng 1994). Indeed, when examining the explanatory styles of people in cultures that promote individuality rather than community, researchers found that causal explanations are more common in individualistic societies, and this difference becomes more pronounced with age (J. Miller 1984).

Malle's categorization also presumes that any explanation that can have an attitude attached to it should be seen as a propositional attitude or reason explanation. Malle claims that mental-state markers are not necessary for identifying something as shorthand for a reason—people infer that the reason is a reason believed by the actor, even if the claim is not made explicit. Malle writes, "In response to the question 'Why did he quit his job?,' the answer "His boss was sabotaging him" is a reason explanation that refers to a belief even though no belief marker is visible" (Malle 2004, 97). But does it? At least two points undermine the inference that all explanations of this sort are shorthand belief attribution explanations. For one, very young children can provide these sorts of explanations in terms of the situation before they understand representational belief. For example, when asked why a girl is looking under the piano, a child can respond by saying "The kitty is under there," and when asked why the boy is looking for his teddy behind the couch, the answer is often "Because that's where he left it" (Bartsch and Wellman 1989; Andrews and Verbeek, unpublished data). However, these explanations should not be understood as truncated belief attributions, given children's difficulty with understanding belief at this age. Instead of explaining what the actor believes, the children could be explaining what she should be doing given her past experience. In this case, the explanation may be more accurately categorized as a causal history explanation than a reason explanation that cites the actor's belief.

A second reason to deny that statements about the situation are always unmarked belief explanations stems from Robert Gordon's analysis of reasons (Gordon 2000). As Gordon argues, facts about a situation, rather than an individual's belief about the situation, can be reasons for action. Recall that Gordon says the fact that it is raining can be the direct cause of Sam's running, rather than necessarily mediated by Sam's belief that it is raining. Young children can explain Sam's behavior by citing the situation, even without an understanding of belief, because they can engage in counterfactual reasoning that leads them to see that if it were not raining, Sam would not be running. Gordon would agree that this explanation does offer a reason, but he would reject the supposition that the explainer is interested in the actor's belief.

We have a couple of reasons to side with Gordon over Malle on this point. Suppose a child explains why another child hit someone by saying that the child was being teased. In Malle's account, that explanation refers to the child's belief that she is being teased. But if she is very young and has no concept of teasing, then this explanation cannot accurately describe the content of the child's belief. This is not to say that the explanation would be incorrect; rather, the explainer cannot have the child's belief in mind when offering this explanation if he knows that the child cannot conceptualize the description of the situation that he offered.

Indeed, this need not only hold for young children. Not all attributions of situational features will reflect the *de dicto* belief of the actor. Consider again Malle's own example: Frank quit his job because his boss was sabotaging him. While Frank's boss may actually be sabotaging him, explaining Frank's quitting in this way may be more of a condemnation of the boss than a description of Frank's belief. Frank might not even know that his boss is sabotaging him. Instead, if the sabotage were successful, Frank may believe that he is terrible at his job, and quit given that belief. Alternatively, the sabotage may have caused Frank to have extremely negative affective responses to going to work, leading him to quit because work made him so miserable. To automatically code this explanation as a belief attribution ignores the other possible interpretations. It assumes that all attributions are *de dicto* attributions, when we often give explanations in *de re* terms. For example, after coming home from the state fair, a mother might tell her daughter, "The judges think that your father bakes the best cake in all of Minnesota," to announce that her husband won the blue ribbon at the cake-baking contest. However, she doesn't really mean to suggest that the judges' *de dicto* belief is "Sally's father bakes the best cake in all Minnesota," given that the judges may not even know that the man has a daughter. While rules of logical inference prohibit us from making inferences from *de dicto* to *de re* attributions of belief, in our folk practices, we violate this rule all the time.

Given that we might benefit from learning under what conditions people explain behavior in terms of personality traits, emotional states, moods, or other nonpropositional mental states, and given that not all statements about the situation can be taken as unmarked belief attributions, we need further research on these questions to uncover the extent of the diversity of the explanations we offer for behavior. In addition, given the variety of functions for explanations, we can also look for differences in explanation type within different kinds of situations. This is a rich area of study that psychologists have only begun to investigate.

Explanatory Pluralism

We are born explanation seekers. Children explore their world from an early age, and they also use the information they gather to more effectively interact with the world. Some of the explanations children seek may be aimed at discovering the causal structure of the world, but others may be aimed at uncovering the normative structure of the world. Causal structures and normative structures can both be used to make predictions about future behavior because they both make generalizations. But normative structures do not offer an explanation at a mechanical level; normative explanations are given to evaluate behavior or to provide statistical information rather than to describe the cause of behavior. While some explanation seeking is directed at uncovering causal structures, children also ask why to learn about the social, cultural, and linguistic features of their society and to learn what behaviors are associated with each other. Like adults, children ask why in the face of violations of expectations, and the answers they find help to resolve the tension and unify their view of the world.

As adults, we give explanations for different reasons, and the reason we have for providing an explanation will help to shape the kind of explanation provided. We offer different kinds of explanations depending on whether or not we approve of the behavior and of who engaged in it. We use our explanations to help understand an action and to make normative judgments about it. We explain by citing propositional attitudes, personality traits, moods, emotions, situational features, causal histories, and enabling factors. And we do not give all our explanations in terms of the event that caused the behavior.

This review of the social and developmental psychology literature on the lay practice of explaining behavior demonstrates that the drive to explain behavior occurs very early in human development, and our explanations take many different forms. The flexible nature of FP explanation further undermines the claim that folk psychology is the attribution of propositional attitudes. Just as we saw for prediction, so FP explanation is not limited to propositional attitude attribution but includes a rich tapestry of explanatory contents.

The empirical evidence also casts further doubt on the central role of the propositional attitudes in folk psychology. Insofar as the folk explain behavior in terms of emotional states, moods, personality traits, enabling features, and situations, they do not limit their explanations to the beliefs and desires that caused the action. And though the folk explain some behavior by citing causes in terms of nonpropositional psychological properties, they also explain behavior by describing noncausal enabling factors. Other explanations take the form of statistical generalizations, which allow people to understand a behavior by seeing it as part of a larger pattern. If we have noncausal explanations for behavior, the accounts of FP explanation offered by the major models of folk psychology discussed in the last chapter will all be deficient in this regard.

In chapter 10 I present my account of pluralistic folk psychology that, I will argue, is a more empirically adequate place to begin to understand our practices of predicting and explaining and our use of propositional attitudes. But before we get to that, I examine some challenges to the account of FP explanation that I have been defending so far.

9 Worries about Explanation and Mental State Attribution

A scorpion and a frog meet on the bank of a stream, and the scorpion asks the frog to carry him across on its back. The frog asks, "How do I know you won't sting me?" The scorpion says, "Because if I do, I will die too." The frog is satisfied, and they set out, but in midstream, the scorpion stings the frog. The frog feels the onset of paralysis and starts to sink, knowing they both will drown, but has just enough time to gasp, "Why?" Replies the scorpion: "It's my nature."
—Aesop, attributed

Explaining Behavior without a Theory of Mind

In the last chapter, we found that the verbal explanations people offer for behavior vary both in terms of their contents and in terms of their forms. While some explanations have propositional attitudes as their contents and are causal in form, other explanations cite nonpropositional mental content, such as emotions or moods, and others refer to no mental content at all. And while some explanations are causal, others are inductive, statistical, or refer to enabling conditions and do not appear to make any claims about causality or laws of human psychology. The varieties of explanatory content and structure suggest that one can be a successful explainer of behavior while lacking the ability to ascribe propositional attitudes.

Before we finally accept that folk psychological practices are possible without needing to attribute propositional attitudes, let us first address some challenges to the last two chapters. Critics may raise a number of concerns. An obvious worry is that I am illegitimately expanding the definition of explanation by allowing that someone without language might be able to explain behavior, and there are at least two reasons to take this position. First, one might think that language is needed for thought, and second, one might think that language is needed to gain the kinds of concepts required for explanations. I will briefly address these concerns.

A second set of worries comes from the idea that our verbal FP explanations at least implicitly attribute propositional attitudes to others. My claim that we offer explanations that do not cite causes or mental states is based on analysis of linguistic behavior. But there are reasons to worry about drawing any conclusions from the empirical data on the verbal explanations we offer, if we can offer explanations without verbalizing them, and if we need not be a competent language user to seek and even produce explanations. Nonetheless I argue that we do not automatically attribute propositional attitudes when we observe intentional action.

Finally, one may worry that nonpropositional and noncausal explanations would be given only for nonintentional behavior. In response, I argue that the folk think that traits cause behavior, and traits are distinct from propositional attitude attributions. The folk's actual behavior suggests that they don't think that all intentional actions are caused by propositions, and they don't think that all intentional actions are caused by some event. Once I show this, I will have the foundation necessary for developing a pluralistic account of folk psychology, which we will turn to in chapter 10.

Nonverbal Explainers

According to my account of a satisfactory FP explanation, the explanation seeker must believe the explanation. But one might worry that without language, an individual lacks beliefs, and hence nonverbal individuals cannot be explainers.

While it might initially seem strange to hold that nonhuman animals and preverbal infants are explaining events in their social (and physical) world, I think that this reaction may stem from the fact that such individuals are not seen as communicating explanations; that is, they do not explain events to others, and in this way they are different from humans whose verbal behavior is rich with explanations. But adult humans, too, explain behavior without verbalizing it. We might explain others' behaviors without communicating that explanation when we try to figure out how to buy a bus ticket when traveling alone in an unfamiliar city, or when observing from afar a person on a beach repeatedly walking a few paces and then stooping down. A person might also explain her own atypical behavior to herself while keeping her explanation secret; think of the self-serving explanation a married woman might offer to herself for a secret adulterous encounter. As such, verbal expression is not necessary for explanation. The mere fact that other species and preverbal infants fail to communicate explanations verbally is not enough to show that they are not generating them.

The more serious criticism along this vein comes from those who argue that having language is necessary for having belief. This is a standard worry among some philosophers. One reason has to do with content. If an individual lacks language, what form does the content of a belief take, and how could we ascribe that content using language? Another worry has to do with the truth functionality of beliefs. Beliefs are taken to be true by the believer, and thus believers must have the concepts of truth and falsity. But these concepts in turn require the concept of belief, since beliefs are the only things that are true or false. Thus, to understand what a belief is, you must be a language user. Arguments such as these have been offered to undermine the claim that animals have beliefs (e.g., Davidson 1975, 1982; Stich 1979). I first briefly consider answers to these two worries and then turn to a more nuanced version of the criticism, according to which language is required to have the concepts or capacities necessary for offering FP explanations.

The argument that one cannot have beliefs without language because language is required to provide content can be addressed by considering alternative vehicles for belief. For one, though an individual may lack an external language, she may still think in a language of thought (Fodor 1975). However, while language is often the default way of thinking about mental content, we have other, less obvious ways of conceiving of representational beliefs. Some philosophers suggest that individuals without language may be able to represent beliefs by using a cartographic structure. It has been argued that beliefs and the rational inference between beliefs can be accounted for by maps or diagrams (Braddon-Mitchell and Jackson 1996; Camp 2007; D. Lewis 1994; Rescorla 2009). For example, mental maps will take the place of mental sentences. A map, like an image, provides a lot of information by virtue of its organization and cannot be divided into a set of semantically meaningful smaller parts. In this way, maps are like words, not sentences: take a point off a map, and you lose all semantic information about that point. Maps are systematic and productive, they have resources that can be rearranged, and they can be rearranged in a potentially infinite number of different ways. Maps can share much of the expressive power of language, including the logical connectives, though they may not be able to accommodate attribution of propositional attitudes (Camp 2007). While this understanding of belief has its limitations, maps are easy to embrace given that not all FP explanations rely on propositional attitudes attribution, and prelinguistic children do not seem to have an understanding of representational belief.

The second argument against nonverbal belief comes from Davidson (1975, 1982). His argument is based on a worry about the truth functionality of beliefs. If you have a belief, you must believe that belief to be true. Davidson thinks that we have no plausible way to understand objective truth without language; truth and falsity apply to propositions only (Davidson 1982). Thus a believer must have an understanding of propositions. This amounts to the requirement that a believer must have metabeliefs about beliefs—something much like a theory of mind. Davidson writes: "My thesis is . . . that a creature cannot have a thought unless it has language. In order to be a thinking, rational creature, the creature must be able to express many thoughts, *and above all, be able to interpret the speech and thoughts of others*" (322–323; italics in original).

The main worry is that Davidson's account of belief leads to conclusions that are prima facie false. For example, we would be forced to say that children who lack a theory of mind have no beliefs, and that even some adults with autism are incapable of thought, although they are competent users of language (Andrews 2002; Andrews and Radenovic 2006). Davidson's account requires that believers must be capable of interpreting the actions of others in terms of their reasons for action, but some children and adults with autism, and most children younger than four, fail to offer explanations in terms of propositional attitudes. This conclusion, I think, is sufficient to undermine Davidson's argument, since the concept of belief that most philosophers operate with would allow us to ascribe beliefs to individuals with autism.

In our paper, Radenovic and I discussed the case of Eric, a high-functioning autistic high school student who was doing well in school and had been mainstreamed into the general classroom. Eric was taking part in applied behavioral analysis therapy to help him learn to stop interrupting in class and during assemblies. In one instance, Eric interrupted a guest speaker in front of five hundred students, shouting, "Yesterday they confused the schedule yesterday. Yesterday they confused the schedule—yesterday." The speaker stopped and looked at Eric, made a joke at Eric's expense, and the entire room broke out into laughter. During the ABA therapy, Eric was asked why the students all laughed. He replied, "They laughed because they felt the same [as I did]" (Gray 1996).

Given Eric's conversation with the therapist, we can easily ascribe to him the belief that people laughed, although Eric is unable to correctly interpret behavior or attribute beliefs. Davidson would have us say that

Eric's inability to accurately interpret others means that he lacks beliefs himself. Not only is this conclusion bizarre, but it is also contrary to a core platitude about beliefs, namely, that people who honestly assert things believe what they say. Davidson's thesis would force us to reject this widely held platitude and, worse, would have us say that Eric is not a rational thinker.

I find the arguments against the possibility of nonlinguistic belief weak. Relying on such arguments to undermine the possibility that one can offer explanations without language is overkill. Instead one might have a more nuanced concern that without language, one lacks the concepts or cognitive capacities needed specifically for explanation. We can turn to address that concern now.

Those who are willing to accept that belief is possible without language may still worry that the kind of beliefs required by FP explanations are not possible in the absence of language. Surely certain beliefs exist for which knowledge of language is necessary, such as beliefs about quantum physics, or the grammaticality of sentences. One might think that beliefs about the explanations of action fall into the same category and are not available to those who lack language.

What are some plausible candidates for such concepts? Certainly the concept of belief is one that some think requires language, as we saw in the previous paragraphs. And reason explanations are, according to standard FP, explanations in terms of beliefs and desires. But this is the very claim that I have offered evidence against, and the critic would be begging the question if she claimed that all FP explanations must include reference to belief. At least the critic would be obligated to confront the empirical evidence before plausibly making such a claim.

Another possible response is to say that one must understand intentionality to offer FP explanations. This view is much more plausible. For an individual to offer an explanation of behavior, it is reasonable to think that she must have some understanding of behavior as distinct from unintentional bodily motion, and also that she must have an understanding of the more general distinction between agents and nonagential entities.

While I agree that explainers must have this ability, we have no reason to think that language is required to make such distinctions. Empirical evidence shows that individuals without language are capable of making such distinctions; as we saw in previous chapters, infants are able to discriminate between intentional and nonintentional action at an early age.

Not only do human infants seem able to understand intentionality before they have any language ability, but this ability is shared with some other apes. Chimpanzees, for example, have been shown to be able to discriminate between a person who was unwilling to give them food and a person who was unable to give them food. If a person had food but couldn't give it to the chimpanzee because the food was too large to fit through the feeding hole or the person couldn't see the food, then the chimpanzee was relatively calm. However, if the person was able to offer the food but refused to do so, the chimpanzee was more likely to demonstrate impatience with the unwilling person by striking the Plexiglas barrier or moving the apparatus (Call et al. 2004).

Another indication that other apes understand intentionality comes from a study of helping behavior in chimpanzees (Warneken and Tomasello 2006). Researchers found that chimpanzees engage in helping behaviors in response to a human caregiver's nonverbal request for an out-of-reach object, similarly to eighteen-month-old children. By responding appropriately to the human's request, the chimpanzees' behavior suggests that they understand human motion as intentional action that has a clear meaning.

These findings suggest that we have no reason to worry about language being necessary for understanding intentionality. Unless some other concept is needed to offer FP explanations (and this seems unlikely), it seems there is no special worry about attributing FP explanatory beliefs to nonlinguistic individuals. If thought without language is possible, then explanations of behavior without language are possible. Unlike, say, thoughts about the grammaticality of sentences, FP explanations are not intrinsically tied to any linguistic concept.

Automatic Mental State Attribution

The second set of concerns stems from a methodological worry; just because we provide verbal explanations that do not make reference to belief doesn't mean that we don't automatically attribute beliefs to agents whose behavior we are explaining. Just because we don't explicitly state the belief doesn't mean that we don't assume it to be present, at least in some implicit sense.

One might object that while our linguistic behavior suggests that we explain action in terms of traits, emotions, enabling features, and situations, the ability to offer such explanations relies on a prior understanding of propositional attitudes. Although FP explanations do not overtly take the form of propositional attitude attributions, they should still be interpreted in terms of the actor's beliefs about the situation. We dealt with a similar concern in chapter 6; perhaps verbal descriptions of behavior are actually shorthand belief-desire attributions, especially in the case of trait attributions.

Note first that if we insist that behind all verbal FP explanations lies an implicit reference to beliefs and desires, we will end up in one of the two following problematic positions. Either we would have to accept that young children have an understanding of representational belief, despite evidence to the contrary, or we would have to conclude that young children do not explain behavior, despite the appearance that they do. In each of the two cases, we would have to face the task of accounting for empirical evidence.

Perhaps more to the point, we have reason to understand belief ascription (and other similar practices) as the result of distinct cognitive capacities, as I have already argued. However, the claim that I rejected is that trait attribution is shorthand for belief and desire attribution, because a double dissociation exists between understanding traits and understanding beliefs. Normal children come to understand personality traits only after they understand the mental states of desire and belief, while some children who cannot attribute beliefs are able to use traits to predict behavior. When impaired children use trait attribution, they are taught to understand traits as dispositions to behave in certain ways. In fact, this is how traits are understood in the psychological literature—as shorthand for kinds of behavior, rather than anything like private states of mind. Unless we are going to return to a behaviorist method of individuating mental states, personality traits should be seen as distinct from any mental states, including beliefs and desires.

Nonetheless the retort that all FP explanations contain at least implicit reference to beliefs and desires is a natural criticism because we can restate many explanations in terms of propositional attitudes, and we can rephrase the reasoning that led to a prediction in terms of propositional attitudes, as well. The explanation "He mugged the woman because he is a drug addict" can be rephrased as "He mugged the woman because he wanted money for drugs, and he believed that the woman had money." But no matter how easy it is to construct these claims in this manner, the mere fact that we can make such a reconstruction does not entail anything about whether that reconstruction is an accurate account of the explainer's cognitive processes.

Of course, this response leaves open the possibility that we are ascribing propositional attitudes when we explain behavior. It is only a response to the worry that, since we can *reinterpret* any verbal explanation in terms of belief and desire attribution, the explainer *is* implicitly attributing beliefs and desires. We now need to address the worry that belief attribution is automatic and drives our folk psychological practices of explanation and prediction, despite the surface features of our explanatory behavior.

To my mind, the main intuition behind this objection is that humans automatically attribute belief whenever interpreting intentional action. The argument goes like this: we do not need to engage in an extra act of reasoning after observing a behavior to determine the beliefs that may have led to the action, because the attribution of belief is the result of cognitive processing that is triggered by the observation. This makes the attribution something that happens very fast, which need not occur at the level of conscious awareness. Thus when we explain intentional action, we automatically infer the actor's belief, even if we do not state that belief in a verbal explanation of the behavior, and even if we are not consciously aware of forming the belief attribution.

This argument is based on an empirical claim about human cognitive processing, and since research has been conducted on this question, we need not rely on our intuitions to conclude one way or another. Evidence suggests that we do not automatically infer beliefs, even when we observe behavior that was caused by an actor's false belief.

In the original study on the automaticity of belief attribution, Ian Apperly and colleagues (2006) compared adult response times to questions asked about a false-belief scenario. Participants were shown a variation of the Maxi task; more specifically, they were shown a video of a woman looking into two open boxes and indicating the box that contains the object with a marker. The woman leaves, and a man changes the position of the boxes or the location of the marker so that the woman has a false belief.

At the beginning of the trial, participants were told that their task was to identify the location of the woman's object at the end of the trial. After watching the man move the object, participants were given one of two possible probes and were asked to indicate whether the probe statement was accurate or not. The belief probe made a statement about the woman's belief, and the reality probe made a statement about the actual location of the object.

The authors reasoned that if belief were automatically ascribed when individuals observe behavior, then even given the instruction to monitor reality, the participants would also be interpreting the woman's belief. Thus there should be no significant difference in response time whether the person is asked about the woman's mental state or about the actual situation, since both pieces of information should be already available to the participants. However, if it takes participants longer to correctly respond to the belief probe, the authors reason that they must be engaging in additional processing, and therefore that belief attribution is not automatic.

What researchers found is that it takes adults significantly longer to attribute a belief than it does to report on reality. This effect was not due to some special feature about belief or an artifact of the study, such as a longer processing time for reading the statement about belief than the statement about the situation. The researchers ran another condition in which participants were instructed before the task to consider the character's belief, and this condition elicited no significant difference in response times between the belief and reality probes.

This finding suggests that adults do not automatically ascribe belief when observing a person's behavior, but attributions of belief are generated in an effortful and deliberate fashion when needed. However, another study challenges this conclusion. Cohen and German (2009) argue that the performance demands on the two tasks are different, since the information about the woman's belief is presumably formed when she marks the location of the object, and the information about the location of the object is given later, when the man moves it. Thus a memory confound might explain Apperly's result.

To test their theory, Cohen and German modified the task so that the last thing the participants see before answering the questions is the woman indicating her false belief by putting a marker on the wrong container. This "short-delay" condition was compared with performance on a replication of Apperly's original "long-delay" experiment. The authors found that belief responses were significantly faster than reality responses in the short-delay condition, and contra the original study, there was no significant difference in the long-delay condition.

While both studies begin to address the question of automaticity in belief attribution, I think it is too soon to draw any solid conclusions about the issue. One might want to interpret Cohen and German's study as evidence that we do automatically attribute belief when we see someone acting on a false belief, but some problems are associated with drawing that conclusion from their study, as they point out. The response times they found were longer than expected for an automatic process, and though the times are inflated (given the time it takes to read the probe and push a button), they think that the belief attribution activated by the task probably involves multiple cognitive processes. Given these methodological concerns, Cohen and German think that for a good study of automaticity, we should turn to the methods of neuroscience.

I see an additional problem with the design of both studies. One concern is that the woman's act of marking the box that contains her object is a symbolic act that primes observers who possess a theory of mind to think about belief. Evidence suggests that using markers such as these improves performance on theory of mind type tasks performed by children younger than four (Hauser 2006). In addition, we know that external markers can help animals perform cognitive tasks. For example, chimpanzees who are trained to use one kind of concrete tag for pairs of similar objects (AA) and another marker for pairs of different objects (AB) are then able to perform analogy tasks that chimpanzees who do not use markers are unable to perform (Thompson et al. 1997). The worry with the present paradigms is that because of the introduction of a marker—a quasi-symbolic element—the participants are no longer automatically inferring belief but are being primed to think about belief. If the woman's act of marking the box is seen as a communicative one, then the natural interpretation of that act is to see it as indicating her belief about the location of the object. If this is right, then the task cannot help us determine whether belief attribution is automatic, any more than would a task in which the woman uttered the sentence "I believe the object is in this box." Rather, to test whether or not we ascribe belief in situations where the actor is not intentionally communicating her belief, we would need a scenario that lacked any such communicative element.

If adults do automatically ascribe beliefs when they observe behavior, then there must be a developmental account of this automatic process. However, no developmental story seems forthcoming. Since children who lack the concept of belief are certainly not automatically ascribing belief to others who act intentionally, it is difficult to see why they would begin to do so once they develop an understanding of representational belief. In some cases, of course, ascribing belief would help the child to understand the behavior. But as I have argued, in most cases ascribing beliefs will not give the child any additional predictive power. If I am right, then those who think that belief ascription is automatic must explain how automatic attributions come to be generalized, and automatized, across all intentional acts. Supporters of automaticity have many questions to answer before we can conclude that adult humans automatically perceive intentional action in terms of the actor's beliefs.

Though the investigation into the automaticity of belief attribution still has a way to go, this discussion does bring home the point that we cannot presume that we automatically mindread from the mere fact that we can reconstruct an explanation in terms of propositional attitudes. The same applies to parallel arguments about the prediction of behavior. The claim that an automatic process takes place is empirical, and it requires empirical investigation. Nonetheless, given the behavioral evidence that individuals can explain behavior without demonstrating any understanding of belief ascription, the burden of proof is on those who think that automatic processes are present.

The critic might still worry that even if we do not automatically attribute beliefs to actors, we do automatically attribute some other kind of mental state. Thus there must be a problem with my account, according to which we can give satisfactory FP explanations in terms of situations or trait attributions that do not explicitly refer to the actor's mental state. While some personality traits, as stable dispositions of an individual, cannot be understood as a mental state of the actor (e.g., honesty, loyalty, pliancy, manipulability), others can (e.g., to call someone a happy person is to say that she is often in a happy mood). Our verbal explanations in terms of behavioral traits, enabling factors, or situations often imply something about the actor's mental state.

Even if this were so, it would still be a conclusion that is inconsistent with SFP, according to which all FP explanations must be at least implicitly propositional. But I think we have reason to reject even this minimal commitment to mental-state reference in an account of FP explanation. For one, as I argued in the previous chapter, situational explanations sometimes cite causes that the actor is not aware of. Recall the example of the employee whose boss is successfully manipulating him to quit, but the employee is unaware of the boss's manipulation. One explanation for the employee's quitting is that the boss is making his working environment extremely unpleasant. The employee may know that his working environment is unpleasant but fail to know that the boss is the cause. Thus this is not the explanation the employee would offer for quitting, since he doesn't know his boss's plan. Sometimes we explain people's behavior in terms of a cause of that behavior, even when the actor is unaware of the causal factor.

The same sort of analysis can be made for trait attributions, insofar as our trait attributions do not always refer to a property that the actor would claim for herself. Or worse, the actor might have specific beliefs about herself that contradict the personality traits. Negative personality traits in particular can be useful for predicting and explaining behavior, though they do not make up a mental state of the individual, and though the individual might deny that the trait term correctly describes her behavior. For example, consider the nonmentalistic trait "self-centered." Seeing Mary enter the elevator I am heading for, I might predict that since she is self-centered, Mary will not hold the elevator for me. I attribute this trait to Mary because of all the other self-centered behaviors she engages in: she always insists we take the speaker to her favorite restaurant, even though it is too expensive for the graduate students; she refuses to come in early for department meetings because she likes to sleep in; when she tires of a task, she quits and forces others to finish it for her. If Mary were asked to explain why she didn't hold the elevator, she might say, "I didn't notice you." However, it was a lack of attention to her surroundings that earned her the reputation of being self-centered to begin with. Or she may not have an answer at all; we need not know all our reasons.

Traits that are societally prohibited, such as being racist or sexist, are often not owned by people who behave in a way that may accurately be described as such. Accompanying the racist behavior may be all the narratives of antiracism, and the unaware racist could firmly believe on intellectual grounds in the equality of the races, to such an extent that she joins antiracist organizations and rallies for equality. However, at the same time, she might unknowingly discriminate against members of another race when they are not part of her social network or class. If someone were to ask her why she discriminated, she may deny that she acted in such a way, claim she doesn't know, or offer an alternative reason explanation for her action. An alternative reason explanation, however, cannot be accepted at face value, given the worries about confabulation, which may be especially strong in situations like this.

Given the tendency to confabulate and our desire to present a positive self-image to an audience, an agent's sincerely stated post hoc reason for her action can be inaccurate. Consider Ted Bundy's claim that his addiction to hard-core violent pornography drove him to murder, or the anorexic's rationalization for her dieting. Sour-grapes situations give rise to another case in which untrustworthy reason explanations are given by an actor—that is, when the fox walks away from the grapevine muttering, "I didn't really want those grapes anyway." Maybe he is just trying to convince himself, but if he succeeds, he will have reconstructed his reason for acting after the fact.

For FP explanations in terms of personality traits denied by the actor, there are no natural interpretations in terms of mental content, and in some such cases, the explanations assume lack of mental content, as in the case of the self-centered person who doesn't notice others. Of course, one might object that in such cases we are not explaining intentional action, since one cannot intentionally not notice things. But I think this response is too simple. These behaviors are considered by the folk to be under control of the actor, and just as our courts hold people responsible for negligence, since we are discussing *folk* psychology, it is relevant that the folk take such actions to be intentional ones. Further, we can cultivate self-centeredness by having intentionally ignored unpleasant situations or people in the past. When a mother tells her son to look away when passing a beggar on the street, she is teaching the boy to become self-centered, and that training can result in the boy growing into a man who actually fails to notice the homeless when he passes them by.

The contents of our verbal FP explanations are diverse, and no evidence supports the idea that all that diversity should be understood as presupposing mental-state ascriptions in all cases. Again, this points to a problem with the claim that folk psychology is the attribution of propositional attitudes. We encountered this tension already in the examination of folk psychological prediction, and here we also see discrepancy between SFP and our actual explanatory practices. At this point, I have offered a number of arguments against the need for the propositional attitudes, and in chapter 10 I argue for a view of folk psychology that accepts that we can be folk psychologists without reading minds. But before going on to that, I wish to examine one more concern about my account of FP explanation.

Explanations, Reasons, and Causes

According to SFP, our explanations are given in terms of beliefs and desires because we take beliefs and desires to be the cause of our behavior. We have already seen that not all FP explanations are causal ones; explanations in terms of enabling features and statistical generalizations do not purport to cite the cause of behavior. Here I want to further argue that the folk also take some intentional action to be caused even when the actor has no primary reason for that action. Rather than thinking all intentional behavior must be caused by reasons, the folk think that some intentional action can be caused by the person as a whole or by some part of her personality.

First, it seems that the folk can take an action to be intentional even when the actor did not engage in that action for a reason. This point is demonstrated by people's response to Joshua Knobe's story about a chairman of the board who doesn't care about the environment but cares only about maximizing profits (Knobe 2003; Malle 2006b). The folk take the chairman to be intentionally harming the environment when such harm is a known side effect of his business decision, though he has no reason to harm the environment; he does not construe his own action as harming the environment but sees it as maximizing profits. He has reasons only for the primary behavior, not the side effect. Side-effect cases, acts of self-centeredness, unconscious bias, and cases that involve acts of negligence or rudeness may all lead to judgments of intentional action, even though no reason explanation for the behavior is evident, because the actor does not construe her action in the same way as the observers do. That the actor does not construe her actions as being caused by a reason may be explained in terms of her personality.

We can understand such cases by extending Rosalind Hursthouse's analysis of intentional actions not done for reasons. She argues that some actions are arational—not done for reasons in the Davidsonian sense—but are still intentional because they would not have been performed had the actor not been in the emotional state that she was (Hursthouse 1991). Hursthouse argues that explanations in terms of an actor's emotional state cannot be understood as shorthand for an explanation in terms of beliefs and desires. Further, she argues that emotion explanations—or arational explanations in general—ought to be seen as an autonomous variety of psychological explanation. An example of arational action is a person's jumping up and down from excitement. We can take the jumping behavior to be intentional and explain it by the person's excitement about some event, yet we cannot offer a traditional reason explanation for the behavior: we cannot "indicate what it was about the action that appealed" (Davidson 1963, 685), we don't know why she jumped rather than smiled, and the actor herself would not be able to answer that question.

Hursthouse argues that the folk understand some intentional actions to be explained not by beliefs and desires but by emotional mental states. I am suggesting that, in addition, we ought to recognize that the folk understand some intentional actions to be explained by nonmentalistic personality traits; some actions are explained by who we are rather than what we think. For example, consider the following explanation for a woman's insistence on a long engagement: "She's a careful person who takes things slowly." This explanation does not imply that the woman doesn't yet believe that her fiancé is the right person for her, nor that she desires more time to assess the relationship. She can be fully committed to her promise and simply be the kind of person who doesn't tend to make changes quickly. In this way, the trait explanation is quite similar to

Hursthouse's arational emotional explanation of behavior. Consider Hursthouse's example of an action explained by anger:

> Jane, who, in a wave of hatred for Joan, tears at Joan's photo with her nails. . . . I can agree that Jane does this because, hating Joan, she wants to scratch her face. . . . I can agree that she would not have torn at the photo if she had not believed that it was a photo of Joan; and if someone wants to say, "So those are the reasons for the action," I do not want to quarrel, for these "reasons" do *not* form the appropriate desire-belief pair assumed by the standard account. On the standard account, if the explanatory desire in this case is the desire to scratch Joan's face, then the appropriate belief has to be something absurd, such as the belief that the photo of Joan *is* Joan, or that scratching the photo will be causally efficacious in defacing its original. And my disagreement is with adherents of the standard account, who must think that some *non*absurd candidates for appropriate beliefs to ascribe to agents performing arational actions are available. (Hursthouse 1991, 59–60)

In both the engagement case and the photograph case, there may be no appropriate set of beliefs and desires that constitute a reason for the action, but these actions are intentional. Given the folk's use of traits to explain behavior, and the finding that that traits cannot always be identified with reasons, it is part of folk psychology that not all actions are explained by reasons. And if the folk think that traits cause behavior, and traits are not propositional attitude attributions, then the claim that the folk think that propositional attitudes are the cause of all behavior is false.

The trait and the emotion explain the behavior; Hursthouse claims that we consider the emotion to cause the behavior, too. In like fashion, one might think that it is part of folk psychology that traits also cause action. For example, a father may attribute his reluctance to let his teenage daughter begin dating to his being old-fashioned, recognizing that he has no rationale for his behavior. Being old-fashioned or conservative may be construed as causing his decision, at least proximately.

These considerations present a further worry. Perhaps folk behavior is inconsistent with not only the idea that all intentional acts are caused by propositional attitudes but also the view that all actions are caused by some event. Important differences exist between causes in terms of emotions and causes in terms of traits. The experience of emotion is an event; it raises no metaphysical concerns to consider Jane's wave of hatred as causing her act of destruction. However, a personality trait, as a stable disposition of a person, is not an event. Traits, unlike beliefs, desires, emotional experiences, or other mental states, cannot have the same sort of efficacy. If it is part of folk psychology that traits cause behavior, as well as explain behavior, then perhaps this metaphysical worry must be addressed.

While I accept that the folk do not think that all actions are caused by reasons, given the multitude of possible accounts of causation, it would be hasty to say that the folk think that some actions are not caused. Rather, the folk sometimes think that actions are due to the person being who she is, not to her having some mental event. This commitment can be analyzed as a causal commitment under a counterfactual view of causation. For example, we would say of the old-fashioned father that, were he not old-fashioned, he would let his daughter date. In such a sense, we might say that it is the father's being old-fashioned that causes him to keep his daughter off the dating scene. Because, according to counterfactual accounts of causation, the counterfactual element could be an enabling condition, a property, a disposition, a historical fact, and so on, such a view is compatible with the pluralism apparent in the practice of folk psychology.

Some might object that counterfactuals provide only a weak sense of causal relevance. However, that charge does not concern me. I am merely trying to describe how the folk understand other people and their actions. What we have found is that the folk think that there are explanations for behavior that are not causally efficacious in the sense of there being an event whose occurrence causes the explanandum. Dispositions, traits, and the person as a whole being are also seen by the folk to explain action, and if we want to understand this explanation as causal, the counterfactual account of causation will suffice.

Toward a New Way

Folk psychology implies that traits, similarly to emotions, can be the cause of behavior as well as the explanation for behavior; folk behavior reflects a commitment that is inconsistent with both the claim that all intentional actions are caused by propositions and the claim that all intentional actions are caused by some event. From a very young age, children have an understanding of others as intentional agents and can differentiate between intentional and accidental movement even before they understand propositional attitudes or personality traits. As adults, our explanations sometimes reflect this natural and early ability to see others as persons, whose behaviors can be explained in terms of who we are, and not in terms of what we think.

Our folk psychological explanations are plural in both content and form, and the diversity that we see in both explanation and prediction is sufficient for rejecting SFP. But if we reject the traditional view, what view should we put in its place?

In the next chapter, I offer a new set of folk psychological principles that is consistent with the pluralism I have been endorsing. First I contrast the commitments of this plural approach to folk psychology with the commitments of standard folk psychology, and I argue that the old research projects must be abandoned. Instead we need a new research program, one that begins with the principles of pluralistic folk psychology and an understanding of folk psychology as more like reading people, and less like reading minds.

IV The Solution

10 Folk Psychological Pluralism: Reading People, Not Minds

Begin with an individual, and before you know it you find that you have created a type; begin with a type, and you find that you have created—nothing. That is because we are all queer fish, queerer behind our faces and voices than we want any one to know or than we know ourselves.

—F. Scott Fitzgerald

The Principles of a Pluralistic Folk Psychology

According to Standard Folk Psychology, human understanding of other people rests on our sense that behavior is caused by beliefs and desires. However, the evidence presented thus far indicates that this view is misguided, because humans use a variety of methods to engage in their folk psychological practices, and not all these methods require seeing others as having reasons for their actions. According to a pluralistic account of folk psychology, while many different cognitive processes facilitate social interaction, what is necessary for being a folk psychologist is the ability to see others as intentional agents. In the standard view, the dividing line between folk psychologists and others is the ability to see others as acting from their propositional attitudes. However, this dividing line underestimates the power of other cognitive processes used in social interaction. Even without a robust understanding of beliefs and desires, agents can predict and explain others' behavior. They can also justify behavior, shape their own behavior to acceptable societal standards, coordinate their behavior with others, identify intentional action, make moral judgments, and engage in a host of other social practices that are arguably as important as predicting and explaining behavior.

Instead of taking folk psychologists to be the class of people who are able to attribute beliefs and desires to others, we can offer a different set of criteria. To engage in our folk psychological practices, we require two capacities. First, a folk psychologist must be able to distinguish agents from nonagents. Second, a folk psychologist must have facility with at least some of the cognitive mechanisms that allow for engagement with some of the practices of prediction, explanation, and so forth. If you want a dividing line, that is the best you'll get. Organisms who are able to differentiate intentional agents from everything else and interact socially with other intentional agents have many of the properties that make us so interested in human mind and action. After that, it is all a matter of degree. Having the concepts of belief and desire does not make for a radical change in social interactions, for as I have argued, it isn't necessary for the ability to predict others' actions, or even for the ability to explain behavior, and as I argue in the next chapter, it isn't necessary for deception, either.

Recall that standard folk psychology is based on the following commitments:

(SFP1) Propositional attitudes are the cause of all intentional behavior.

(SFP2) Folk psychology is the attribution of propositional attitudes.

(SFP3) One needs to be a folk psychologist to have robust success in predicting, explaining, and interpreting behavior.

(SFP4) The method that allows us to predict behavior is also the method that allows us to explain behavior.

Given the centrality of (SFP3) to the definition of folk psychology, I have argued that we should preserve this principle, but in so doing, we are forced to reject all the others. I propose that we replace the principles of SFP with another set of principles that are consistent with both (SFP3) and the descriptive account of social cognition that I have presented. Let us replace them with the principles of a Pluralistic Folk Psychology, as follows:

(PFP1) One needs to be a folk psychologist to have robust success in predicting, explaining, and interpreting behavior.

(PFP2) Folk psychology is a social competence, which includes the ability to identify behavior, predict behavior, explain behavior, justify behavior, normalize behavior, coordinate behavior, and so on.

(PFP3) The social competences of folk psychology are supported by a number of different cognitive mechanisms, and one's degree of success as a folk psychologist is a function of the number of competences mastered and the degree of facility with the different competences.

(PFP4) Intentional behavior is seen as sometimes caused by any number of factors, such as moods, propositional attitudes, emotions, and so on, and sometimes influenced by other factors such as personality traits, dispositions, or historical facts.

(PFP5) The requirement for being a folk psychologist is the ability to recognize that intentional agents exist, and to fare well in discriminating intentional from nonintentional agents.

(PFP1) is identical to (SFP3), given its status as the core commitment of folk psychology. The other principles are meant to elaborate on the first principle in a way that is empirically adequate given the discussions of the previous chapters while retaining enough of the flavor of SFP to avoid the accusation that this is merely a change of subject. This chapter begins with a defense and discussion of the last four elements of PFP. I then argue that none of the standard theories of folk psychology can easily be modified to remain consistent with these principles. I conclude that the old project of trying to find a single model of folk psychology is misguided and should be replaced with a new project—one that starts by rejecting the claim that our folk psychology consists of seeing others primarily as receptacles for propositional attitudes, and replaces it with a more holistic approach, according to which we see others as persons.

(PFP2) Folk psychology is a social competence, which includes the ability to identify behavior, predict behavior, explain behavior, justify behavior, normalize behavior, coordinate behavior, and so on.

The second element of PFP is meant to draw attention to the functions of folk psychology beyond prediction and explanation. The emphasis on prediction and explanation, to the exclusion of other folk psychological practices such as gossiping, justifying, condemning, evaluating, manipulating, coordinating, and so on, may be seen as a legacy that philosophers inherited from Hempel's emphasis on prediction and explanation, an influence that was subsequently passed on to psychologists. As we begin to leave behind the influence of the logical empiricists on the structure of folk psychology, and the notion that our social interactions are much like the interaction between scientist and subject, we can leave behind their influence on the scope of folk psychology, as well.

Theories about the structure and nature of folk psychology have relied heavily on evidence about our ability to predict behavior that came from the false-belief task. While prediction has been of primary interest in the folk psychology literature, with explanation of secondary interest, it has long been noted that the practices of folk psychology extend much further. Churchland points out, "We use the resources of folk psychology to promise, to entreat, to congratulate, to tease, to joke, to intimate, to threaten, and so on" (Churchland 1989, 231; see also Wilkes 1981, 1984). Others have emphasized different roles for folk psychology, including coordinating behavior (Morton 2003), making judgments of moral responsibility (Knobe 2003; Morton 2003), identifying intentional action (Knobe 2003), perceiving intentions (Gallagher 2004), understanding others (Hutto 2004; Gallagher 2001), justifying behavior (Davidson 1963; Andrews 2004), regulating behavior (Hobson 2007; Mameli 2001; McGeer 2007; Zawidzki 2008), and providing reasons (Davidson 1963; Hutto 2008). Each of these views stems from an insight about one or more of the myriad ways in which we interact with others, and I propose that they all be included, along with the standard practices of prediction and explanation, in any complete account of folk psychology.

Not all the authors mentioned in the previous paragraph would be welcoming of this inclusive approach; some argue that folk psychology is fundamentally used for a particular practice, and that other practices are merely derivative. For example, Daniel Hutto argues that folk psychology is fundamentally for offering reasons for behavior, and since to have reasons one must have language, in his view it follows that a folk psychologist must have competence with a natural language. Once language is in place, we develop the ability to act from reasons, and to see others as acting from reasons, because we have been exposed to stories and conversations about people acting for reasons (Hutto 2008).

In addition, Hutto, like many of these authors, is committed to an understanding of folk psychology as the attribution of the propositional attitudes. For Hutto, it is clear that folk psychology provides reasons for behavior in terms of the propositional attitudes. In Tadeusz Zawidzki's account of the evolutionary function of folk psychology, he focuses on the attitudes and argues that the evolutionary function of propositional attitude attribution could not have been to predict behavior but may plausibly have been to help regulate social behavior to facilitate coordination (Zawidzki 2008). In Peter Hobson's account of the development of folk psychology, he too relies on the propositional attitudes when he suggests that infants come to grasp mental-state concepts in terms of a biologically based identification mechanism, which allows individuals to assimilate the mental properties they see in others (Hobson 2007).

Since many of these authors are concerned about folk psychology as the attribution of the attitudes, and so far I have only argued that folk psychological prediction and explanation can be accomplished without appeal to the attitudes, one might worry that some other practices, such as regulating behavior, might require propositional attitude attribution. However, we can easily call to mind examples of these sorts of practices that do not rely on propositional attitude attribution. For example, we can condemn a person for being a jerk (trait attribution), and we can coordinate behavior with another if we know her habits (inductive generalization over past behavior). We can justify behavior by pointing out the situation the person was in, or showing that it is consistent with an ethical principle. We can regulate others' behavior by obeying the norms of society. We also can identify a person's goals long before we gain facility with propositional attitude attribution, as we know from studies of human infants and chimpanzees.

By expanding the practices associated with our folk psychology abilities to include all the competencies associated with social interaction, we are able to draw on a greater data set in developing a theory of how we understand other minds. While some might worry that such an inclusive approach will muddy the waters, no one has denied that we use our competence as folk psychologists in a number of different social contexts, and for different purposes.

While facility with prediction and explanation is certainly part of what it means to be a folk psychologist, an individual who possesses only those folk psychological competences would lack many paradigmatic features of a folk psychologist. Consider someone who is able to predict and explain by attributing propositional attitudes but cannot identify personality traits or perceive another's emotional state. While children with autism are often presented as a good example of individuals who lack the ability to attribute beliefs and desires, high-functioning adults on the autistic spectrum who gain some competence in making predictions in false-belief situations can still have some facility with understanding others' character traits or emotional states. And among those people with autism who pass false-belief tasks there can be severe social impairments; successful performance on the task does not track successful social interactions in ordinary contexts (Happé 1994; Ozonoff and Miller 1995). To account for this deficit, Happé and Frith have hypothesized that due to weak central coherence (the ability to take into account the context when interpreting social as well as nonsocial situations), children with autism cannot use their knowledge of other minds in everyday life, although they can use this knowledge in context-free and limited experimental settings (Frith et al. 1994; Happé 1994). If this account is correct, then the ability to recognize the salient features of the situation may cause folk psychological deficits, even if the target's beliefs and desires are correctly understood, and when predictions can accurately be made in cases where the salient features of the situation are made explicit.

In addition, having the ability to ascribe propositional attitudes is insufficient for making accurate predictions of behavior. For example, adults with Asperger's syndrome often have problems with small talk, and they know that they have this problem. What is a simple task for neurotypicals is often experienced as a deliberate engagement with a quasi-logical problem for people on the autistic spectrum. In his autobiography, John Elder Robison, who was diagnosed with Asperger's later in life, illustrates this struggle by describing a conversation he had with a friend:

> Last week my friend Laurie said, "One of my girlfriends is having an affair. And the guy rides a motorcycle just like yours!"
>
> Laurie's statement posed a problem. Unlike most interactions, ours had not started with a question. Should I respond with an opinion about the statement? Or should I ask a question myself? I considered what I had just heard:
>
> Laurie has a girlfriend. *Yes, Laurie has lots of girlfriends. Which one is she talking about?*
>
> The girlfriend's having an affair. *Why tell me? Do I know her? Do I know the guy? Is this a convoluted way of suggesting that I should have an affair, since I have a motorcycle?*
>
> The boyfriend has a motorcycle. *Well, that narrows it down. Most potential boyfriends have cars, not bikes. So this boyfriend is one of the 5 percent, as opposed to the 95 percent of the motoring public. Do I know him?*
>
> The motorcycle is just like mine. *How much does Laurie know about bikes? Does she mean he rides an Electra Glide Classic, or does she just mean his motorcycle is black?*
>
> . . . I knew she wanted a relevant response—something connected to what she had just said, more than just "Oh." I also knew from experience and observation that a statement like "I went to Newport to see the Jazz Festival last weekend" would not be an appropriate answer. It occurred to me that what I needed to do was to keep gathering information until I could frame an intelligent conversation. The successful conversational computer programs did that. So I asked a question.
>
> "Which girlfriend is that?"
>
> Laurie looked surprised. "Why would you want to know that?" she said. (Robison 2008, 189–90)

This incident illustrates Robison's failure to accurately predict how Laurie would respond to his question, and the heroic measures he undertook to figure out an appropriate response. From his description of his thought processes, it is clear that he is able to attribute beliefs and desires to Laurie. But that ability doesn't allow him to be a successful conversational partner

Folk Psychological Pluralism

in this situation. Robison says he later realized what he should have said, but only after overhearing a similar conversation. Because he lacks the ability to read social cues, Robison's conversational successes depend on his ability to observe conversations and find patterns. Before he began studying conversations, his facility for small talk was much worse, so bad that people took his inappropriate responses as evidence he was a psychopath.

A familiar caricature of a person with autism is someone who cannot pass the false-belief task and hence cannot attribute beliefs and desires. Not only is this picture misleading in its interpretation of passing the false-belief task, but it also presents an extremely simplistic picture of the range of deficits found in people on the autistic spectrum. In fact, 20 to 35 percent of children diagnosed with autism pass the false-belief tasks (Baron-Cohen 1995). The impairments associated with autism span the range from failure to recognize other people as agents to difficulty knowing *what* (and not *that*) others are thinking or feeling—a lack of empathic accuracy. At one end of this continuum, we have individuals who would likely not be characterized as folk psychologists, insofar as they are unable to recognize others as agents. At the other end, we have people like John Elder Robison, who clearly *is* a folk psychologist, although he is not terribly sensitive to other people's emotions or goals. We all sometimes fail in our folk psychological practices by making false predictions, offering implausible explanations, or failing to coordinate, and we all on occasion are unable to figure out what others are thinking. While people on the autistic spectrum have a greater problem with this than do neurotypicals, it is still a matter of degree.

By including a host of abilities as part of folk psychology, we better capture the myriad ways in which people might use propositional attitudes, but we also better capture how minds understand minds in different ways and with varying degrees of success. That is, the individual differences we see in people's folk psychological competencies are more consistent with this inclusive approach to folk psychology. Some people are fine at predicting behavior but offer explanations that others see as nonsensical or simplistic. A narcissist falsely thinks that the thoughts of others are always focused on her, but she still has no problem with quotidian predictions and justifying others' actions. The depressed person will explain her successes as the result of the situation and not take credit even when credit is due, but she may perform perfectly in empathic accuracy tests. As long as an individual can engage in some of these practices to some degree of success, he is a folk psychologist.

(PFP3)   The social competences of folk psychology are supported by a number of different cognitive mechanisms.

As we have seen already, folk psychology is not exhausted by the attribution of propositional attitudes, but the practices of prediction and explanation, as well as the other practices of folk psychology, are made possible by a host of cognitive capacities. While I have focused on a small set of rather well-known and well-studied cognitive capacities, by no means do I think that these exhaust the methods we use when engaging in the folk psychology practices. The question of which other cognitive mechanisms are involved in these and other practices is one that I take as an ongoing research project. My discussion has focused on the behavioral research on understanding minds, but as I stated in previous chapters, the current discussion only scratches the surface of what is involved in even just our folk psychological practices of prediction and explanation. As I stated, additional research on emotion and mood perception will be relevant to a fuller picture. Furthermore, we have much to learn from other scientific disciplines.

The current attention to social neuroscience is another means for uncovering the mechanisms that allow us to be successful folk psychologists. For example, the discovery of the mirror neuron system may help to explain the phenomenon of social resonance, or coming to think and feel what others close to you think and feel. Because of the work of Rizzolatti, Gallese, and their colleagues, we now know that neurons in the ventral premotor cortex of monkeys discharge both when a monkey is witnessing another engage in a goal-related action and when the monkey engages in that action itself (Rizzolatti et al. 1996; Gallese et al. 1996). Using imaging techniques, researchers have detected mirroring regions in the human brain, as well (Fadiga et al. 1995). The mirror neurons are part of larger mirror systems and may serve as one of the mechanisms involved in our automatic folk psychology judgments (Gallese and Goldman 1998; A. Goldman 2006). While the relationship between folk psychology and mirror neurons is still undetermined (Dinstein et al. 2008), the field of social neuroscience promises to offer much information about the brain areas and other cognitive processes associated with our folk psychological practices.

Research in the burgeoning field of social endocrinology can also help us understand the mechanisms that are involved in successful folk psychological behavior by demonstrating how hormones, together with our sensitivity to others' hormones, are related to social cognition. While much is already known about levels of testosterone and sexual behavior, other research is looking at the role of hormones outside the domain of sexuality. For example, in one study, researchers found that when playing an investment game, participants who were exposed to oxytocin were more likely to give all their money to an unseen trustee; almost half of the oxytocin group made the full commitment, compared to a quarter of the control group (Kosfeld et al. 2005). Another group of researchers suggested that women are judged to be more attractive when they are fertile, based on a study that found exotic dancers receive larger tips just before they ovulate (G. Miller et al. 2007). Such studies suggest that without knowing why we are so affected, our folk psychological practices are constrained by exposure to some hormones.

The roles of these different systems in the production of folk psychological behavior must be extraordinarily complex. Given the complexity already apparent, the expectation that we can model folk psychology in terms of a flow chart should be discarded. The dynamic sophistication involved in our practices should lead us away from trying to understand folk psychology in terms of functional models (e.g., Stich and Nichols 1995; Nichols and Stich 2003). Such models cannot represent the phenomenon accurately, since they do not include the varieties of cognitive processes and heuristics involved in our social practices.

In my view, no one path exists for a particular folk psychology behavior or judgment. Rather, we have *folk psychological styles*, with individuals differing in style from one another and from case to case. When you need to predict whether your colleague will meet you after the conference, you might rely on her verbal promise, but that alone may not be enough to solve that predictive problem. You might also consider personality traits such as attentiveness, punctuality, or reliability; you might consider some of her personal circumstances, such as her having a young infant that needs to be fed, or an alcohol problem; and you might consider some of the situational factors, such as the conference being in a big hotel that is difficult to navigate. Whether or not you rely on one of these pieces of information—or some combination of them—to formulate your prediction, it will be based on the kind of folk psychologist you are, what you notice about the situation, how you understand the person, and your mood, among other factors.

Explanatory style has been investigated by social psychologists who have found that people vary even in how they explain their own behavior, depending on things such as their mood or stress level. For example, people who are depressed tend to attribute their successes to some unstable cause outside of themselves. Depressed people tend to think that their successes are the result of some accident, but their failures are their own fault, caused by their own internal stable features. People who are not depressed are much more likely to explain their successes in terms of internal and global personality traits and to dismiss their failures as accidental and caused by external features (Buchanan and Seligman 1995). Such differences in how individuals explain their own behavior provide just one example of how factors such as hormones interact with cognitive mechanisms when we engage in some folk psychological practices.

No general flow chart will be possible in my account, for the particulars of the case and one's facility with the different cognitive capacities will lead to a complex interaction that guides one's decision-making process. This means that we will observe both individual differences between folk psychologists and situational differences for an individual in any predictive situation. We should also expect different capacities to play a more or less central role in the different folk psychology practices. As I have argued, while we should not expect that our quotidian predictions rely on propositional attitude attribution, we will see a much greater reliance on propositional attitudes when explaining behavior.

To make this point, we can look again at the abilities of people on the autistic spectrum. While some argue that a theory of mind can never be taught, as we have seen, a variety of therapies have been used to help individuals on the autistic spectrum engage in the folk psychological practices. Therapists are able to help autistic children to behave appropriately in social situations by making accurate predictions, coordinating their behavior, and so on, but the end of a successful therapy is not to make the children use the same cognitive mechanisms as typically developing individuals; rather, it is likely that people with autism gain these competencies by relying on psychological processes different from those used by typically developing individuals. One reason to think this is so is that autistic children rarely develop anything like the typical interest in social interaction. A number of language-based therapies aim to improve social interaction and social understanding of high-functioning children with autism, although these children have already been through applied behavioral analysis (ABA) therapy, speak language, and are often placed in the classroom with normally developing children. Such therapies involve explicit explanations of socially relevant concepts such as friendship, causes of different emotions, emotional expressions, and the like. This means that while normally developing children intuitively grasp these concepts, a child on the autistic spectrum must have them broken down and analyzed for her.

Therapy can explicitly teach a child to label simple emotions (e.g., sad, happy, afraid, angry) via explicit teaching of the emotion and can teach how to recognize these emotions in self and others by identifying the ways people usually express them. For children who learn about emotions through such therapies, the emotion concepts are not given. Rather, the concepts are analyzed for them and taught to them through therapies such as the picture exchange communication system (PECS) or Carol Grey's social stories therapy. In ABA therapy, the child is trained to use symbols that refer to mental states and to use the correct symbol in the correct situations. Given the developmental differences, however, we have no reason to suspect that the mechanisms involved in these behaviors are similar to those used by a child who develops language normally. Though the child may learn how she ought to behave, and how others should behave, there is reason to think that she does not understand *why* she ought to act in this way.

Individuals rely on different capacities to engage in folk psychological practices, whether they are depressed people explaining their own behavior, or people with Asperger's trying to figure out how to hold a conversation. The capacities we rely on vary among individuals, and even within individuals across contexts, and these facts support the move away from a single model that captures all our folk psychological practices.

That individual differences exist among folk psychologists reflects our natural tendency to see people as more or less socially skilled. Some people lack social graces; we take others to be skilled socializers, and we rely on those individuals not only to make our social interactions delightful but also to contribute to our society as helpful psychotherapists, good teachers, and effective political leaders.

(PFP4) Intentional behavior is seen as sometimes caused by any number of factors, such as moods, propositional attitudes, emotions, and so on, and sometimes influenced by other factors such as personality traits, dispositions, or historical facts.

The fourth principle of a pluralistic folk psychology rejects the familiar claim that the folk take behavior to be caused by propositional attitudes. In the last chapter, I argued that people see intentional behavior as caused by nonpropositional mental states, and by other mental properties such as personality traits or dispositions. We also see some behavior as primarily caused by a person's past history rather than anything more internal. And in a radical departure from the traditional picture, the folk see that some intentional behavior is not caused by anything resembling a reason. As

Hursthouse argues, an arational action can be intentional and caused by emotions rather than reasons. We jump for joy, we tear up a photo in anger, we tousle someone's hair in love, and those actions can be intentional even if there are not reasons that led us to engage in them (Hursthouse 1991). We can provide a similar analysis of intentional actions that are caused by things other than reasons, including personality traits or past experience. Ending a yoga pose can be an intentional act, even if one did not have a reason for stopping at that particular moment. An early move out of the pose is sometimes seen as resulting from a lack of self-discipline, and thus something the yogi is responsible for, unlike an early move out of the pose caused by a physiological response such as losing balance. Some actions we do before we know it, and without having reasons for them, but we still take ownership of those actions and see them as intentional acts. So maybe the next time your teenager answers, "I don't know" when you ask, "Why did you do that?" you should consider that she may be telling the truth.

Once we allow that things other than reasons cause some intentional actions, this offers a serious challenge to any of the major theories I group together under SFP. At the least, the existence of arational intentional actions shows that the accounts generated by those operating under the framework of SFP are incomplete.

Theory-theorists cannot account for such behaviors; arational actions are left out of the framework altogether. For example, Nichols and Stich's (2003) model of folk psychology as (primarily) theory assumes that intentional human action is caused by beliefs and desires inputted into a practical reasoning system. Correspondingly, their third-person mind-reading system operates on others' beliefs and desires to output the expected behavior. In accounts such as this one, arational actions fall outside the scope. There is no entryway for an action that is not caused by a belief or a desire in models of folk psychology that ignore the causal role of emotions, personality traits, and so forth. If a person does not have a reason for acting, then your prediction or explanation of her behavior would not count as a folk psychological act according to this model.

In some accounts, simulation theorists fare better. Early characterizations of simulation theory describe simulation as feeding pretend beliefs and desires into one's own (off-line) practical reasoning system, and these models suffer from the same inability to account for actions that are not caused by reasons. Alvin Goldman's early work on mental simulation falls neatly into the SFP model. However, Goldman's more recent development of simulation includes what he calls low-level mind reading, and we could see this view as allowing us to predict, and even to some extent to explain, some arational actions. While Goldman does not address this issue directly, it is a simple matter to expand his view to permit such behaviors. In his account of low-level mind reading, we engage in a face-based simulation of others' emotional states (A. Goldman 2006). When we observe another's facial expression, our mirror-neuron system is activated, which causes activation of the neural substrate associated with the target's emotion. That is, to some degree, I share the emotion of the target when I see her facial expression, and I can read her emotion off my own experience.

Goldman relies on the claim that there is a human mirror system sensitive to facial expressions, concluding that this system is responsible for our ability to understand others' emotions. Having the right kind of mirroring system in place is not sufficient for mind reading, Goldman is quick to point out, but should only be seen as the basis for what he characterizes as low-level emotion reading.

Following Goldman, mirroring may be at play in our understanding of some arational actions. Suppose you see a person jumping up and down, your mirror system is activated, and you automatically see that she is jumping for joy, not disgust or fear. Knowing the emotional state she is in helps you to explain her behavior and can lead you to ask the right kind of questions—perhaps "You got the job?" However, the mirror system cannot work for all kinds of arational action. For example, the system should not be expected to be involved in our recognition that a behavior is caused by a personality trait; there is almost certainly no mirror system for personality.

Goldman is right to recognize that cognitive systems do much of the work of understanding other minds without having to appeal to mental states such as belief and desire, but he doesn't go far enough. The folk think that behavior is caused not only by emotions and propositional attitudes but also by personality traits and situations. Mirroring alone cannot account for our recognition of someone's personality trait, so we need some other explanation for our ability to recognize someone as selfish or generous from a small set of behaviors.

Model theorists are even better at accounting for our understanding of arational actions, since their models can include emotions, moods, and sensations, as well as propositional attitudes (Godfrey-Smith 2005). Insofar as we can expand the model view to include additional elements, such as personality traits and a person's past history, model theory should be able to accommodate intentional action that isn't done for a reason.

(PFP5)   The requirement for being a folk psychologist is the ability to recognize that intentional agents exist, and to fare well in discriminating intentional from nonintentional agents.

The final principle of a pluralistic folk psychology specifies a necessary condition for being a folk psychologist, which is needed to limit the class of folk psychologists to something generally consistent with our intuitions about the extension of the category. To be sure, I do not want to define away the possibility that some nonhuman creatures are folk psychologists, but I also don't want to allow everything into the category so as to make it empty. One reading of the debate about chimpanzee theory of mind is to see it as a question about whether chimpanzees see other apes as intentional agents with mental lives. If the recognition that other agents exist is considered a necessary condition for being a folk psychologist, this debate remains a live one.

The folk notion of agency to which I am appealing here rests on the flexibility of cognition. When we observe something acting differently in extremely similar situations, we suppose that the behavior is due to the thing's agency and is not a direct result of external stimuli. Where we see inflexibility, we assume that no agency exists. To take a familiar example of cognitive inflexibility, consider the ant's response to dead conspecifics. When an ant dies, it excretes folic acid, which acts as a cue for the other ants to take the corpse out of the nest. But when a live ant is painted with folic acid, its nest mates will drag the struggling body away. As far as carting away the dead goes, the ants do not enjoy a flexible cognitive system that allows them to distinguish between live and dead ants, and this suggests they lack an ability to distinguish agents from nonagents. Their behavior is determined by the existence of the folic acid stimulus.

While I do not have much more to say about this principle, let me end by pointing out that the characterization of people with autism as impaired folk psychologists can be traced back to this requirement. In his early classification of autism as a disorder, Leo Kanner described children who had impairments so extreme that it is not an exaggeration to say that they sometimes lacked the ability to distinguish intentional agents in the world. For example, he says of one child:

On a crowded beach he would walk straight toward his goal irrespective of whether this involved walking over newspapers, hands, feet or torsos, much to the discomfort of their owners. His mother was careful to point out that he did not intentionally deviate from his course in order to walk on others, but neither did he make the slightest attempt to avoid them. *It was as if he did not distinguish people from things or at least did not concern himself about the distinction.* (Baron-Cohen 1995, 61; italics mine)

Even highly verbal people with autism have impairments that are better described as a failure to recognize others as persons than as a failure to attribute beliefs. In many self-reports, people on the autistic spectrum describe the difficulty they have in seeing others as agents. For example, Peter Hobson (2004) quotes one autistic youth as saying, "I really didn't know there were people until I was seven years old. . . . I then suddenly realized there were people. But not like you do. I still have to remind myself that there are people."

When an individual fails to recognize others as agents, that individual is more accurately described as people-blind than as mind-blind. While people have minds, they also have intentional actions, personality traits, mannerisms, and emotions. They joke, tease, gossip, and share conspiratorial stories and moral judgments with others around them. They are sad, happy, fearful, in love, or grumpy. When someone fails to see any of this, they are failing to see a whole person, not just a set of propositional content.

Folk Psychological Pluralism

The principles of pluralistic folk psychology provide us with a basic framework for the revised project of determining the nature of folk psychology. They show that the explanations for how we predict and explain behavior will differ from the explanations for our attribution of propositional attitudes, for example. These principles provide us with a starting point in that they are descriptively adequate, unlike the principles of Standard Folk Psychology. With this new foundation, we can also ask new questions and give new answers to the old ones. For example, these principles suggest a new answer to the question about possible ultimate explanations for propositional attitude attribution, which I examine in chapter 11. They also suggest new ways of examining the question of whether other species are folk psychologists, and whether they use the same processes that humans use to predict and explain behavior, questions I discuss in chapter 12.

Importantly, these principles suggest that the explanandum in the metaphysics of mind does not reflect the folk understanding of mind and action. The metaphysician's emphasis on questions about the nature of belief—whether a belief is identical to a brain state, a functional state, or something else; the individuation of beliefs; the ontological status of belief;

the causal powers of belief—reflects the view that beliefs are the central element of mind, despite the interest in emotion, embodiment, and environment found in other quarters within the philosophy of mind. The study of how the folk actually see others as agents who act not just from reasons but also from emotions, moods, personality traits, experiences, and so forth, suggests a different emphasis may be warranted for philosophers aiming to uncover the nature of mind.

How Do the Traditional Accounts of Mind Reading Stack Up?

Folk psychology, theory of mind, and mind reading are all terms that have been used in SFP to refer to our ability to interpret others as having beliefs and desires and acting for reasons. These terms and their general approach present human social cognition as a sparse and intellectual exercise in which mind is divorced from the person. When we are reading minds, the focus narrows such that information about the person is lost. This includes information about what kind of person the target is, what her personality is, what kinds of behaviors she engages in, what sort of emotional responses she tends to have, what her social status is, and what her current mood is. Mind reading looks only at mental content; in so doing, it overlooks the vast array of information that we use when making social judgments about others.

I have argued that this sort of information about the person is central to our ability to predict and explain behavior. Mindreading sheds the messy business of dealing with the person when it focuses on the content of mind, and the accounts consequently suffer.

Consider simulation theories. For the simulation theorist, the folk perception of others is based on an ability to determine what we ourselves would think if we believed and desired the things that the target believes and desires. Remember that the simulation theorists do not argue that we sometimes use simulation for our folk psychological practices; rather, they claim that simulation is necessary for *any* degree of folk psychological understanding. Over time, use of simulation might lead to other shortcut heuristics, but those methods are merely derivative.

Accepting such claims requires that all the additional methods for predicting behavior can only be used by those who are good enough simulators to have developed shortcuts. That would seem to include predictions in terms of stereotypes, personality traits, past behaviors, and social norms. But children can use some of these methods to predict behavior before they are successful at standard simulation tasks. Furthermore, we have no prima facie reason for thinking that one must simulate to understand stereotypes, personality traits, or social norms. We do not simulate when determining what personality someone has, and insofar as we might mentally transform ourselves into someone having trait T when simulating a target with trait T, that transformation rests on additional knowledge about the trait and the kinds of behavioral tendencies associated with it. As we saw, the simulation theorist cannot retort that traits are merely shorthand for mental states, since a disassociation exists between trait attributions and belief attributions.

Theory theories fare even worse. According to theory-theorists, our ability to accurately predict behavior relies on our ability to correctly attribute beliefs and desires; people who suffer from deficits in folk psychology lack the ability to attribute such mental states and may not even understand they exist. As we saw in the previous section, theory-theorists are also unable to account for the folk acceptance of intentional action that is not caused by propositional attitudes.

Neither of these accounts of the cognitive architecture underlying our folk psychology can be modified to incorporate the facts about pluralism. And the trend toward hybrid views does not solve the problem. The recent SFP literature recognizes the strengths and weaknesses of each theory, but this recognition has not led to a critical reassessment of the general approach; instead it has produced a trend toward the development of different hybrids of the two theories. Josef Perner was one of the first to argue that we should move beyond the dichotomy when he wrote: "The future must lie in a mixture of simulation and theory use. However, what this mixture is and how it operates must be specified in some detail before any testable predictions can be derived" (Perner 1996, 103). A survey of the published SFP literature shows that the hybrid view is now dominant. Goldman, another early advocate, writes, "Some kind of *mixed* theory, I suspect, is unavoidable" (A. Goldman 1995b, 192), and his recent book is widely taken to be a defense of a simulation-theory hybrid. Others such as Currie and Ravenscroft (2002) and Nichols and Stitch (2003) have identified weaknesses in their prior views and have modified those to include elements of the alternate theory.

However, no hybrid account is going to avoid the limitations of both theories if neither approach recognizes that our social practices of predicting and explaining behavior are possible without a concept of representational belief, and without having to attribute propositional attitudes. The hybrid accounts, like the traditional ones, still fail insofar as they focus on propositional mental contents rather than on a more integrative notion of the person acting in society. They fail in taking a homogenized view of our acts of social prediction, and in assuming that we use one method in all cases (even if they accept that this method might include elements of both simulation and theory). And they fail to recognize that prediction and explanation are not symmetrical.

I have shown no single method exists for predicting or explaining behavior, and thus we should reject the question "What is the architecture of folk psychology?" on the basis of its false presupposition, namely, that we engage in folk psychological practices in only one way. I have argued that this is true not only between categories of folk psychological practices (i.e., there are differences in how we predict and explain behavior) but also within categories. In addition, I have argued that there are folk psychological styles, and individuals do not always use the same methods to predict behavior; thus we must reject the general question "How do we predict others' behavior?" as being based on a false assumption. A better question, one that accepts individual differences and differences between the various folk psychology practices, would be something like "What are the cognitive strategies involved in predicting behaviors?"

Simulation theorists, theory theorists, and theorists of resulting hybrids might protest that their models are not designed to deal with folk psychology in the broad sense I have led us to; they might claim only to offer models of how we predict and explain behavior when we do attribute propositional content. If these accounts are taken to be so limited in scope, they are still uninformative without an accompanying theory about how to determine under what conditions we make predictions and explanations in terms of propositional content. Furthermore, the pluralism inherent in our predictive practices is an interactive pluralism; we do not use just one method at a time but apply some combination of methods to arrive at our predictions. Even more problematic for this response is the existence of folk psychological styles; not everyone will use the same combination of methods to make the same prediction.

What simulation theory and theory theory are both guilty of is an overly intellectualized view of human social cognition according to which we cannot help but think of peoples' beliefs and desires when we are interacting with them, and our understanding of others, our ability to predict their behavior or to explain it, fundamentally rests on what they *believe* rather than on who they are. At bottom, the problem with both simulation theory and theory theory comes from their reluctance to see our folk psychological practices as engagements with socially situated people—agents with personalities, pasts, and ways of being. Instead such approaches portray our social lives as a manipulation of sets of disembodied propositions.

Model theory fares better than simulation theory or theory theory insofar as it allows for the inclusion of elements other than propositional attitudes in our understanding of others. Model theory, like theory theory, is an information-rich account of folk psychology, and we have seen that many of the methods used to engage in folk psychological practices require a rich body of knowledge. This includes specific knowledge about the person, as well as general knowledge about traits, stereotypes, social norms, past behavior, and so on.

To see how well model theory fares with the principles of PFP, we can examine two versions of the theory. Recall that in Godfrey-Smith's account, we have a general folk psychological model, and we use that model to construct additional models of individuals given their particularities; the individual model might include information about the individual's personality, emotional tendencies, past behaviors, social standing, and so forth, and these elements are connected by logical relations (Godfrey-Smith 2005).

In Maibom's account of model theory, our social practices are made possible by the existence of at least two kinds of models: models of general information about social practices, which she calls social models, and models of particular individuals, which she calls folk psychology models and takes to be limited to the target's beliefs and desires (Maibom 2007).

Both accounts move closer to an empirically adequate account of how our folk psychology practices are possible. Both are consistent with our judgments of others as influenced by elements other than propositional attitudes. And both are consistent with the notion that folk psychology is a social competence and is not limited to predicting and explaining behavior. Maibom argues that one benefit of model theory over theory theory is the emphasis model theory places on the practice of folk psychology, and its contention that theoretical knowledge without the know-how needed to apply that knowledge should not be seen as knowledge of the empirical world (Maibom 2009). And Godfrey-Smith (2005) emphasizes that folk psychological competence is really facility with manipulating the relevant models.

Though it is an improvement, model theory, in both these versions, is less amenable to the third and fourth principles of pluralistic folk psychology. The third principle states that a number of different cognitive mechanisms are at work in our folk psychology practices, but according to model theory, all these practices can be described as represented theoretical information. The claim might be understood as a general claim about human cognition and representation, and as consistent with the analysis of human cognitive architecture as neural networks in the brain. If that is the position, then model theory does little more than tell us that our understanding of human behavior can be theoretical, though we have a nonpropositional cognitive architecture.

In addition, the characterization of our folk psychological practices as *theorizing* forces a cognitive distance between individuals that does not appear to be there. Some of the mechanisms involved in our folk psychological judgments are automatic, and we respond to stimuli that we are not even aware of. Take our sensitivity to information from others' endocrine systems. Our tendency to judge someone who has sprayed himself with oxytocin as trustworthy is not plausibly seen as theoretical knowledge, but this response to the hormone interacts with other mechanisms that are more heavily information based. For example, since I know that oxytocin sprays are on the market, I might start to question my natural reactions to people and worry that someone may be using the spray to manipulate me.

Or consider how simple touch can have an effect on one's folk psychological judgment. While we all recognize that touch plays an important part in building bonds between infants and caregivers and between individuals developing intimate relationships, the effect of a discrete touch by a stranger may not be so well known. But touching affects our interpersonal relationships in many ways; evidence suggests that people who are touched briefly demonstrate a greater willingness to help the toucher, to feel increased gratitude toward her, and to share more information with her. People are more persistent in working on a difficult task when lightly touched, and customers give bigger tips when touched. Touch encourages children to perform better in an educational setting, by increasing their willingness to come to the blackboard. These sorts of effects are found even when one does not know that one was touched (see Guéguen 2010 for a review). Why do people respond differently when touched? Evidence suggests that in certain contexts and cultures, people make more positive folk psychological judgments about those who touch them, describing the toucher as more friendly, helpful, patient, and honest than individuals who performed the same role without touching (Erceau and Guéguen 2007; Fisher et al. 1976; Steward and Lupfer 1987). These kinds of phenomena do not leave much room for any theoretically mediated information processing.

Our understanding of others' emotions or moods based on their facial expressions, and our perception of some motions as goal directed, further undermines any account of folk psychology that is based entirely on theoretical information. We understand some things about other people with the same immediacy with which we understand some things about ourselves, without requiring a theoretical lens.

In addition, the story I have been telling emphasizes the complexity involved in folk psychology. Models are typically described as simplifying that which they represent, minimizing the variables and running in an idealized problem space. But the dynamic involved in coming to some conclusion about human behavior, given both the automatic processes and the more controlled, information-heavy processes, is unlikely to be easily idealized or simplified. If so many variables are inherent in every act of social judgment, the model theory owes us an account of how we are able to limit those variables and decide which ones to ignore and which ones are salient whenever we construct a model.

Maibom and Godfrey-Smith may have different responses to such concerns. Maibom emphasizes the knowledge implicit in social models, which provide us with procedural information about social norms; she might argue that we don't need to construct new models for each situation, because many of our quotidian acts of prediction are based on the social models. While I agree that we do have such procedural information and we rely heavily on it, relying on social norms alone cannot help us when we are forced to make judgments in cases of deviation from the norms. According to Maibom, in such cases we resort to folk psychological models, which represent the same information that is represented in the theory-theory account. However, as I have argued, we do not need propositional attitude information to predict all deviant behavior. While Maibom's account of folk psychology adds nonpropositional information to the folk theory of human action, it still relies heavily on propositional attitude psychology.

Godfrey-Smith takes folk psychology as fundamentally a skill in manipulating models of individuals and social generalizations, and his view is perhaps more compatible with an approach that takes the person as central:

Folk-psychological interpreters can rapidly put together specific, filled-out psychological profiles, to explain and predict the actions of individual agents. Some of these specific psychological profiles are extremely fragmentary and minimal, while others are rich and detailed. They are put together out of a repertoire of standard elements, including states like beliefs and preferences that take that-clauses and are linked by logical relations, along with such things as emotions, sensations, and moods. (Godfrey-Smith 2005, 5–6)

While still holding a theory-based view, Godfrey-Smith acknowledges that our understanding of many aspects of folk psychology, such as emotions or moods, is not theoretically posited but known directly through experience. Only once we introduce those elements into a folk psychology model do they become part of an information-rich theory given their relations to other elements of the theory, including theoretical entities.

In addition, though he seems to place primary importance on the SFP notions of belief and desire, his reliance on the construal of a model allows us to understand belief in ways that may be more amenable to the PFP approach. Godfrey-Smith tells us that the model can be seen as a realist map or as an instrumentalist input–output box or as something in between. By allowing different construals of the model, we are also allowing very different ways of conceptualizing belief.

It is here that the view becomes especially promising. I suggest that if we combine Godfrey-Smith's model theory with Schwitzgebel's phenomenal dispositional account of belief, we could avoid some of the problematic consequences of the view that belief attribution is needed to predict and explain behavior. Recall that in Schwitzgebel's view, a person believes *that p* if she behaves according to, and experiences enough of the stereotypic elements associated with, the belief *that p* to satisfy the attributor and her audience, and if any missing elements important to the attributor and her audience can be excused due to some aspect of the situation (Schwitzgebel 2002). So in this view, the belief attribution is shorthand for disposition plus phenomenal experience, and in a folk psychology model, we can construe the beliefs in this way. The belief elements in the model could be read as shorthand descriptions of behavioral dispositions plus phenomenal experience.

If we were to accept a version of Godfrey-Smith's model account and construe the folk psychology models according to a Schwitzgebelian account of belief, this would be a radical deviation from the SFP model: children who lacked a concept of representational belief could still be relying on beliefs in the form of behavioral and affective tendencies when understanding other people and their action. Thus it is consistent with Godfrey-Smith's account that one can use a folk psychology model without having the concept of belief. Rather than seeing others in terms of what they believe, we can see others in terms of what they do and what they feel.

Given the flexibility inherent in this account due to the role of construal, and its ability to accommodate an asymmetrical model of how we explain behavior (as I argued in chapter 7), Godfrey-Smith's version of model theory may be consistent with PFP. However, as we add traits, social norms, people's past behavior, and so on, to the model, in addition to the propositional attitudes and the emotions and moods, we need to know more about the relationship between these elements and how to manipulate such a model. We are told that logical relations hold between the elements, and those relations will do the major work in providing us with an output. But it isn't clear that we will find logical relations connecting and weighing disparate elements such as personality judgments, social-norm roles, knowledge of past behavior, endocrine or mirror system responses, and so forth. We might not even find that probabilistic relations connect these elements. Human folk psychology is not only complex but also not the result of logical processes; we have seen that our folk psychological practices are marked by pragmatism and bias. Our judgments are influenced by what we want to be the case, and by what we have experienced recently. The messy facts are what are supposed to be smoothed over by models that operate in context-free space, and while that might work for some folk psychological practices such as explanation, it isn't clear how it would work for other folk psychology practices, such as prediction, for example. If we don't have the theoretical knowledge to connect all the elements in our model, and we don't know how to weigh the variables, we won't be able to manipulate the model in a useful way.

Another worry about the model theory is that it seems not to leave room for some of the automatic processes involved in our folk psychology practices. Our unmediated responses to others' facial expressions, hormones, movements, and touches suggests an immediacy in our folk psychology that is not reflected by any exhaustive theoretical account. Our automatic willingness to trust others or to see others as attractive, honest, or likable is not accurately characterized as an act of interpretation, because we are not making inferences but simply seeing the individual as trustworthy as immediately as we see his gender. Of course, once we know that the target is a man, and is trustworthy, we can appeal to some theoretical information about what such people tend to do in certain circumstances. However, the model theory has nothing to say about a simple folk psychology judgment that this man is trustworthy.

Model construction and manipulation may accurately describe some subset of our folk psychological practices. However, any account of folk psychology that presents it as nothing more than theoretical knowledge will be hard pressed to accommodate the immediacy and automaticity of many of our folk psychological practices. The theoretical distance between the knower and the known does not reflect the closeness so often experienced between mothers and children, lovers, and good friends. To really know someone is more than being able to manipulate logical principles to predict or explain their behavior; it involves having a seemingly effortless sense of the person.

Reading People, Not Minds

The shift away from propositional mental contents and toward understanding others more holistically as persons better reflects the way we relate with other people. As very young children, we lack general knowledge about human personality types, normal behavior, stereotypes, and how beliefs and desires relate to behavior; at the beginning, our knowledge of others is individualistic. Infants know a limited number of individuals, and through experience they develop expectations about how those individuals behave. When these expectations are not met, this background allows infants to begin to wonder why. As infants gain experience with people's behavior, they add to (and take away from) the profiles they have built of the first people in their lives. Our earliest folk psychological interactions are with the individuals we typically come to know the best, and it is from this early recognition of our caregivers as persons that our folk psychological practices spring forth.

Rather than beginning with generalizations of behavior, as the standard folk psychology story goes, we begin by understanding individuals as persons. It is from our early experience with individual characters we can later form generalizations about people, though we also form generalizations when we learn things about people from our mother's knee, directly through stories about normal and abnormal behavior, through statements about types of people, and indirectly by observing our caregivers' responses to others. But for most human infants, the root of all folk psychology is the early understanding of the person who takes care of us.

As a child's social domain expands, she builds additional psychological profiles and uses them to understand the people she comes to know well, and these new profiles provide additional information to use in formulating general knowledge. When she meets new people, she understands them first via a combination of automatic processes that let her make initial judgments about a person's traits and status, and the general principles she has generated from previous individual personality profiles.

As children gain more experience with people, they gain a greater array of both particular character knowledge and generalizations about normal behavior. This leads adults to have both individual knowledge of persons and general knowledge of character types and normal behavior.

Accordingly, when we make sense of people we know, we use a different approach from the one we use to make sense of those we don't know much about. Those we know we see as well-developed characters, while those we don't know well are seen as types. There is a difference in degree, but also a difference in kind. Those we know are our in-group, and there is an acceptance of the practices of our in-group that is not reflected in our understanding of those we don't know. Metaphorically, the farther away we are from someone, the less likely we are to see him as a person with a fully developed character, and the more likely we are to see him as a type. Our folk psychological engagements are based on our sense of how close we are to the target, and the strategies we use to predict, explain, justify, normalize, coordinate, and so forth, vary accordingly.

The mindreading approach to folk psychology misses the richness and variety in our social interaction. The old project of developing a model of how we mindread should be replaced with a new approach that focuses on our understanding of others as persons, and on the differences between how we know friends and strangers.

Folk psychology as person reading is consistent with the principles of a pluralistic folk psychology and is consistent with the developmental picture, as well as the real differences we see in our engagements with those we know and those we do not. Mindreading accounts do not naturally capture this real-world relationship with other people. For one thing, the standard approaches do not naturally account for the difference in kind in the folk psychological engagements between strangers and intimates, because according to those views, we understand others as containers for sets of propositional attitudes, rather than as fleshed-out people with smells, tics, cultures, status, and various idiosyncrasies.

Our social engagement with others is possible due to a rich set of predictive and interpretive cognitive processes, as I have been arguing. But it also rests on something more rudimentary, namely, our ability to see others as persons. Persons, in contrast with nonintentional objects or artifacts, have a host of interesting properties. They are self-propelled. They are conscious beings, with phenomenological awareness. They have personalities. They are subjects rather than objects, and because of this, they are objects of moral (and legal) concern.

The normativity of personhood is an essential part of our folk psychology. When we are explaining behavior, justifying behavior, or coordinating behavior, we are thinking about what the individual ought to be doing given her personality, her social position, and our relationship to her. Our explanations for out-group members and for people we have already deemed to be worthy of disapprobation will reflect that prior judgment, just as we explain our own behavior, and the behavior of people we approve of, so as to put it in a positive light. These findings from social psychology and the explanatory-style research program force us to reject any assumption that folk psychology is completely value neutral. Even our quotidian predictions of others are based on what we think others should do; the driver should stop at the red light, and the couple walking toward me on the narrow sidewalk should move to let me pass. When such quotidian predictions turn out to be false, and an individual violates our expectation, we see that person as worthy of disapproval, however slight.

When we interact with people face-to-face, we are more likely to see them holistically, and as such we sense that we have a better understanding of them. When we are distanced from others with whom we are engaged, our sense of them as a person is reduced. This is apparent in a classic study of social cues and e-mail. The authors of the study found that given the weak social-context cues in e-mails, people focus more on themselves than on others, and this changes the content of communications. For example, people are more likely to disclose extremely personal information via e-mail, are more inclined to give bad news, and in general are more likely to behave irresponsibly (e.g., by flaming) (Sproull and Kiesler 1986). New e-mail users are less likely to respond to the recipients of their e-mails as persons, not because they are unable to gauge what someone would think or feel in response to an irate note but because they lack the subtle behavioral and social-context cues needed for a fleshed-out character profile.

Our physical interactions benefit from a rich array of information that comes from body movements such as gait and facial expression, hormonal information, and all the information about a person's social standing and group membership that we gain from their appearance, style of speech, and movements. With this additional information, we are able to build richer psychological and character profiles for the individual, and with this additional information we have more data to use when predicting, explaining, and engaging in other folk psychology practices.

While individuals on the autistic spectrum are often described as having an impairment of mindreading, they can also be described as having a problem with person reading. People on the autistic spectrum might be a bit more like people using e-mail for the first time, given their difficulties with understanding body language, emotional expressions, and other social cues. High-functioning autistics and many people with Asperger's learn how to respond appropriately through therapy or through observation of others, as people who spend much time communicating via electronic media learn to respond appropriately by creating techniques to provide and read the kind of information lost. This way of seeing the deficit is consistent with the hypothesis that autistic spectrum disorders are due to weak central coherence.

Take, for example, the story about John Elder Robison's problem with small talk. He says that when he later overheard two women talking in a restaurant about another's affair, he realized what his friend Laurie was up to in telling him about her girlfriend's affair (or at least he thought so):

> When I heard them talk, I suddenly understood that Laurie's statement had been meant to entertain or impress me, and that my response should have been an expression of admiration or excitement. However, that never occurred to me at the time. It's clear to me that regular people have conversational capabilities far beyond mine, and their responses often have nothing at all to do with logic. I suspect normal people are hardwired to develop the ability to read social cues in a way that I am not. (Robison 2008, 191)

As is apparent from this passage, Robison can ascribe beliefs and desires to others and can gain greater competence at ascribing plausibly correct ones, as well. He understands that Laurie desires to impress him, and that she thinks he should respond with admiration or excitement. But note that even before he knew her mental content, he also knew that there was some mental content. He is not mind blind. Rather, what he didn't know was what was on her mind, so to speak, because he wasn't sensing the cues she was giving. We are all in that position from time to time. It is just much more common for people like John Elder Robison, and at least part of his social impairment comes from the inability to relate to others as well-developed characters. The difficulty some have with small talk and casual conversation is a problem with understanding the subtle social cues that successful conversational partners use to figure out when to interject a comment, when to make a joke, and when to laugh at another. Conversation also involves knowing how to tease without hurting, and how to respond to others when they tease you, something Robison also had much difficulty with as a child.

Skilled folk psychologists know how to read what is going on in a conversational exchange in a way that is richer than knowing what the others believe and think. In contrast, an impaired folk psychologist might see a conversational partner as a type rather than a person, like a one-dimensional character in a bad novel. While knowing personality types and behavioral patterns is part of folk psychological competence, it does not get you very far. As F. Scott Fitzgerald wrote, "Begin with an individual, and before you know it you have created a type; begin with a type, and you find you have created—nothing."

The analogy between folk psychology and fiction is apt. Skilled folk psychologists are like skilled novelists, who are able to construct the kind of personality profile needed to engage in the folk psychology act or to tell a compelling story. The adage for novice writers has long been "Show, don't tell." A novel that shows rather than tells does not draw characters as sets of beliefs and desires; rather, it places the characters in situations and has them act accordingly, and the more skilled the novelist, the better the reader sees the character as a person. A one-dimensional character is one result of poor storytelling, and poor storytelling is often the result of describing only a character's mental contents. A good storyteller paints us a portrait of the character by showing us the topography of her behavior: how she speaks, how she responds to different people and different situations, and her mannerisms. A skilled folk psychologist will be sensitive to these same elements when interacting with other people.

Since understanding others as persons involves so many factors, and our understanding of others as persons is key to our folk psychological practices, the old project of determining the structure of our folk psychological practices needs to be replaced with an entirely new project. This new project is based on an understanding that folk psychology is heterogeneous in terms of the practices it includes and the cognitive and biological mechanisms involved. This means that the new project can take a more piecemeal approach, asking questions that range from the general ("How do we come to see another as having a personality trait?") to the specific ("What is involved in predicting what a serial killer will do next?"). To understand folk psychology better, we can examine general differences between prognosticating predictions and quotidian ones, and general differences between explanation and prediction. We can also examine how we engage in other folk psychological projects by determining how we evaluate, justify, negotiate, manipulate, and so on. The project is collaborative, and with researchers in psychology, neuroscience, endocrinology, anthropology, and philosophy working together, we might hope to find better answers to questions about the structures of our folk psychology.

At this point, advocates of SFP might be thinking that my critique and proposed course of action are all well and good but do not address folk psychology, understood narrowly as the attribution of beliefs and desires. I take up this concern in the next chapter by offering a theory of the function of our ability to ascribe such mental content to others. My answer is a departure from the usual story about the function of propositional attitude attribution.

The mindreading approach to folk psychology should be replaced with a research program shaped by an understanding of folk psychology as person reading. Person reading is a holistic approach to folk psychology and promotes an understanding of others as whole people rather than sets of propositions. Taking a person-reading approach opens up new avenues of research in folk psychology; it invites researchers to uncover folk psychological styles, to look for groups of actions that are predicted using the same cognitive mechanisms, and thereby uncover similarities between kinds of actions that may not have been previously recognized as such. It also offers promise for people with social impairments by identifying specific practices and tailoring therapies for the particular deficit shown by the individual. It might also offer insight into our folk psychology failures, as well as our successes, and illuminate how the various processes involved in our acts of predicting and explaining interrelate.

My intention has not been to offer anything like a theory of folk psychology but rather to lay out a set of principles to structure a new research program. In the next two chapters, I aim to show how this new approach can help to answer two questions about folk psychology and phylogeny. One is the functional question about the attribution of the attitudes. If we do not need to attribute beliefs and desires to others to predict much behavior, what do we need them for? The other is the question of theory of mind in other species. What is a theory of mind from the perspective of Pluralistic Folk Psychology, and do apes, dolphins, or members of any other species mindread?

V Implications of the Account

11   Social Intelligence and the Evolution of Theory of Mind

If a social animal is to become—as it must become—one of "Nature's psychologists" it must come up with the appropriate ideology for doing psychology; it must develop a fitting set of concepts and a fitting logic for dealing with a unique and uniquely elusive portion of reality.

—Nicholas Humphrey

The Social Intelligence Hypothesis

Humans can do a lot socially without having to think about others as receptacles for beliefs and desires. Yet most adult humans are able to consider people's mental content. If we can accomplish most of our social goals without ascribing propositional content—without mindreading—why is this skill so widespread? Why is it that attributing propositional attitudes is ubiquitous among adult humans?

As young children, before we have the set of attitude concepts and the fitting logic that connects those concepts to action, we are still able to predict behavior, explain behavior, make judgments about the acceptability of behavior, coordinate behavior, and so forth. I have argued that we are even able to act deceptively and predict behavior when others have false beliefs without appealing to any representational belief concept. But these claims fly in the face of what has long been given as an evolutionary story about the function of the ability to attribute beliefs and desires.

The Social Intelligence Hypothesis provides a well-received answer about the evolution of our ability to attribute propositional attitudes. Varieties of this hypothesis suggest that we must attribute propositional attitudes to succeed in a complex social environment. The hypothesis, which originates with Alison Jolly (1966) and Nicholas Humphrey (1976), attempts to explain the perceived difference in intelligence between species and at first focused on the differences between primates and other taxa.

The difference was mysterious, since while many activities in primates' daily lives require sophisticated cognitive ability (e.g., navigating, processing food, remembering what food is available when), these tasks are not unique to the primates and other species who are considered to have sophisticated cognitive abilities, so ecological demands could not alone account for the difference in cognitive capacity between species.[1]

What could account for the difference is the corresponding complexity of these species' social environments, or so Humphrey and Jolly independently proposed. Apes and monkeys live in intricate social groups that require substantial cognitive commitment; they must be able to recognize individuals (visually, aurally, and perhaps via other modalities as well), they must keep track of kin relations (especially in matrilineal species such as baboons), they must keep track of dominance relations and alliances, and they must be sensitive to possible defections. They must be able to remember who did what to whom and when, and who should care about it. In addition, they must decide what to do in the face of such actions and make judgments about whether they should, for example, challenge a dominant, join a coup, or court the dominant's mate. They must decide when to let others know they have found food, and when to keep it for themselves.

The family feuds, social climbing, and power struggles of primate social living make for much cognitive work, work that humans are all too familiar with. Not for nothing are the interactions of ape and monkey societies often portrayed as if they were pages from a novel. Researchers have called this primate political landscape Machiavellian (Whiten and Byrne 1988) and have likened it to something out of a Jane Austen novel (Cheney and Seyfarth 2007). In his book *Chimpanzee Politics*, Frans de Waal (1982) emphasizes the cognitive demands created by chimpanzees' need for competition and deception. To thrive in this cutthroat environment is to come out on top of what has been called an evolutionary arms race (Whiten and Byrne 1988).

According to Humphrey, the function of primate cognitive ability is to give individuals the ability to construct complex decision trees for predicting how one's own behavior will affect others. Given the fierce primate social environment, making better predictions of behavior was instrumental for gaining greater resources; better predictions were used to better manipulate others' behavior. As individuals gain a more sophisticated theory of social action and greater predictive success, they up the stakes for other members of their community, thus creating an evolutionary arms race. Since attributing propositional attitudes is needed for making the most accurate predictions of behavior, the arms race led to the development of mental-state concepts such as belief, and a theory of how beliefs and desires cause behavior. Developing these abilities takes sophisticated cognition, because they require the postulation of theoretical entities such as belief and desire, and also require the development of some mechanism for using these theoretical entities to make predictions of behavior. Thus we would expect that any species that was engaged in the evolutionary arms race would demonstrate greater general cognitive sophistication than species that were not (Humphrey 1976).

The Social Intelligence Hypothesis is premised on the theory that sophisticated cognition must be adaptive, given the high costs associated with developing a large brain. Evolution is not optimizing, and we should not expect creatures to be cleverer than they need to be. From this, it follows that primates developed sophisticated cognitive abilities for some particular function.

Current supporters of the Social Intelligence Hypothesis have expanded its focus from primates versus nonprimates, and the hypothesis is thought to be a general-purpose explanation for differences in cognitive capacities. Species with sophisticated cognitive capacities are those who live in complex social groups, whereas most asocial species have less in the way of cognitive ability. Evidence for this hypothesis comes from a number of different arenas. Neurological evidence is provided by correlations between social group size and the relative size of the neocortex in a number of different taxa, including humans, cetaceans, insectivores, carnivores, and bats (Dunbar 1998), though the correlation does not appear to hold for some species, such as orangutans, who are large brained and semisolitary. Behavioral evidence also supports the hypothesis; Kamil (2004) argues that the degree of social acuity correlates with reproductive success in social animals, based on his studies of baboons. Three degrees of sociality (spatial proximity to other adults, being a recipient of grooming, and grooming others) are strongly correlated with offspring survival rate in baboons, independent of dominance ranks (Silk et al. 2003). Supporters of the Social Intelligence Hypothesis take the neurological and behavioral data to represent strong evidence of a correlation between sociality and cognitive ability among species, and the hypothesis is thought to explain the correlation.

However, if I am right to question the assumption that attribution of propositional attitudes leads to greater predictive power, this version of the social intelligence hypothesis lacks motivation. We have cheap heuristics for predicting and deceiving, and they do not require the ability to attribute propositional attitudes. Our ancestors who lacked a theory of mind did not need it to predict the behavior of friends and foes who themselves lacked a theory of mind, nor did they need one to deceive them.

If mindreading is adaptive, there is likely a different explanation. I suggest that a better account of the function of mindreading is the development of sophisticated moral abilities such as the justification of behavior, which helps to explain both how a theory of mind facilitates group living and how it facilitates the development of technological advances. The hypothesis I propose is that our species developed moral understanding *before* we developed the ability to attribute propositional attitudes and gained a theory of mind. If this is right, then the moral sense is more primitive than theory of mind.

Deceiving without a Theory of Mind

We take advantage of a number of different cognitive mechanisms when we predict behavior, but can we deceive without having a theory of mind? In one sense, the answer is obviously yes. Across species, animals survive by deceiving others, from the piping plover's broken-wing ploy to the little green frog who lowers his voice to sound bigger. But no one argues that these creatures have a theory of mind; simple heuristics are available to explain these behaviors, and simple plausible evolutionary stories can be told.

In another sense, the answer is obviously no. If deception involves intentionally creating in another a false representation of the world, then of course theory of mind is needed for deception. Since the little green frog is protecting his territory by warding off potential competitors with his deep croak, he needs *at most* the ability to consider how his actions affect the actions of others. (Of course, he doesn't even need that; the behavior might be nothing more than a noncognitive evolved strategy, one of the happy accidents that the green frog's ancestors happened upon.) There is no need for the frog to consider the beliefs of his competitors, so he isn't really deceiving the other frogs, much less lying to them, as the popular press reported (Zimmer 2006).

These two answers correspond to two types of deception, as identified by the primatologists Richard Byrne and Andrew Whiten. They describe the common animal deception as an example of tactical deception, which they define as "acts from the normal repertoire of the agent, deployed such that another individual is likely to misinterpret what the acts signify, to the advantage of the agent" (Byrne and Whiten 1991, 127). What we might call *true deception*, on the other hand, requires that the deceiver intends that another has a false belief.

True deception is often taken to be one of the technological advancements in the social cognition arms race. However, a theory of mind offers an advantage only when predicting the behavior of someone else with a theory of mind; when predicting the behavior of others who lack a theory of mind, attributing beliefs will normally offer no additional predictive power. Let us return to the example of how someone without a theory of mind might learn not to utter the standard call associated with finding food. First of all, the individual must recognize that every time he finds food, he makes a certain sound, and when he makes that sound, everyone else comes and takes away some of the food. Upon noting this correlation, he takes it to be a causal relationship. Subsequently, when he finds food and wants to keep it for himself, he doesn't make the cry. This individual is manipulating the behavior of others without considering the content of their minds, and he is able to do so because he has noticed the relationship between two variables. But he does not need to know why the others come when he calls, and he does not need to know anything about their beliefs or desires. This behavior is a form of tactical deception, though, and does offer advantage to the individual in a world of food scarcity.

Recall that I made a similar move in chapter 2 and argued that a child could pass the false-belief task without a representational theory of mind. We also saw from the infant research that it is possible to track false belief and intentions well before developing this ability. The more evidence we have that sophisticated behaviors, including deception and performance of "theory of mind" tasks, do not require inferences about propositional attitudes, the less plausible Humphrey's story becomes. In addition, if other species predict, manipulate, deceive, compete, and so forth without mindreading, then we have no reason to think that humans need to do so. While it is true that evolution is not a tidy process, we should avoid postulating the development of a unique cognitive process to make better predictions of behavior when the current mechanisms work just fine.

Humphrey's story is based on the assumption that having a theory of mind permits greater success in deceiving those who *lack* a theory of mind. For a theory of mind to offer a competitive advantage, it would have to be widespread, since in a community that is not rife with individuals who already have a theory of mind, no competitive advantage exists to having one; methods of deception that do not require a theory of mind already exist. On the other hand, in a community that does have many individuals with a theory of mind, it would be a disadvantage to lack it. Clearly it can be advantageous to have a theory of mind to deceive others who can consider your thoughts and motivations. In addition, we need to appeal to mental states in situations that are about mental states to begin with (e.g., when teaching someone how to meditate, or determining how to convince someone that he or she wants to buy a house). But since having a theory of mind does not help to predict the behavior of those without a theory of mind, and yet today adults have one, there may be another story to be told about theory of mind acquisition. In what follows, I propose a different kind of social intelligence story to account for the evolution of theory of mind in humans.

Predicting with a Theory of Mind

In developing the framework for a pluralistic folk psychology, I have emphasized that humans can predict behavior without having the ability to attribute beliefs and desires. Nonetheless I have been careful not to deny that we sometimes do mindread when anticipating what others will do next. At this point, we can examine under what conditions an individual needs a theory of mind to predict behavior. Because quotidian predictions can be made using various methods that do not require understanding representational belief, we need to look toward the more unusual predictions to find cases in which having a theory of mind would be beneficial. When we need to make predictions in unfamiliar situations, about unknown actors who are not easy to categorize, or about known actors who are behaving atypically, the methods we use to make quotidian predictions will often fail. Given these considerations, I suggest that our ancestors would have benefited from having a theory of mind to predict behavior in anomalous situations. When faced with an anomalous situation, we cannot appeal to our experience or someone's past behavior to predict what is going to happen next. We cannot rely on our knowledge of traits or stereotypes or social norms. Instead we need to engage in a more effortful cognitive act that begins with coming to grips with the situation. When we recognize an anomaly in behavior or situation, we are immediately thrown into a state of affective tension. Seeing something as an anomaly and wanting to act appropriately in the situation (to make a correct prediction, or coordinate behavior, or so forth) require that one first seek to understand the situation. Understanding the situation involves formulating a construal of the situation's elements, including the target's behavior, the environment, other actors, and so forth. This means that an individual who recognizes an anomalous situation is thrown into a state of explanation seeking.

What sorts of explanations are available to the explanation seeker in an anomalous situation? Since the case falls out of the normal repertoire of behaviors, then neither causal-history explanations nor enabling-factors explanations will be of much use. A potential predictor does not understand anomalous behaviors, and without understanding a behavior, it is even more difficult to determine what caused the behavior. To understand an anomalous behavior, we have to seek a reason for the behavior that will make sense of it.

Let me give an example of a situation in which a behavior might be seen as anomalous. Suppose that all adult members of a community gather leaves for bedding every evening. The leaves make for a soft place to sleep, but since the leaves dry out during the day, a new bed needs to be made each evening. Adult females build nests for their offspring, and adolescents begin gathering their own leaves after they are weaned. One day, an adolescent who has made her own nest several times already does not join the rest of the community in gathering leaves. Instead she leaves the group, only to return the next morning none the worse for wear. Night after night, the adolescent disappears without building a nest and reappears in the morning. This behavior makes no sense to the other group members, who follow a well-established pattern of behavior without any deviations. No individual differences, nothing about the adolescent's personality, help her group members make sense of the behavior; she isn't antisocial, she isn't consorting with new friends outside the group—that is, none of the standard causes of such behavior make sense here.

To explain this behavior, an observer has no recourse but to consider the actor's reasons. As we know, observers more often explain behavior by appealing to the causal history of the individual, and actors more often explain their own behavior by appeal to beliefs and desires. However, some conditions arise in which observers explain others' behavior in terms of reasons—when they are motivated to portray the behavior in a positive light (Malle 2004; Malle et al. 2007). While it may be easy to disapprovingly explain out-group behavior or condemn anomalous behavior by referring to a negative personality trait or stereotype (e.g., she ate her child because she is crazy), one cannot offer a positive explanation for an in-group member so easily. In the nest-building example, the deviant is a fully accepted group member, so the group members may be motivated to portray her behavior in a positive light and hence will tend to explain the behavior in terms of the actor's beliefs and desires.

Given the underdetermination of propositional attitudes by behavior, these explanations may not be accurate. But seeking to understand a state of affairs involves asking for an explanation of what led to the current situation, and this leads us to consider the beliefs and desires that the actor might have had. After developing a plausible explanation that cites an actor's beliefs and desires, we can use that attribution to make a prediction. In an anomalous situation, a prediction of future action can only come after an explanation for the agent's past behavior because predicting behavior based on the attribution of beliefs and desires relies on a prior ability to explain or construe behavior as being caused by beliefs and desires. This suggests that before our ancestors began explaining behavior, they lacked the ability to attribute propositional attitudes. In this view, it is in offering *reasons*, not predictions, where we should expect to see the evolution of theory of mind.

Norms and Theory of Mind

If humans did not develop the concepts of belief and desire to better predict behavior but rather developed the ability to resolve the affective tension that came with wondering why someone acted in an anomalous way, then our human ancestors must have had some way to identify these behaviors as anomalous. The sensitivity to behavior that is bizarre or otherwise out of the ordinary makes sense only against a background expectation about normal behavior. What this means is that our ancestors had an understanding of something like norms before they had a theory of mind.

Social norms are both action guides and tools for anticipating others' behaviors. However, they are more than merely statistical regularities. For example, since most North Americans choose to drive a car with an automatic transmission, the person who buys a car with a manual transmission is violating a statistical norm. However, because driving a manual is not a behavior that the community will view with disapproval, it does not violate a normatively salient statistical regularity, or a social norm.

A social norm is based on one's expectations in cases where violating the norm results in a negative consequence for the transgressor, either in the form of disapproval from the community or in the form of negatively valenced emotional responses in the actor, such as secret guilt. Community disapproval varies in its form; on the mild end of the continuum, disapproval may be expressed as simple puzzlement, but in more dramatic cases, the transgressor may be injured or killed. Adherence to the norm solidifies one's membership in the community and invites acceptance and protection by the other community members.

Not only human societies have social norms; many animal societies do, as well. Perhaps the most common norms surround the distribution of food and sex. Chimpanzees, for example, have norms about how to divide meat after a hunt (Boesch 2002), how rank influences access to provisioned food (Hare et al. 2000), and how to treat offspring (de Waal 1996) and sexual partners (Goodall 1971). Violations of these norms can result in physical harm toward the transgressor.

Other animal norms appear to have a purely social function. Susan Perry discovered an interesting set of norms within a community of capuchin monkeys related to social games:

> All of these behaviors occur in relaxed social contests, in which the participants are typically somewhat isolated from the rest of the group. . . . The participants move slowly (which is highly unusual for a capuchin) and have trancelike expressions on their faces, staring out into space or else looking at their fingers. . . . All of them [the activities] involve a certain amount of risk or discomfort to one or both participants. Handsniffers have one another's fingernails delicately lodged in their nostrils, which restricts their movements; tail-sucking and the finger-in-mouth game involve placing a body part between the sharp teeth of the partner (since many capuchins are missing digits and tail tips, it is reasonable to assume that this is risky); the hair-passing game involves yanking significant amounts of hair out of the face and shoulders, which cannot be very comfortable. Perhaps these conventions are ways of testing the bonds between individuals. (Perry et al. 2003, 254)

Because such behavior has no obvious purpose, Perry thinks that these hand-sniffing games may have a derivative function of building trust and strengthening bonds between individuals. It takes a lot of time for two monkeys to get to the point when they will calmly permit a partner to insert her finger deep into a nostril or eye socket. This suggests that hand sniffing and other capuchin games are social norms; they are behaviors that are created and enforced by the community. Perry thinks that these rituals may be used to signal commitment to the social relationship, and failure to perform the ritual may have long-term negative consequences for the pair. Individuals must coordinate with each other to touch in ways that involve risk, and in ways that are not extendable to just anyone in the community. In addition, the games involve turn taking and role switching, suggesting that the players are following well-developed rules. If the norm is violated, a capuchin will be injured, losing a fingertip or sustaining damage to an eye. Moreover, if the social-bonding interpretation is correct, violations could also lead to emotional distress over the deterioration of the bond.

Since monkeys almost certainly do not attribute representational beliefs to others, the development of social norms in monkeys demonstrates their ability to develop variations of the behavioral repertoire that involve creating, following, and violating social norms having to do with trust, harm, and cooperation. Recognizing a norm violation is an implicit acknowledgment that social norms exist, and is based on an expectation about normal behavior. The norms need not be declaratively represented; the rules may take the form of some implicit knowledge *how* rather than propositional knowledge *that*.

What this suggests is that rather than developing a theory of mind to predict behavior, humans may have developed a theory of mind to explain norm violations. First, I have argued that before humans needed to explain behavior, there was little driving the need to develop a theory of mind. In addition, I suggested that the need to explain people's actions was driven by others' anomalous behaviors. But to perceive a behavior as anomalous, one needs to have an understanding of normal behavior, and to understand behavior as normal is to have at least an implicit understanding of the relevant social norms. Insofar as this account is correct, before the human species developed a theory of mind, humans had an understanding of social norms.

An Adaptive Function of Explaining Behavior

This discussion suggests that Humphrey's story gets things backward; understanding of beliefs and desires could not have been an adaptation for making better predictions of behavior, because before they began offering additional predictive power, the belief and desire concepts would already have been part of the cognitive repertoire. Given the assumption that developing a theory of mind comes at great cost, we might expect it to have some adaptive function. If this is so, then the account I have provided suggests that the adaptive function of a theory of mind has something to do with explaining behavior, rather than predicting it.

A different version of the Social Intelligence Hypothesis is compatible with this account. In her initial presentation of some of the ideas that led to the hypothesis, Alison Jolly suggests that cooperative social learning, not fierce social competition, led to greater cognitive capacity. For many species, social learning involves a close observation of what another is doing. My hypothesis can be seen as an extension of Jolly's version of the

Social Intelligence Hypothesis, since an individual is in a better position to learn a new behavior when she knows what the behavior is for. This is not to say that a theory of mind evolved to promote social learning, since the ability to explain behavior is not necessary for a great deal of social learning. Many different species learn to engage in behaviors simply as a result of observing someone in their social group performing those behaviors. Birdsongs are a good illustration; male white-crowned sparrows, for example, sing different mating songs depending on whether they live in Berkeley or Sunset Beach, California (Marler and Tamura 1964). These sparrows learn to sing the song they were exposed to as fledglings, without any need to understand anything about song dialects. In other instances, however, knowing why someone is engaged in a behavior can be an important step in learning the behavior oneself.

Social learning in animals is currently of great interest to those researching animal culture and innovation. In this field, a cultural behavior is understood to be one that is transmitted repeatedly until it becomes widespread throughout the population (Whiten et al. 1999). New sets of behaviors may be introduced to the community's behavioral repertoire by immigrants or innovated by community members. Innovation is "the process that generates in an individual a novel learned behavior that is not simply a consequence of social learning or environmental induction" (Ramsey et al. 2007, 395; see also Reader and Laland 2003). Thus an innovative behavior is anomalous and is not comprehensible either in terms of what others are doing or in terms of obvious environmental features. I suggest that having the ability to understand why another is engaged in an innovative behavior, as well as social learning of beneficial innovations, is what drove the evolution of a theory of mind.

Others have postulated a relationship between theory of mind and technological developments, as well. For example, some argue that a theory of mind was needed for Oldowan tool manufacture via stone-knapping techniques to become cultural (e.g., Mithen 2000, 2002). However, social learning need not require a theory of mind when the affordances of the new behavior are obvious; seeing how a tool helps to butcher an animal much more quickly and efficiently is reason enough to make such a tool for oneself. My point is not that theory of mind is needed to engage in any social learning; rather, I argue that the development of a robust culture with both technological advancements and social norms requires the ability to recognize the reasons individuals have for acting in novel ways.

In the biological anthropology literature, culture is defined as not only the way we do things (McGrew 1992) but also the norms and standards of one's community (McGrew 2009). Cultural traditions involve the existence of implicit codes of behavior, because they refer to population-specific differences in behavior that (a) are not ascribable to purely ecological differences between communities, (b) are socially learned, and (c) persevere for some time. Thus social learning is an essential part of the development of a culture, but culture, as a *collection* of norms and standards, exists only in a subset of animal species that engage in social learning.

Arguments in favor of culture have been made for a number of species; collaborative research has demonstrated the existence of culture and community-specific behavior in chimpanzees (Whiten et al. 1999), orangutans (Van Schaik et al. 2003), capuchin monkeys (Perry et al. 2003), and whales and dolphins (Rendell and Whitehead 2001). For example, the chimpanzee project continues with 571 candidate behaviors as culturally variant (Whiten 2007). Many of the behaviors on this list are related to different methods of food processing, though other cultural behaviors appear to have purely social benefits, such as the chimpanzee handclasp grooming seen in some communities.

Innovation is an essential aspect of culture and of individual intelligence (Reader and Laland 2002; Piaget 1936/1952). The cognitive processes involved in the development of culture must account for both the individual innovation and the spread of the innovation inside the group. Candidate processes for innovations include exploration, neophilia (attraction to novelty), and learning (Reader 2003). Reader gives the example of the British titmice who learned to open milk bottles by piercing the foil at the top of the bottle and eating the cream off the top (Fisher and Hinde 1949; Hinde and Fisher 1951). To innovate this behavior, the titmice had to explore a novel area (the doorsteps where the bottles were left), investigate a novel object (the milk bottles), and try a new food (the cream). The titmice may have invoked learning to improve their technique by adjusting their grip on the bottle and to discover that the foil cap is easily pierced (Reader 2003).

Because cultural behaviors result from some innovative behavior that spreads throughout a social group, a community that has a robust culture must also have some mechanism for identifying and promoting useful innovations. Social learning is thought to play an important role here. In the titmouse example, naive birds that come across opened bottles can learn about the affordances of the bottle: it contains food and can be opened via piercing with the beak. They can also observe other birds opening and drinking from the containers.

It is in identifying the benefits associated with such novelty that the ability to explain behavior may be adaptive. In the case of the titmouse, it does not require much of an imagination for the naive bird to discover why his conspecifics are opening the bottles; the affordances are too strong. But as culture develops, the innovations are less likely to be so obviously beneficial to group members. Take, for example, the handclasp grooming first identified in chimpanzees at Mahale (McGrew and Tutin 1978). When two chimpanzees handclasp groom, they sit facing each other, holding each other's hand or wrist over their heads. This behavior is considered a cultural one because it is not common across chimpanzee communities, and we know of no ecological reasons for the behavior. When a naive chimpanzee sees others engage in handclasp grooming, the worth of the behavior is not as immediately obvious as the worth of the titmouse's opening the milk bottle. The function of social traditions, like chimpanzee handclasp grooming or the capuchins' finger-in-nostril game, may require a bit more attention on the part of the naive individual.

As early hominids innovated behaviors whose functions were not transparent to observers, it is likely that group members needed to understand the reasons behind the new behaviors for the innovation to be adopted by the community. One such innovation was surely the use of fire for cooking food, which is a clear case of a beneficial innovation (Wrangham 2009). However, the benefits of cooking meat were unlikely to be apparent to our human ancestors. Fire, which would have been known as a destructive force, and food, which is needed for energy, might have seemed an unlikely combination. It is not wild speculation to suggest that the first individuals who cooked and ate meat were seen as engaging in a truly bizarre behavior, one that may even have violated the norms associated with meat eating and sharing. In response to this novel behavior, group members could have taken one of two general strategies: they could have punished or ostracized the innovator for violating the norm, thereby stopping the transformation of the behavior into a cultural tradition, or they could have tried to understand the anomalous behavior and sought to justify the individual's actions. The willingness to take the second option and to justify a bizarre (and, on the face of it, destructive) act demonstrates the kind of openness to novelty that is necessary for technological advancement. Such reasoning suggests a potential adaptive function for explaining behavior: it allowed the development of innovative technologies and social behaviors that have benefits not immediately obvious to naive individuals.

While the development of culture depends on the neophilia of the individuals who first innovate, it also depends on the willingness of the community to tolerate norm violations.

A community that ostracized individuals for acting outside the norm would have fewer innovations. When people are shunned for acting abnormally, they are transformed from in-group members to out-group members. However, when community members seek an explanation for an individual's abnormal behavior, they are seeking reasons for the action that will serve to justify it. The close relationship between the practices of explaining and justifying behavior bolsters this hypothesis. We often use the terms *explanation* and *justification* interchangeably. When the teenager says, "I can explain!" in response to her mother's disapproval of some action, she means that she can justify her action in her mother's eye. Moreover, when attempting to justify an action, we often provide only an explanation and leave the normative claim unstated. For example, if I try to justify why I ran a stop sign, I might merely point to my bleeding passenger without trying to convince the officer that getting a bleeding person to the hospital trumps stopping at a residential stop sign at 3 a.m. If the first instances of explaining behavior in terms of reasons were also attempts to justify behavior, this would help explain the close connection we still see between these two practices.

Communities that tolerate abnormal behaviors and seek to see the worth in them are more likely to develop technologically in the way that the *Homo* line did. They are also more likely to develop a sophisticated moral sense. The explanations of abnormal behavior that transformed them into cultural traditions and hence normalized them would function as justifications. Having a community with a developed moral sense will be beneficial insofar as it helps with the cohesion of social groups. A moral sense combined with an openness to innovation will allow for the construction of a more complex society that involves things like turn taking, sharing, and property. Behavioral innovations that assist the survival of a group can be refined and promoted once individuals develop the ability to justify behavior. For example, one might be able to convince conspecifics to take turns serving as sentry, or to build group shelters, once members of one's society are able to understand behaviors in terms of reasons, justify behavior, and analyze the arguments given for novel behaviors. Living in large social groups will be beneficial to individuals if they can expect aid from others. Novel behavior that promotes long-term gains over short-term gains can be adopted by the group once that behavior is seen as being done for a (good) reason.

Social innovations can create or strengthen an emotional bond between conspecifics, and this bond can be seen as the glue that holds the community together, even when its members do not see one another for long periods of time. In chimpanzee societies, for example, out-group males and infants may be killed, and this indicates that real survival value accrues from making sure that your community members understand that you are one of them. Having shared explanations or justifications for culturally specific behaviors, even if these explanations are no more than confabulations, may be essential in a community that makes life-and-death decisions based on whether an individual is one of them or not.

Thus we get a twofold adaptive benefit from explaining behavior: it promotes both technological development and social-moral development. I have argued that some understanding of social norms is the likely precursor of a theory of mind used to explain behavior. The adaptive worth of explaining behavior and justifying behavior in terms of others' beliefs and desires should be clear; it leads both to the drive to understand abnormal behavior and to the acceptance of the kinds of innovations that have a real impact on fitness and thus drive the species' evolution and ecology.

Social Intelligence as Explaining Behavior

Explaining behavior in terms of one's reasons for action, I suggest, offers real benefits to individuals and species, much more so than predicting behavior based on someone's reasons. If there is an evolutionary story to be told about our coming to see others as having propositional attitudes, it is likely to be a story about the cognitive capacities that allow one to recognize that an anomalous behavior has some purpose behind it.

This view has at least two interesting implications. One is that species without a theory of mind could still have some normative or quasi-ethical systems, and such individuals may be considered something like a moral agent (Andrews 2009). For a person to be a moral agent, at minimum, two things must hold: the individual must be autonomous, and the individual must understand the consequences of her actions. For each condition, some think that having a theory of mind is required. For example, Christine Korsgaard (2006) argues that autonomy is a form of normative self-government that requires that the actor have self-awareness of the grounds of action as grounds—that is, one must recognize that her reasons serve to justify the action. This suggests that theory of mind is necessary for autonomy, since even to realize that one has reasons for actions requires metacognitive understanding of one's own propositional attitudes. However, an individual without a theory of mind can still recognize that a behavior is a norm violation, can recognize that others will respond negatively to norm violations, and can choose whether or not to violate that norm given those consequences. Whether one wants to call such a creature of full-blown moral agent or not is a matter of discussion, but since the individual has some understanding of social norms, and understanding social norms is a form of moral understanding, individuals without a theory of mind could still have moral knowledge. Having such knowledge opens a door into the sphere of the normative.

In the next chapter, I explore a consequence of this view. If the human understanding of belief was used to explain behavior before it was used to predict behavior, then when we turn to examine theory of mind in other species, we should consider whether critters are seeking explanations of behavior.

12 Being a Critter Psychologist

Comparative researchers have never specified "the unique causal work" that representations about mental states do.
—Derek Penn and Daniel Povinelli

Problems with the Chimpanzee Theory of Mind Research Program

I have argued that being a folk psychologist does not depend on having a theory of mind, and that, for the most part, we do not need the ability to attribute propositional attitudes to predict behavior. I have also suggested that the evolution of theory of mind in humans was not driven by a need to improve behavioral predictions. These views have implications for the ongoing research program on chimpanzee theory of mind. This research program, though moribund for twenty years after Premack and Woodruff first introduced the question, has seen an explosion of interest in recent years. However, it is not entirely clear what the current generation of researchers are after when they ask, "Does the chimpanzee have a theory of mind?"

As was discussed in chapter 2, Premack and Woodruff understood the term *theory of mind* to refer to the ascription of mental states to others to predict and explain their behavior. Premack made this definition explicit in 1988 when he said that he and Woodruff were originally interested in the question "Does the ape do what humans do: attribute states of mind to the other one, and use these states to predict and explain the behavior of the other one?" (Premack 1988, 160). However, given our discussion about the role of belief attribution in prediction and explanation so far, it is clear that Premack and Woodruff's question itself conflates a number of issues, and the question requires some revision.

First, we must address the false presuppositions in the question. In formulating it, Premack and Woodruff assumed that humans attribute mental states when both predicting and explaining behavior. We have seen that this is not necessarily the case. The question also fails to distinguish between prediction and explanation, and I have argued that it is more natural to find mental-state attributions in explanations than in predictions. Yet the research paradigms designed to test the question focus on prediction; to my knowledge, no one has studied chimpanzees' social explanation-seeking behavior. I see this as an implicit endorsement of the symmetry thesis, which I rejected in chapter 3.

Another problem with the question is that it is ambiguous. *Theory of mind* has meant both attributing mental states to predict and explain and more specifically attributing belief and desire to predict and explain. Worse, given the philosophical debates about the nature of belief, researchers may be working under different conceptions of what it is to have a belief.

To avoid the ambiguity, some researchers have suggested that we understand the term as a "generic label" for a number of different cognitive processes involved in social cognition (Tomasello et al. 2003b, 239), a view that fits nicely into a PFP approach. Today the dominant view is that chimpanzees understand a variety of nonpropositional mental states, such as seeing (Hare et al. 2000; Plooij 1978; Goodall 1986; de Waal 1996; but see Povinelli and Eddy 1996), hearing (Melis et al. 2006), goals (Uller 2004), intentionality (Tomasello and Carpenter 2005; Warneken and Tomasello 2006), and even knowledge (Kaminski et al. 2008; Hare et al. 2001). However, even scientists who are happy to explain the behavior of chimpanzees in terms of sophisticated cognitive mechanisms show little willingness to see chimpanzee social cognition as mediated by concepts such as belief. For example, while they think that chimpanzees can ascribe perceptual states to others, Tomasello, Call, and Hare believe that "there is no evidence anywhere that chimpanzees understand the beliefs of others" (Tomasello et al. 2003a, 156). Even David Premack today admits that chimpanzees do not have a theory of mind in the sense of being able to attribute beliefs, because "creatures without language cannot attribute belief" (Premack and Premack 2003, 149).

Not everyone agrees with this position. Some are boosters; given her decades of work with Kanzi and other symbol-trained chimpanzees and bonobos, Sue Savage-Rumbaugh writes, "There is no doubt that Kanzi attributes intentions and feelings to others and that he recognizes the need to communicate things about his own mental state to others" (Savage-Rumbaugh et al. 1998, 56). And some are critics; Daniel Povinelli and his colleagues think that all chimpanzee behavior can be accounted for without postulating that they understand anything about others' mental states.

Rather, chimpanzees can solve the purported theory of mind tasks by constructing behavioral abstractions rather than relying on mentalistic concepts such as *seeing* (Povinelli and Vonk 2003, 2004).

The claim that chimpanzees do not understand belief is far too hasty. For one thing, it reflects an implicit commitment to the symmetry thesis, which we have seen to be false. The symmetry thesis states that prediction is backward explanation. If this thesis were true, it would be methodologically appropriate to use only predictive tasks to test chimpanzee theory of mind, since you would also be testing their ability to explain, albeit in a forward-looking way. That researchers have only tested for theory of mind in predictive tasks suggests that they at least implicitly accept the symmetry thesis. Otherwise they would also have attempted to determine whether chimpanzees attribute beliefs to explain behavior. The ability to attribute beliefs will not be fully examined in chimpanzees until someone is able to test chimpanzee explanatory behavior, and while it may be true that we have no evidence that chimpanzees do understand others' beliefs, this may be due to the researchers' theoretical assumptions and not a reflection of the chimpanzees' capacities. When we look for something where we don't expect it to be, we are not really looking at all.

In addition, I am concerned that the definition of the term *belief* (or perhaps just its extension) is more constrained when it comes to questions of chimpanzee belief. As we saw in chapter 2, we can analyze belief in a number of different ways, and there should be different ways of examining whether chimpanzees understand that others have beliefs given those different accounts.

The lack of agreement about meanings, the ambiguity, and the false presuppositions lead me to conclude that the question "Does the chimpanzee have a theory of mind?" should be rejected and replaced with more specific questions about the nature of chimpanzee social cognition. The original question allows for a yes–no answer, but either answer merely invites more questions about what the answer actually means. I suggest that we replace the original question with other, more productive questions, such as the following: Is the chimpanzee a successful predictor of others' behavior, and in which contexts? Do chimpanzees seek explanations for behavior? Do chimpanzees recognize others as intentional agents? Do chimpanzees have any understanding of representational belief? Do they engage in joint attention with any other chimpanzees (e.g., is joint attention limited to mother-infant dyads?) or with any humans? Do they have any understanding of personality traits? Might chimpanzees construct dispositional stereotypes?

To demonstrate how this investigation might go, I will start by suggesting ways to answer the first four of these questions. My aim is not only to help steer the ongoing debate about the chimpanzee's social cognitive abilities but also to demonstrate the fecundity of the PFP framework for researchers.

Chimpanzee Critter Psychology

Starting from the position that chimpanzees, like other animals, have minds, we can ask whether chimpanzees are critter psychologists, that is, whether they recognize that other critters are intentional agents, and whether they have robust success in any of the folk psychological practices. I argue that like some children younger than three, many chimpanzees can also be considered folk psychologists, given the PFP framework. The requirements for being a folk psychologist in my account are having the ability to recognize that intentional agents exist and having success in some of the folk psychological practices of predicting, explaining, or interpreting the behavior of an intentional agent; such an individual is at least a minimal folk psychologist. We can define a *critter psychologist* as a nonhuman animal who, minimally, understands that others are intentional agents and can successfully engage in some folk psychological practices.

I first argue that chimpanzees recognize that others are intentional agents, and from there I examine the extent to which they engage in predictive, explanatory, and interpretive practices.

Intentional Agency

To see someone as an intentional agent, we must see the agent as the origin of her behavior, as having some flexibility in behavior, and as having behavioral goals. A number of different comparative studies demonstrate that chimpanzees, like human infants, naturally perceive certain kinds of movement as purposeful. We know that chimpanzees perceive a difference between intentional behavior and unintentional body movement and are more impatient with humans who are unwilling to give them food than with those who are unable to give them food (Call et al. 2004). We also know that chimpanzees help humans achieve their goals; in the course of normal social interaction with a human caregiver, chimpanzees pick up an object the caregiver accidentally dropped (Warneken and Tomasello 2006). In addition, we know that chimpanzee infants, like human infants, perform on violation of expectation tasks in ways that suggest an understanding of agency (Uller 2004).

The original chimpanzee theory of mind study is now seen by Premack as evidence that chimpanzees understand goals. In the original study, the chimpanzee Sarah was shown videotapes of humans working to achieve some goal such as trying to play an unplugged record player or trying to light a gas heater (Premack and Woodruff 1978). In discussing that study, Premack writes:

> To consistently choose photos depicting the proper "solutions" to particular problems, as Sarah did, one must first see a "problem." But what is a "problem"? A videotape depicts merely a sequence of events, not a problem. A "problem" is produced by a reader who interprets a videotape. The reader must see the actor as being goal-directed, as *trying* to reach inaccessible food or *trying* to rectify malfunctioning equipment. Sarah's consistent choice of solutions to the actor's problems demonstrated that she did interpret the videotapes, attributing mental states to the actor. (Premack and Premack 2003, 146)

Premack's depiction of this study as requiring the perception of a problem is interesting. If Sarah interpreted the human as having a problem, and her action as helping him solve the problem, she must certainly have seen the human as an agent with a goal. However, Premack is too quick to conclude that this means that Sarah attributed a mental state to the actor, since one might be able to see someone as having a goal without seeing them as having a desire; having the concept of desire may not be necessary to recognize behavior as goal oriented.

Another reason to think that chimpanzees understand agency comes from their imitative behavior. Evidence suggests that chimpanzees are able to imitate intentional behaviors and can even act out a model's intended action when that behavior has not been displayed (Myowa-Yamakoshi and Matsuzawa 2000; Tomasello and Carpenter 2005). Further, chimpanzees, like eighteen-month-old human infants, also appear to know when they are being imitated. In a study with a chimpanzee named Cassie, Nielsen and colleagues (2005) found that Cassie responded differently when being imitated by his caregiver than he did when his caregiver engaged in nonimitative behavior. Like human infants, Cassie would systematically vary his behavior while closely watching the imitator. Nielsen and colleagues describe one bout of behavior while Cassie was being imitated: "Cassie poked his finger out of the cage, wiped the ground in front of him, picked up a piece of straw and placed it in his mouth, pressed his mouth to the cage, then poked his finger out of the cage again" (Nielsen et al. 2005, 34). Such repetitive sequences were the norm when Cassie was being imitated, but not when the caregiver engaged in nonimitative behavior or no behavior at all. Cassie's response demonstrates that he was aware that his caregiver was acting purposefully, further evidence that the chimpanzee has a notion of agency.

In contrast to these findings, one published study concludes that chimpanzees do not understand capability, or what others can and cannot do (Vonk and Subiaul 2009). Since an individual who does not understand capability would not be able to distinguish between an intentional and unintentional action, this study offers a challenge to the dominant view. However, I see reason to reject the authors' interpretation of their findings.

In the study, chimpanzees are given the opportunity to beg for food from one of two humans, one of whom is unable to supply the food. Across a number of experimental conditions, the researchers found that the chimpanzees did not beg from the capable human significantly more often. However, we do not know whether the "incapable" human was seen as incapable by the chimpanzees. The human was rendered incapable of supplying the food owing to her placement in a series of apparatuses that either hid her limbs completely or served as a barrier to movement.

For example, a person is incapable of delivering food because there is a bar in front of his ankles, so he cannot use his foot to push the tray toward the chimpanzee, or in front of his arms, so he cannot reach ahead with a tray of food. However, a bar in front of the ankles need not deter a determined provider from delivering food, since he can lift his feet over the bar, and the same goes for a bar in front of the wrists. A chimpanzee might be especially unimpressed by the barrier, given chimpanzee physiology. Chimpanzee limbs are largely interchangeable, such that a leg may be used to perform a function for which humans would only use an arm. Given the disanalogy between the motor capabilities of humans and chimpanzees, asking the chimpanzee to report on the capability of humans requires them to suppress any knowledge they might have about chimpanzee capability, or any cues they might use when predicting the behavior of a chimpanzee, and develop new cues or a new understanding of human ability.

Another problem with this study is that the experiments required the chimpanzees to make a further inference: if a limb was not visible, it could not be used. The subjects had to realize, for example, that the experimenters with arms held behind their backs were not just holding their arms out of sight but were unable to use their arms in any way. Both issues make this set of studies a problematic test of sensitivity to capability, and given the previous evidence suggesting that chimpanzees are sensitive to what others can and cannot do, it seems likely that task demands were the cause of the poor performance in this experiment rather than an insensitivity to causally relevant observable cues.

The studies just discussed offer evidence that chimpanzees have an understanding of agency. Chimpanzees realize that other chimpanzees and humans engage in purposeful action that is goal directed, and while this is sufficient for us to say that they have an understanding of agency, it does not allow us to say much about how they understand agency, what the chimp understanding of agency consists of, and how they discriminate agents from nonagents. Our understanding of the infant understanding of agency is perhaps a bit more developed, but similarly, we do not know, for example, why infants are more likely to see an ungloved hand as an intentional actor, compared to a gloved hand. Comparative research on the folk and the critter understanding of agency is needed if we want to understand whether the mechanisms used by humans and chimpanzees are the same, or whether these behaviors are merely analogous. Regardless of mechanism, however, the function is the same across species: humans and chimpanzees see others as intentional agents engaged in purposeful behavior.

Predicting and Coordinating

Support for the idea that chimpanzees see one another as intentional agents also comes from evidence that they are able to successfully predict and coordinate behavior with others. Of the host of data on predicting and coordinating, the most impressive comes from behavioral observations of chimpanzees in their natural habitat. I will briefly describe two behaviors common among some communities of chimpanzees—hunting and border patrols—as evidence of their ability to predict and coordinate behavior.

During his thirty years observing chimpanzees at Taï National Park, Côte d'Ivoire, the ethologist Christophe Boesch has documented the chimpanzees' sophisticated ability to cooperate to hunt colobus monkeys (Boesch 1994, 2002). Unlike in other chimpanzee communities, where an individual can succeed in a hunt alone, in the Taï forest, single hunters rarely succeed. This drives the Taï chimpanzees to use group hunting strategies, involving up to four individuals in a single hunt. Boesch and colleagues describe the four roles in a group hunt: the driver initiates a hunt by forcing the prey to move through the trees in a single direction; the blocker will climb trees to keep the prey from deviating from the driver's path; the chaser will climb under the prey and attempt to capture it; the ambusher will quietly climb in front of the prey to block escape and form a trap.

When the prey is spotted, each of the hunters takes on one of these roles, based on their location in relation to the monkey and the location and behavior of the other chimpanzees. The behavior is carefully synchronized among the chimpanzees, and the hunters have to behave flexibly, for they will change roles as necessary. Each of these roles is quite sophisticated, and it can take the Taï chimpanzees twenty years to become proficient in the more sophisticated hunting roles.

Once the hunt is concluded, the hunters receive different amounts of meat depending on their role at the end of the hunt. The drivers and the ambushers rarely capture the prey, and they usually receive about three times less meat than the captors (Boesch 2002; Boesch and Boesch-Achermann 2000). However, if an ambusher accurately predicts the prey's behavior, and the behavior of the other hunters, then the ambusher receives just as much meat as the captors. Bystanders receive significantly less meat than do the hunters, so it benefits the chimpanzee to join a hunt, even in the face of danger (Boesch 1994). Hunters, unlike bystanders, are permitted early access to the carcass.

The ability of chimpanzees to coordinate their behavior to achieve a goal that can only be achieved by a group is indicative of their ability to predict behavior—not only the behavior of the prey but also the behavior of the other hunters. This is true both during the hunt, when the movements of all the hunters have to be carefully choreographed, and also after the hunt. For example, the driver, who rarely makes contact with the prey and almost never makes the kill, must anticipate that he will be rewarded by those who do make the kill. The group hunting dynamic also suggests that chimpanzees are able to identify when others make good predictions, given that an ambusher who correctly anticipates the movements of the prey and the other hunters is given more meat than one who does not.

Chimpanzees also demonstrate their ability to coordinate behavior in their border patrols. Chimpanzees are one of the few species known to form coalitions to engage in large between-group hostile encounters. Such intergroup aggression has led to the extermination of one known chimpanzee community at Gombe (Goodall et al. 1979). When males form patrol groups, their behavior changes dramatically. John Mitani describes the behavior of chimpanzees in Kibale National Park, Uganda: "Males are silent, tense, and wary. They move in a tight file, often pause to look and listen, sometimes sniff the ground, and show great interest in chimpanzee nests, dung, and feeding remains" (Mitani et al. 2002, 18).

These patrols move along the periphery of their territory, sometimes making incursions into neighboring territories to hunt colobus monkeys, and often they run across members of the other community. Depending on the size of the patrolling group and the size of the group they encounter, the patrol may either back away quietly or attack. When hunting outside their territory, they are silent and quickly take the prey back into their own territory. However, when intergroup encounters result, the chimpanzees have been observed to kill infants and adult males. David Watts and his colleagues describe one example of an intergroup encounter:

> As they reentered the forest, the Ngogo chimpanzees met chimpanzees from another community . . . two females with infants, one juvenile, and one adult male that immediately fled northeast with the Ngogo chimpanzees in pursuit. The Ngogo chimpanzees caught up to the strange adult male after chasing him for about 100 m and surrounded him. Adult Ngogo male EL began to pummel the intruder, and adults BF, BRU, LO, and MO quickly joined him. The strange male tried to escape down a small hill but could not elude these five Ngogo males and others that joined them. The Ngogo males, led by EL, continued to beat, bite, and kick him for 20 min, and dragged him farther down this hill into a small stream valley about 50 m away from the spot of his initial capture, where he died during or shortly after the attack. All of the Ngogo males remained in the area after the stranger was killed. Several circled his body and some sniffed it, while others sat nearby. After about 30 min, all of the Ngogo chimpanzees moved southwest, angling toward the center of their range. (Watts et al. 2006)

These kinds of aggressive intergroup encounters are almost always won by the attacking group. When the patrols cross into another community's territory, it appears that they will attack only when they outnumber the groups they come across; otherwise they retreat. The patrolling chimpanzees are able to coordinate their behavior, as in the case just presented, acting as a group to kill another chimpanzee. The researchers also believe that the chimpanzees are able to recognize low-cost versus high-cost opportunities, and that they will make opportunistic attacks when costs are low. If so, chimpanzees are also able to gauge the likelihood of success of their actions.

Given both the naturalistic data and the experimental findings, we can conclude that chimpanzees are critter psychologists, given their ability to predict and coordinate behavior with others they see as agents. However, we still know little about the mechanisms they use to engage in these behaviors. In particular, we do not know whether the means they use to predict behavior can also be used to explain behavior. To better understand the mechanisms that chimpanzees use to engage in these behaviors, we need to know what else they can do. One way of determining whether chimpanzees only anticipate others' behavior in terms of behavioral regularities is to examine whether they also act to understand others' behavior by looking for explanations. If chimpanzees are able to engage in folk psychological practices in anomalous situations in which prior behavioral regularities are lacking, then we have reason to think that chimpanzees may be able to explain behavior.

Explanation Seeking
While it is uncontroversial to say that chimpanzees predict the behavior of conspecifics and prey, explaining behavior is another matter entirely. We don't yet know much about the chimpanzee ability to seek explanations. Little research has been done on this issue, and the studies that have been conducted focused on explanations of physical events (e.g., Povinelli and Dunphy-Lelii 2001).

This oversight should be remedied. Given my account of the elements involved in explaining behavior, we can examine whether chimpanzees seek explanations in terms of (a) having a curiosity state directed at some unexpected state of affairs, and (b) engaging in exploratory behavior associated with the state of affairs. We can also look for evidence that chimpanzees accept an explanation by looking for indications that the curiosity state has been resolved. Just as we were able to examine preverbal children's ability to seek explanations, we can use methods like those presented in chapter 8 to examine the chimpanzee's ability to explain.

We have prima facie reason to suspect that chimpanzees might seek explanations for behavior. Chimpanzees engage in a great deal of exploratory behavior, and they are able to learn from observing others engaging in novel actions. Moreover, the previous discussion of whether chimpanzees understand agency offers suggestive evidence that they might also seek explanations of behavior.

In the Nielsen study, upon noticing the behavior of his caregiver, Cassie began to systematically alter his behavior, all the while watching his caregiver's movements, as though he were trying to figure out whether he was being imitated. Similar studies on children are interpreted as the child's testing the hypothesis that she is being imitated, and are seen to offer convincing evidence of imitation recognition (Asendorpf et al. 1996; Meltzoff 1990). If we interpret the results of this study in the same way, we will be compelled to accept that Cassie engaged in some explanation-seeking behavior. To test a hypothesis about human behavior, he would have been in a curiosity state to drive the hypothesis generation, and he would have created an interpretation of the human's behavior that he could then test.

Though the study is suggestive, the need remains to directly examine whether chimpanzees explain others' behaviors. Evidence that the chimpanzee is explaining someone could come from looking at the topography of chimpanzee behavior: a facial expression or body posture indicating an affective curiosity state; then directed exploratory behavior; and finally a resolution of the curiosity state, as indicated by a satisfaction facial expression or body posture.

Finding evidence of a chimpanzee curiosity state might sound like a difficult task, but current developments in chimpanzee emotion research have simplified this problem. Chimpanzees express emotions by their facial expressions, and following Ekman's work in emotion in human facial expressions, Lisa Parr and Kim Bard have created the Chimpanzee FACS (Facial Action Coding System). They use this system to construct models of chimpanzee expressions to determine the configuration of muscle movements that chimpanzees find salient in their perception of emotion, and the researchers have found that chimpanzees are sensitive to others' emotional responses, as indicated by their facial expressions. For example, Lisa Parr's research demonstrates that chimpanzees are able to categorize facial expressions associated with different emotional responses (Parr 2003).

We have evidence of a chimpanzee affective state that we can categorize as a curiosity state, and we have evidence of chimpanzee affective states of satisfaction, and we have evidence of chimpanzee exploratory behavior. But what we do not yet have is a systematic way to examine whether these three elements arise together in a pattern suggesting explanatory behavior. One way of finding the pattern is to make a formal observational study of chimpanzee behavior in the field and hope to observe incidents that fit the proposed pattern of behavior. This may be our best bet, since we are most likely to see explanatory behavior in the face of anomalous behavior.

It may be possible, however, to set up an anomalous event in an experimental context. This would require making another animal appear deviant to the subject. For example, consider the following scenario. Chimpanzee B observes an anomalous behavior: chimpanzee A screaming at what appears to be a banana. Chimpanzee B is in a curiosity state, as indicated by his facial expression. Next chimpanzee B moves toward chimpanzee A and explores the surroundings. After removing the barrier hiding the snake, chimpanzee B understands why chimpanzee A is screaming, and his curiosity state is resolved.

Some problems arise with the details of this experimental setup. For one, when chimpanzee B sees the snake, he is unlikely to be satisfied; he is more likely to be terrified and run away. And unless chimpanzee A is constrained, it is likely he would run away, too, as soon as he saw the snake. But something like this setup could help to provide experimental evidence that chimpanzees explain behavior. We know that chimpanzees are interested in deviancy. In a personal communication, Frans de Waal says that chimpanzees will run toward their screaming cohorts to see what the trouble is. However, that behavior may be an example of information seeking rather than explanation seeking. What is the difference? When an individual is seeking information, she lacks the affective state that drives the search for an explanation. For example, when a chimpanzee looks in the direction another is looking, or looks to see what is causing someone to make an alarm call, but does not express curiosity, she may just be seeking information. Information seeking is not associated either with a puzzled affective state or with a conflict between the situation and the appropriate behavior from the animal's behavioral repertoire. And it is likely that information seeking is not the only goal in anomalous situations. When the actor is truly deviant, and the behavior is outside the norm, an observer may be driven to seek an explanation.

A drug addict is one example of a deviant. As we know from the early research on chimpanzee addiction, a chimpanzee addicted to morphine will prefer to seek drugs over food (Spragg 1940). The lack of interest in food is highly unusual for a chimpanzee, and were a naive chimpanzee to be placed in a food competition study with an addict, the naive chimpanzee should show some surprise at the addict's behavior. For example, consider the following experimental setup. The addict is familiar with the morphine delivery system in an opaque box, and the addict and a naive subordinate chimpanzee both witness the baiting of a container in the room with a banana. Both chimpanzees are released into a room that contains the containers baited with the banana and the morphine. We expect that the addict would ignore the food in favor of the morphine, and the naive chimpanzee would get the food without altercation, to his surprise. However, if the naive chimp was surprised by the addict's lack of interest in the food and wanted to explain the addict's behavior, he might engage in some exploratory behavior (examine the other chimp, examine the box containing the morphine delivery system). In a second trial, both chimpanzees would witness the room being baited with a papaya. If in this case the naive chimpanzee were to seek the food without concerning himself with the addicted chimpanzee, it shows that he predicted that the chimp would not seek the food because of the preference for morphine. This prediction could not be made using simple induction, since the situations would be different insofar as the food item was different. The naive chimpanzee would therefore have learned that the addicted chimpanzee prefers the drug to all else, and would have used this information about the addict's desire to predict his future behavior.

While this should remain a thought experiment, given the moral repugnance of addicting a chimpanzee to morphine, it is one example of where we might see explanation-seeking behavior. Deviance is something that humans seek to explain, and when researchers are in a position to introduce naive chimpanzees to deviants, they could do so. The proceeding behaviors might suggest that the chimpanzee is explanation seeking, but, as with prelinguistic children, it will be difficult to conclude that a chimpanzee has successfully generated an explanation.

Whether or not chimpanzees seek to explain behavior is an open research question, and an area rich with opportunity for learning about what chimpanzees think about the chimpanzee mind. So far, all the studies of chimpanzee theory of mind have focused on prediction. But prediction is easily accomplished without considering the contents of mind. If we want to know whether chimps understand others' mental states, we should examine their ability to explain behavior.

Belief Attribution
Despite interest in the topic, I believe that the issue of whether chimpanzees understand belief remains underexplored, given the confusion about the nature of belief and the role it plays in human folk psychological practices. The received view is that chimpanzees do not understand belief (or at least no evidence demonstrates that chimpanzees understand belief). For example, in their review of the theory of mind research program, Call and Tomasello (2008) conclude that while chimpanzees understand perceptual states, knowledge, goals, and intentions, they do not understand false belief (which, if true, let me note, would strongly suggest that chimps do not understand true belief, either). Instead Call and Tomasello claim that "chimpanzees understand others in terms of a perception-goal psychology, as opposed to a full-fledged, human-like belief-desire psychology" (187).

If a "full-fledged human-like belief-desire psychology" is what the SFP view says it is, then one concern with Call and Tomasello's conclusion is that they, like Premack and Woodruff, are mistaken about human psychology. However, another worry arises about this conclusion, and that comes from a potential contradiction in the claim that chimpanzees understand seeing and knowledge but do not understand belief.

Let us look at the problem with seeing first. The suggestion is that chimpanzees understand that others have mental representations of their perceptions of the world, and that those perceptions can vary from one individual to the next. In addition, chimpanzees are able to use their understanding of others' mental representations to predict their behavior. But to predict behavior, the chimpanzee's understanding of seeing must be holistically connected to a host of other concepts—for example, the chimpanzee must understand that seeing a desirable food item will make an individual want that item, and unless some defeating desire or defeating observation intervenes, the individual will seek out the food item. A defeating desire might be the desire not to be beaten by the alpha, and a defeating observation might be an observation that an alpha is present. What is the difference between this perception-desire account and a belief-desire account? Very little indeed. The story sounds plausible to supporters of a belief-desire psychology simply because the human concept of seeing is intimately connected to believing, so much so that we say "seeing is believing."

Seeing does the same work as *believing*, because someone who sees something happen will then be in a doxastic state regarding that event, whereas someone who does not witness the event will not share that doxastic state (ceteris paribus). Likewise the success of a child's performance in the false-belief task can be ascribed to her developing understanding of seeing just as easily as it can be ascribed to her developing understanding of belief. The child who passes the false-belief task understands that Maxi did not see his mother move the chocolate to the cupboard, and therefore she understands that Maxi will not look for the chocolate in the cupboard.

Our concept of seeing has behaviors associated with it, in addition to having connections with other concepts. Since in humans the category of behaviors we call seeing is associated with the doxastic category of believing, to say that a chimpanzee has anything like the human understanding of seeing, we would be compelled to accept that she also understands belief.

The claim that chimpanzees understand knowledge but not belief is likewise conceptually problematic. According to the traditional account of knowledge as justified true belief, a known proposition must be believed because taking a proposition to be true involves believing it. The act of taking something to be true is an act of believing it, just as the act of rejecting a proposition as false requires believing the negation of it. The justified true belief analysis of knowledge has been challenged, given the Gettier counterexamples (1963), which suggest that justified true belief is not sufficient for knowledge. However, for the most part, epistemologists have not given up on the belief condition for knowledge (but see Williamson 2000).

Thus to claim that chimpanzees understand seeing and knowledge but not belief is fundamentally problematic. One way to resolve this tension would be to reject the claims about the chimpanzee's understanding of seeing and knowledge. However, overwhelming evidence demonstrates that chimpanzees understand seeing. Naturalistic data include reports that adult chimpanzees monitor gaze, while infant chimpanzees do not (Plooij 1978). Infant chimpanzees, like infant children, do not attend to gaze when making requests from their mothers, and do not begin to look at their mother's face before making a request until around ten and a half months. Chimpanzees seem to develop a sophisticated understanding about what others can see, as they are able to anticipate others' behaviors based on what they can and cannot see. For example, low-ranking chimpanzees act differently when they are out of the dominant's sight. When a lowly chimpanzee is invisible, he will take advantage of his situation by mating with a preferred partner or by eating food that would not be available to him if the dominant were present (Whiten and Byrne 1988). As we have seen, chimpanzees express emotion via their facial expressions, which are understood by others. And like humans, chimpanzees sometimes find it useful to hide their expressions from others. De Waal reports that in one case, when a chimpanzee began fear-grinning in response to threatening vocalizations from another chimpanzee, he literally wiped the expression off his face before turning to face his rival. It took him three tries (de Waal 1996). And while laboratory experiments have found mixed results, recent studies defend the claim that chimpanzees do understand seeing (Hare et al. 2000; Tomasello et al. 2003a). Brian Hare and colleagues found that when a subordinate and a dominant chimpanzee are both released into a room baited with food, the subordinate will avoid the food if the dominant can see it. In the conditions under which the dominant chimpanzee cannot see the food, the subordinate will eat it. The chimpanzees are across the room from each other, so the subordinate has to consider a different visual perspective to judge what the dominant can see.

The claim that chimpanzees understand knowledge is based primarily on experimental evidence. Let me briefly describe one study (Kaminski et al. 2008). Two chimpanzees take turns pointing at opaque buckets to gain food rewards that may be hidden inside. In this experiment, the subject observes that two buckets are baited, but the naive competitor only observes the baiting of one bucket. What the researchers found was that when the subject was allowed to make the second request, she tended to choose the bucket that the competitor did not see baited. (Unlike adult humans given a similar task, the chimpanzees allowed to make the first request did not tend to choose the bucket that the competitor knew was baited, thus maximizing their chances of gaining a food reward on their second turn.) Note that neither chimpanzee witnessed the other's first choice, so the subject's choice was influenced not by what her competitor did in fact do but rather by what she expected her competitor to do. The authors claim, "These results suggest that, at least in some situations, chimpanzees know what others know, in the sense of have seen" (Kaminski et al. 2008, 229).

The conclusion that chimpanzees understand knowledge has been derived from studies about auditory awareness as well as visual perception (Melis et al. 2006). Insofar as such claims are warranted, they entail something about the chimpanzee's ability to understand another's epistemic state, and understanding another's epistemic state requires understanding something more general about knowledge that is common to evidence gathering via both visual perception and auditory perception. In the human case, we would say that what is common to our understanding of others' epistemic states, given their perceptual experiences, comes from an understanding of knowledge. And since, in our best analysis, understanding knowledge requires understanding belief, if the chimpanzees understand knowledge, they must also be seen as understanding something about belief.

This argument cuts both ways. Those who think that chimpanzees do not understand the concept *belief* will simply claim that they do not understand the concept *knowledge* or the concept *seeing*, either. The critic might say that these studies show that the chimpanzee is sensitive to another's knowledge or perceptual state without understanding that he is sensitive to it—without any conceptual metacognition involved.

Instead of looking toward the predictive paradigms for evidence of chimpanzees' understanding of belief, we should turn toward the explanatory paradigms. However, here too difficulties arise. In the fearful-banana paradigm described earlier, the topology of explanatory behavior does not indicate the attribution of a belief. Recall that kinds of explanations are pluralistic, too. Chimpanzee B may well explain chimpanzee A's behavior in terms of the situation (there is a snake there) or in terms of a perceptual state (he sees a snake). The best nonverbal evidence that a chimpanzee understands belief would consist of the topology of explanatory behaviors in a situation that does not permit an explanation in terms of anything other than belief state. And to devise an experiment like this requires more knowledge about normal chimpanzee social behavior, and knowledge about instances of deviance in natural chimpanzee society.

Moving Forward

To make greater progress in studying chimpanzee theory of mind, we need better conceptual analysis of the relevant concepts, including knowledge, belief, and seeing. In addition to the conceptual work, methodological work must also be done. We can make progress by recognizing that humans do not appeal to beliefs nearly as often as thought. If humans do not predict much behavior by attributing beliefs, we have no reason to think that other species would. I suggest that we are likely to move ahead on this question of chimpanzee belief attribution only through dedicated field research by primatologists interested in the question of explanation-seeking behavior. The work is laborious and time-consuming, but field researchers are privy to a wider array of natural behaviors than are researchers working with chimpanzees in a laboratory setting. In the field, a variety of social and ecological conditions cannot be replicated in a laboratory. For example, the intergroup conflict behavior described earlier is unique to the field; certainly no researcher would be granted ethics approval to reproduce such interactions in captivity, and where serious conflicts do arise among captive chimpanzees, caregivers separate the individuals. In addition, in the field we find seasonal differences—rainy seasons and dry seasons—that affect animal mobility and the availability of different food items. The field is a much richer environment for a chimpanzee, no matter how much enrichment he has in captivity. Differences in terrain, food, building materials, potential tools, social partners, and so on, all provide more opportunity for discovering novelty than does a captive situation.

If explanatory behavior is evolutionarily beneficial because it promotes the development of technologies, then looking for the topology of explanatory behavior in the field makes sense. The work on chimpanzee cultures has uncovered technological differences in tool use and construction among different groups of chimpanzees, and these findings indicate that chimpanzees have mechanisms for the social transmission of novel behaviors. A close examination of those mechanisms may help us discover whether the need to explain behavior naturally arises for the chimpanzees. If it doesn't, then we have reason to conclude that chimpanzees do not naturally understand belief. But from that conclusion, it does not follow that chimpanzees cannot be given the opportunity to learn about belief in a human enculturation situation. Savage-Rumbaugh's conviction that Kanzi understands others' minds may indicate something about Kanzi's uniqueness, rather than point to a generality about bonobos. Without fieldwork, however, we cannot know this. We must observe first; then we can think again about experiments testing for belief attribution.

Chimpanzees are folk psychologists who see others as intentional agents with goals. They predict and coordinate behavior, and they may even seek explanations for anomalous behavior. What we don't yet know is whether chimpanzees understand others as having representational beliefs. We need more research to answer this question, but we need to do the right kind of research. Predictive experimental paradigms cannot hope to supply an answer, given the ubiquity of alternative explanations. Rather, we must first determine whether chimpanzees seek to explain behavior.

If chimpanzees do not seek to explain behavior, then they will probably not have an understanding of belief, given the fundamental nature of explanation for the development of the belief concept. I have argued that the traditional understanding of the relationship between prediction and explanation should be turned on its head. Prediction in terms of belief is derivative of explanation in terms of belief, and so if someone understands belief, she is also explaining behavior. Given the PFP account, methodological changes are necessary in the chimpanzee theory of mind research program. We should decenter the role of prediction, just as we have decentered the role of propositional attitude attribution in folk psychology. Chimpanzees are folk psychologists, but they may still know nothing about belief.

13 Conclusion

Seeing People

In one of his last collections of oral histories, Studs Terkel spoke to Harvard students and employees who had been involved in a campaign to increase wages for custodians, cooks, and other workers. One not surprising fact that emerges from these stories is that before the beginning of the campaign, the workers and the students were quite alienated from one another. Bob Kelly, a building manager at Harvard, said, "When I first came, I didn't like the students at all. I resented them a great deal, and I just looked at them as wealthy snobs. They don't see you. Some of them won't speak to you. If they see you in the street, they don't see you" (Terkel 2003, 301).

As the campaign started, students and workers began relating to one another differently. Greg Halpern, one of the students who occupied Massachusetts Hall to protest Harvard's labor policy, described the transition:

> I think students began to see custodians differently. When you look through someone, when you pass someone in the hallway and don't make eye contact and you don't say hi, and in four years you don't go up and talk to the same person who cleans the dining hall or your room, you're clearly not respecting them, you're not thinking of them as a person. After the campaign, there were plenty of students who finally began to think of workers as people they could know. And so there were friendships formed. We have barbecues at my house now where workers come, and we go out together to bars or just hang out. That certainly never happened before. Maybe we earned their respect. (Ibid., 309)

Kelly described the transition from the workers' perspective:

> I'd notice those students working nights and days, they'd be here running off copies and have meetings all night. They'd be in here at seven-thirty in the morning, going out postering. They were doing something that they would gain nothing from. . . . The workers who did the work around the university, I noticed, got to like the

students. Instead of "We're taking care of spoiled little rich kids" it's "Can you believe they're doing this for us?" . . . Boy, people can surprise you. (Ibid., 301–302)

As a result of the campaign, some social relationships and behaviors changed. Two groups of people from different backgrounds who did not relate to one another well came to feel a resonance. Both Kelly and Halpern describe this process in terms of *coming to see the other*. They began to treat one another like people, but the transition was not due to understanding one another's reasons for action. Describing it as an improvement in mindreading clearly misses the point; the shift in the way the students and the workers were perceiving each other cannot be accounted for in the framework of Standard Folk Psychology. In fact, it becomes apparent in the interviews that neither side came to accurately know the others' reasons for actions. Halpern suspects that the improved relationships between students and workers may be due to the students earning the workers' respect. The workers were surprised by the students' behavior and couldn't believe what was happening. Kelly thinks that the students did not have anything tangible to gain from their actions, but when he asks himself what selfless action gives you, he suggests perhaps that the students gained hope.

As the workers and students began to see one another as persons, their attitudes changed, and they noticed more similarities than differences. Liliana Lineares, a custodian at Harvard, said:

What happened between the students and the workers was an emergence of a really tight relationship, a sort of common affection rose between us. Before the taking of Massachusetts Hall, I didn't have this feeling. When it happened, when the sit-in happened, at first really nobody could believe it. It was almost like a form of salvation that the students had finally become conscious of our problems. Before the student strike, I definitely saw them as privileged people who were very different than me. After the sit-in, I saw that it wasn't like that. (Ibid., 298)

When alienated individuals come to see one another as persons, they see them as embedded in an environment, with personal relations, economic realities, past histories, personalities, moods, physical limitations, future goals, and social contexts. The students and the workers came to see others as people, not robot slaves, and not just as other minds. To describe the transition in the relationship between students and workers at Harvard during this period as a change in the beliefs and desires that the individuals attributed to one another is misleading; it substitutes one form of alienation for another.

A similar worry about overly intellectualizing human beings has been raised in the domain of ethical theory. Ethicists debate whether consequentialism, deontology, and virtue ethics are incompatible with personal relationships, because such theories require that people act from duty, obligation, or some other objective principle, rather than from a subjective feeling of love or friendship. As Michael Stocker (1997) argues, ethical theories for the most part are concerned with justification and reasons for action, rather than motives, and living the good life requires harmony between reasons and motives. By focusing on reasons and ignoring motives, Stocker thinks that most ethical theories ignore the person, both in terms of the actor and in terms of the target, and the advice offered by such theories is ultimately unable to lead one toward the good life.

The contemporary discussion of folk psychology has largely ignored such worries while suffering from the very malady Stocker identifies in most ethical theorizing. This is particularly problematic given that the study of folk psychology is a descriptive endeavor, as opposed to a normative one. Accounts of folk psychology should portray actual, as opposed to ideal, action; but the standard accounts focus on reasons for action while ignoring the less intellectual, affective, habitual, or cultural forces that influence how we see others. When we come to understand that our consideration of others' beliefs takes up less of our cognitive energy than the standard accounts suggest, there will be no motivation to portray people as alienated individuals calculating one another's future behavior as if we were physicists looking at particles. In our social relationships, we have love and affection, laughter and teasing, playful games, and furious fights; there is hasty generalizing, accurate stereotyping, and implicit bias—these are all part of our interpersonal engagements. While standard views of folk psychology, which focus solely on the attribution of propositional attitudes, leave out the richness of our practices and engagements, the pluralist approach is able to account for it.

Replacing Standard Folk Psychology with Pluralistic Folk Psychology can help to improve our empirical investigation into theory of mind in children and critters, which in turn can offer a fresh start in our attempts to describe the cognitive architecture subsuming our folk psychological practices. It also invites empirical research on a wider array of folk psychological practices, including explaining, justifying, regulating, and coordinating behavior. But it also brings to light the need for greater conceptual contributions. For many, belief is assumed to be a representational state of an organism, and this view is imported into much of the empirical research. However, other accounts are on offer, and there are methodological consequences to adopting one account over the other. What one thinks about the nature of belief will have implications for the philosophy of mind in the debates about eliminative materialism, identity theory, functionalism, and ecological approaches to cognition. But the conceptual analysis should not be seen as a purely philosophical practice. Just as the philosophical accounts should help to shape the research programs in psychology, so the empirical results should inform the philosophical accounts. This process of theorizing, testing, and revising should be part of an interdisciplinary collaboration that incorporates the strengths of philosophical analysis and empirical investigation.

By introducing persons into our study of folk psychology and by refusing to portray the diverse practices of folk psychology as amounting to a third-person act of telepathy, not only do we start down a path that leads to a better understanding of our folk psychological practices, but we also gain a better understanding of the similarities and differences between humans and other species in the full range of life engagements—from birth and the connection between caregiver and child, through the various relationships we have at different developmental stages, to the very end of life. The folk, and the critters, have much left to teach us.

Notes

1 Do Apes Read Minds?

1. I understand Standard Folk Psychology (SFP) to include the traditional theory-theory accounts of folk psychology found in D. Lewis 1972 and Churchland 1981 and some versions of simulation theory, such as A. Goldman 1995a. SFP also refers to theories of folk psychology that incorporate elements of theory theory and simulation theory, such as Nichols and Stich 2003 and A. Goldman 2006. SFP does not include Gordon's (1986, 1995a, 1995b) account of mental simulation, nor does it include challenges to SFP advocated by philosophers including Gallagher (2001, 2006), Hutto (2004, 2008), Zawidzki (2008), or the other authors in Hutto and Ratcliffe 2007.

4 How Do You Know What I'm Going to Do? You Know My Beliefs

1. The main problem with Gordon's view, as I see it, is that to get a simulation started, one needs to know what features of the situation are relevant—which properties would actually affect the person's behavior. We cannot simulate every property a person has, and we need to find some way of determining which ones are salient. Without a method for understanding which properties, including the features of a person's environment, are salient and necessary inputs for the simulation, simulation could not account for our ability to predict behavior. For example, the behavior of a racist would be quite different from my behavior in certain circumstances, but it would also be easy to predict his behavior, because I know the nature of his strongly held beliefs. But in recognizing the person's racism, it seems I am acknowledging his beliefs and using them to modify my beliefs for the purpose of the simulation. To imaginatively identify with the racist, I would need to know he was a racist, and I would have to use beliefs regarding the superiority of one race over another as part of the input. Thus the environmental input version of simulation theory cannot avoid attribution of beliefs or desires in at least some cases. Because of this, my discussion of simulation theory involves only those versions that include beliefs and desires as inputs.

5 How Do You Know What I'm Going to Do? You Know Me

1. The authors offer two explanations for this result. First, it supports the view that stereotypes are hypotheses, and data are needed to test the applicability of the hypothesis to an individual. Subjects who did not see the video of Hannah taking the test did not have the evidence that they needed to generate predictions about academic success. Alternatively, the subjects may have made automatic predictions about academic performance given the stereotype but were unwilling to state these predictions given the stigma against using stereotypes in this way. That is, the subjects may have recognized that they did not have the evidence needed to justify any prediction of behavior, so they consciously decided to withhold judgment. The performance of the subjects who saw the test videotape suggests that they made at least an implicit prediction of behavior after viewing the context video.

8 The Science of Folk Psychological Explanation

1. Bloom and colleagues argue that the order of acquisition is due to the syntactic complexity of the different terms, not semantic complexity of the concepts associated with them. Since the early *wh*-questions (what, where, who) can serve as major sentence components in conjunction with the copula (e.g., "What's that?" "Who's that?"), and the later *wh*-questions (why, how, when) cannot, these later *wh*-questions are syntactically more complex (L. Bloom et al. 1982).

11 Social Intelligence and the Evolution of Theory of Mind

1. While the Social Intelligence Hypothesis is widely accepted, alternative accounts also describe primate cognitive uniqueness. For example, Povinelli and Cant (1995) argue that the morphological features of the great apes create unique kinesthetic problems that need to be solved. In their view, as apes evolved greater body mass than the other arboreal primates, their usual methods of locomotion through the trees were compromised owing to the greater weight. Arboreal apes had to spend ever-increasing amounts of time determining how to get from one place to another, and they had to find paths through the trees that would hold their bulk. As the apes became better at solving this locomotion problem, they developed an understanding about their body, which Povinelli and Cant hypothesize may have sufficed to establish an explicit concept of self. Another competitor is the view that the need to create mental maps to keep track of the distribution of food across a large territory led to the developed primate brain (Clutton-Brock and Harvey 1980).

References

Allison, Scott T., and David M. Messick. 1985. The group attribution error. *Journal of Experimental Social Psychology* 21 (6): 563–579.

Allison, Scott T., Leila T. Worth, and Melissa W. Campbell King. 1990. Group decisions as social inference heuristics. *Journal of Personality and Social Psychology* 58 (5): 801–811.

Ambady, Nalini, and Robert Rosenthal. 1992. Thin slices of expressive behavior as predictors of interpersonal consequences: A meta-analysis. *Psychological Bulletin* 111 (2): 256–274.

Ambady, Nalini, Frank J. Bernieri, and Jennifer A. Richeson. 2000. Toward a histology of social behavior: Judgmental accuracy from thin slices of the behavioral stream. In *Advances in Experimental Social Psychology*, vol. 32, ed. Mark P. Zanna, 201–272. San Diego: Academic Press.

Ames, Russell, Carole A. Ames, and Wayne M. Garrison. 1977. Children's causal ascriptions for positive and negative interpersonal outcomes. *Psychological Reports* 41 (2): 595–602.

Andersen, Susan M., and Roberta L. Klatzky. 1987. Traits and social stereotypes: Levels of categorization in person perception. *Journal of Personality and Social Psychology* 53 (2): 235–246.

Andersen, Susan M., Roberta L. Klatzky, and John Murray. 1990. Traits and social stereotypes: Efficiency differences in social information processing. *Journal of Personality and Social Psychology* 59 (2): 192–201.

Andersen, Susan M., Serena Chen, and Christina Carter. 2000. Fundamental human needs: Making social cognition relevant. *Psychological Inquiry* 11 (4): 269–275.

Anderson, D. Eric, Bella M. DePaulo, and Matthew E. Ansfield. 2002. The development of deception detection skills: A longitudinal study of same-sex friends. *Personality and Social Psychology Bulletin* 28 (4): 536–545.

Andrews, Kristin. 2002. Interpreting autism: A critique of Davidson on thought and language. *Philosophical Psychology* 15 (3): 317–332.

Andrews, Kristin. 2003. Knowing mental states: The asymmetry of psychological prediction and explanation. In *Consciousness: New Philosophical Perspectives*, ed. Quentin Smith and Aleksandar Jokic, 201–219. Oxford: Oxford University Press.

Andrews, Kristin. 2004. How to learn from our mistakes: Explanation and moral justification. *Philosophical Explorations* 7 (3): 247–263.

Andrews, Kristin. 2005. Chimpanzee theory of mind: Looking in all the wrong places? *Mind and Language* 20 (5): 521–536.

Andrews, Kristin. 2009. Understanding norms without a theory of mind. *Inquiry* 52 (5): 433–448.

Andrews, Kristin, and Ljiljana Radenovic. 2006. Speaking without interpreting: A reply to Bouma on autism and Davidsonian interpretation. *Philosophical Psychology* 19 (5): 663–678.

Andrews, Kristin, and Peter Verbeek. N.d. Does explanation precede prediction in false belief understanding? Unpublished data.

Apperly, Ian A., Kevin J. Riggs, Andrew Simpson, Claudia Chiavarino, and Dana Samson. 2006. Is belief reasoning automatic? *Psychological Science* 17 (10): 841–844.

Apperly, Ian A., and Elizabeth J. Robinson. 1998. Children's mental representation of referential relations. *Cognition* 67 (3): 287–309.

Apperly, Ian A., and Elizabeth J. Robinson. 2001. Children's difficulties handling dual identity. *Journal of Experimental Child Psychology* 78 (4): 374–397.

Apperly, Ian A., and Elizabeth J. Robinson. 2003. When can children handle referential opacity? Evidence for systematic variation in 5- and 6-year-old children's reasoning about beliefs and belief reports. *Journal of Experimental Child Psychology* 85 (4): 297–311.

Apperly, Ian A., Dana Samson, Naomi Carroll, Shazia Hussain, and Glyn Humphreys. 2006. Intact first- and second-order false belief reasoning in a patient with severely impaired grammar. In *Theory of Mind*, special issue, *Social Neuroscience* 1 (3–4): 334–348.

Aristotle. 1987. *De anima*. New York: Penguin Putnam.

Asendorpf, Jens B., Veronique Warkentin, and Pierre-Marie Baudonnière. 1996. Self-awareness and other-awareness II: Mirror self-recognition, social contingency awareness, and synchronic imitation. *Developmental Psychology* 32 (2): 313–321.

References

Ashton, Michael C., and Victoria M. Esses. 1999. Stereotype accuracy: Estimating the academic performance of ethnic groups. *Personality and Social Psychology Bulletin* 25 (2): 225–236.

Atance, Cristina M., and Daniela K. O'Neill. 2004. Acting and planning on the basis of a false belief: Its effects on 3-year-old children's reasoning about their own false beliefs. *Developmental Psychology* 40 (6): 953–964.

Baillargeon, Renée, Rose M. Scott, and Zijing He. 2010. False-belief understanding in infants. *Trends in Cognitive Sciences* 14 (3): 110–118.

Baird, Jodie A., and Louis J. Moses. 2001. Do preschoolers appreciate that identical actions may be motivated by different intentions? *Journal of Cognition and Development* 2:413–448.

Baker, Lynne Rudder. 2001. Folk psychology. In *The MIT Encyclopedia of the Cognitive Sciences*, ed. Robert A. Wilson and Frank C. Keil. Cambridge, MA: MIT Press.

Baron-Cohen, Simon. 1995. *Mindblindness: An Essay on Autism and Theory of Mind*. Cambridge, MA: MIT Press.

Bartsch, Karen, and Henry Wellman. 1989. Young children's attribution of action to beliefs and desires. *Child Development* 60 (4): 946–964.

Bartsch, Karen, and Henry Wellman. 1995. *Children Talk about the Mind*. New York: Oxford University Press.

Behne, Tanya, Malinda Carpenter, Josep Call, and Michael Tomasello. 2005. Unwilling versus unable: Infants' understanding of intentional action. *Developmental Psychology* 41:328–337.

Bennett, Jonathan. 1978. Some remarks about concepts. *Behavioral and Brain Sciences* 1:557–560.

Berlyne, D. E. 1954. A theory of human curiosity. *British Journal of Psychology* 45:180–191.

Berlyne, D. E. 1960. *Conflict, Arousal, and Curiosity*. New York: McGraw-Hill.

Berscheid, Ellen, William Graziano, Thomas Monson, and Marshall Dermer. 1976. Outcome dependency: Attention, attribution, and attraction. *Journal of Personality and Social Psychology* 34 (5): 978–989.

Birch, Susan A. J., and Paul Bloom. 2003. Children are cursed: An asymmetric bias in mental-state attribution. *Psychological Science* 14 (3): 283–286.

Birch, Susan A. J., and Paul Bloom. 2004. Understanding children's and adults' limitations in mental state reasoning. *Trends in Cognitive Sciences* 8 (6): 255–260.

Bloom, Paul, and Tim P. German. 2000. Two reasons to abandon the false belief task as a test of theory of mind. *Cognition* 77 (1): B25–B31.

Bloom, Allan, Marcella Wagner, Larry Reskin, and Anna Bergman. 1980. A comparison of intellectually delayed and primary reading disabled children on measures of intelligence and achievement. *Journal of Clinical Psychology* 36 (3): 788–790.

Bloom, Lois, Susan Merkin, and Janet Wooten. 1982. "Wh"-questions: Linguistic factors that contribute to the sequence of acquisition. *Child Development* 53 (4): 1084–1092.

Boesch, Christophe. 1994. Cooperative hunting in wild chimpanzees. *Animal Behaviour* 48 (3): 653–667.

Boesch, Christophe. 2002. Cooperative hunting roles among Tai chimpanzees. *Human Nature* 13 (1): 27–46.

Boesch, Christophe, and Hedwige Boesch-Achermann. 2000. *The Chimpanzees of the Tai Forest: Behavioural Ecology and Evolution*. Oxford: Oxford University Press.

Braddon-Mitchell, David, and Frank Jackson. 1996. *The Philosophy of Mind and Cognition*. Oxford: Oxford University Press.

Brandone, Amanda C., and Henry M. Wellman. 2009. You can't always get what you want: Infants understand failed goal-directed actions. *Psychological Science* 20 (1): 85–91.

Bromberger, Sylvain. 1966. Why-questions. In *Readings in the Philosophy of Science*, ed. Baruch A. Brody, 66–84. Englewood Cliffs, NJ: Prentice Hall.

Brooks, Rodney. 1991. Intelligence without representation. *Artificial Intelligence* 47:139–159.

Brown, Roger. 1968. The development of wh questions in child speech. *Journal of Verbal Learning and Verbal Behavior* 7 (2): 279–290.

Buchanan, Gregory McClellan, and Martin E. P. Seligman, eds. 1995. *Explanatory Style*. Hillsdale, NJ: Lawrence Erlbaum.

Budesheim, Thomas Lee, and Kathleen Bonnelle. 1998. The use of abstract trait knowledge and behavioral exemplars in causal explanations of behavior. *Personality and Social Psychology Bulletin* 24 (6): 575–587.

Burgess, Diana, and Eugene Borgida. 1999. Who women are, who women should be: Descriptive and prescriptive gender stereotyping in sex discrimination. *Psychology, Public Policy, and Law* 5 (3): 665–692.

Buttelmann, David, Malinda Carpenter, and Michael Tomasello. 2009. Eighteen-month-old infants show false belief understanding in an active helping paradigm. *Cognition* 112:337–342.

Byrne, Richard, and Andrew Whiten, eds. 1988. *Machiavellian Intelligence: Social Expertise and the Evolution of Intellect in Monkeys, Apes, and Humans*. New York: Oxford University Press.

Byrne, Richard, and Andrew Whiten. 1991. Computation and mindreading in primate tactical deception. In *Natural Theories of Mind: Evolution, Development, and Simulations of Everyday Mindreading*, ed. Andrew Whiten, 127–141. Oxford: Blackwell.

Cain, Kathleen M., Gail D. Heyman, and Michael E. Walker. 1997. Preschoolers' ability to make dispositional predictions within and across domains. *Social Development* 6 (1): 53–75.

Call, Joseph, Brian Hare, Malinda Carpenter, and Michael Tomasello. 2004. "Unwilling" versus "unable": Chimpanzees' understanding of human intentional action. *Developmental Science* 7 (4): 488–498.

Call, Joseph, and Michael Tomasello. 2008. Do chimpanzees have a theory of mind: 30 years later. *Trends in Cognitive Sciences* 12:187–192.

Callanan, Maureen A., and Lisa M. Oakes. 1992. Preschoolers' questions and parents' explanations: Causal thinking in everyday activity. *Cognitive Development* 7 (2): 213–233.

Camaioni, Luigia. 1993. Continuità versus discontinuità nello sviluppo comunicativo pre-linguistico e linguistico [Continuity versus discontinuity in the development of prelinguistic and linguistic communication]. *Sistemi Intelligenti* 5 (2): 189–197.

Camp, Elisabeth. 2007. Thinking with maps. *Philosophical Perspectives* 21:145–182.

Campbell, Donald T. 1967. Stereotypes and the perception of group differences. *American Psychologist* 22 (10): 817–829.

Capitanio, John P. 2004. Personality factors between and within species. In *Macaque Societies: A Model for the Study of Social Organization*, ed. Bernard Thierry, Mewa Singh, and Werner Kaumans, 13–32. New York: Cambridge University Press.

Carey, Susan. 1985. Are children fundamentally different kinds of thinkers and learners than adults? In *Thinking and Learning Skills*, vol. 2, ed. S. Chipman, J. Segal, and R. Glaser, 485–517. Hillsdale, NJ: Lawrence Erlbaum.

Carlson, Stephanie M., and Louis J. Moses. 2001. Individual differences in inhibitory control and children's theory of mind. *Child Development* 72 (4): 1032–1053.

Carnap, Rudolf. 1956. *Meaning and Necessity: A Study in Semantics and Modal Logic*. 2nd ed. Chicago: University of Chicago Press.

Cartwright, Nancy. 1979. Causal laws and effective strategies. *Noûs* 13:419–437.

Cartwright, Nancy. 1983. *How the Laws of Physics Lie*. Oxford: Oxford University Press.

Chak, Amy. 2007. Teachers' and parents' conceptions of children's curiosity and exploration. *International Journal of Early Years Education* 15 (2): 141–159.

Chandler, Michael J., and David Helm. 1984. Developmental changes in the contribution of shared experience to social role-taking competence. *International Journal of Behavioral Development* 7 (2): 145–156.

Chen, Xin, Vincent M. Reid, and Tricia Stiano. 2006. Oral exploration and reaching toward social and non-social objects in two-, four-, and six-month-old infants. *European Journal of Developmental Psychology* 3 (1): 1–12.

Cheney, Dorothy L., and Robert M. Seyfarth. 2007. *Baboon Metaphysics: The Evolution of a Social Mind*. Chicago: University of Chicago Press.

Chouinard, Michelle M. 2007. *Children's Questions: A Mechanism for Cognitive Development*. Boston: Blackwell.

Churchland, Paul M. 1981. Eliminative materialism and the propositional attitudes. *Journal of Philosophy* 78 (2): 67–90.

Churchland, Paul M. 1989. Folk psychology and the explanation of human behavior. *Philosophy of Mind and Action Theory* 3:225–241.

Churchland, Paul M. 1991. Folk psychology and the explanation of human behavior. In *The Future of Folk Psychology: Intentionality and Cognitive Science*, ed. John D. Greenwood, 51–69. Cambridge: Cambridge University Press.

Clancy, Patricia M. 1989. Form and function in the acquisition of Korean wh-questions. *Journal of Child Language* 16 (2): 323–347.

Clark, Andy, and Josefa Toribio. 1994. Doing without representing. *Synthese* 101 (3): 401–431.

Clements, Wendy A., and Joseph Perner. 1994. Implicit understanding of belief. *Cognitive Development* 9 (4): 377–395.

Clutton-Brock, T. H., and Paul H. Harvey. 1980. Primates, brains, and ecology. *Journal of the Zoological Society of London* 190:309–323.

Cohen, Adam S., and Tamsin C. German. 2009. Encoding of others' beliefs without overt instruction. *Cognition* 111 (3): 356–363.

Cousins, Steven D. 1989. Culture and self-perception in Japan and the United States. *Journal of Personality and Social Psychology* 56 (January): 124–131.

Cross, Susan E., Michael L. Morris, and Jonathan S. Gore. 2002. Thinking about oneself and others: The relational-interdependent self-construal and social cognition. *Journal of Personality and Social Psychology* 82 (3): 399–418.

Csibra, Gergely, and György Gergely. 1998. The teleological origins of mentalistic action explanations: A developmental hypothesis. *Developmental Science* 1 (2): 255–259.

Currie, Gregory. 1995. Imagination and simulation: Aesthetics meets cognitive science. In *Mental Simulation*, ed. Martin Davies and Tony Stone, 151–169. Oxford: Blackwell.

Currie, Gregory, and Ian Ravenscroft. 2002. *Recreative Minds*. Oxford: Oxford University Press.

Darley, John M., and C. Daniel Batson. 1973. "From Jerusalem to Jericho": A study of situational and dispositional variables in helping behavior. *Journal of Personality and Social Psychology* 27 (1): 100–108.

Darley, John M., and Paget H. Gross. 1983. A hypothesis-confirming bias in labeling effects. *Journal of Personality and Social Psychology* 44 (1): 20–33.

Davidson, Donald. 1963. Actions, reasons, and causes. *Journal of Philosophy* 60 (23): 685–700.

Davidson, Donald. 1973. Radical interpretation. *Dialectica* 27 (3–4): 313–328.

Davidson, Donald. 1975. Thought and talk. In *Mind and Language*, ed. Samuel Guttenplan, 7–24. Oxford: Oxford University Press.

Davidson, Donald. 1982. Rational animals. *Dialectica* 36 (4): 317–327.

Davidson, Donald. 1991. Three varieties of knowledge. In *A. J. Ayer: Memorial Essays*, ed. A. P. Griffiths, 153–166. Cambridge: Cambridge University Press.

Dawes, Robyn M. 1989. Statistical criteria for establishing a truly false consensus effect. *Journal of Experimental Social Psychology* 25 (1): 1–17.

Dawes, Robyn M., and Matthew Mulford. 1996. The false consensus effect and overconfidence: Flaws in judgment or flaws in how we study judgment? *Organizational Behavior and Human Decision Processes* 65 (3): 201–211.

Deaux, Kay, and Laurie L. Lewis. 1984. Structure of gender stereotypes: Interrelationships among components and gender label. *Journal of Personality and Social Psychology* 46 (5): 991–1004.

Dennett, Daniel C. 1978a. *Brainstorms: Philosophical Essays on Mind and Psychology*. Cambridge, MA: MIT Press.

Dennett, Daniel C. 1978b. Beliefs about beliefs. *Behavioral and Brain Sciences* 4:568–570.

Dennett, Daniel C. 1987a. Designing intelligence. In *Creative Intelligences*, ed. Richard Langton Gregory and Pauline K. Marstrand, 19–30. Westport, CT: Ablex.

Dennett, Daniel C. 1987b. *The Intentional Stance*. Cambridge, MA: MIT Press.

Dennett, Daniel C. 1991. Real patterns. *Journal of Philosophy* 88 (1): 27–51.

Dennett, Daniel C. 1996. *Kinds of Minds: Towards an Understanding of Consciousness.* New York: Basic Books.

Desrochers, Stéphan, Paul Morissette, and Marcel Ricard. 1995. Two perspectives on pointing in infancy. In *Joint Attention: Its Origins and Role in Development,* ed. Chris Moore and Philip J. Dunham, 85–101. Hillsdale, NJ: Lawrence Erlbaum.

Diekman, Amanda B., Alice H. Eagly, and Patrick Kulesa. 2002. Accuracy and bias in stereotypes about the social and political attitudes of women and men. *Journal of Experimental Social Psychology* 38 (3): 268–282.

Dinstein, Ilan, Cibu Thomas, Marlene Behrmann, and David J. Heeger. 2008. A mirror up to nature. *Current Biology* 18 (1): R13–R18.

Dunbar, Robin I. M. 1996. *Grooming, Gossip, and the Evolution of Language.* Cambridge, MA: Harvard University Press.

Dunbar, Robin I. M. 1998. The social brain hypothesis. *Evolutionary Anthropology* 6 (5): 178–190.

Dunn, Judy. 1988. *The Beginnings of Social Understanding.* Cambridge: Harvard University Press.

Dunn, Judy, and Jane R. Brown. 1993. Early conversations about causality: Content, pragmatics, and developmental change. *British Journal of Developmental Psychology* 11 (2): 107–123.

Dunning, David, Dale W. Griffin, James D. Milojkovic, and Lee Ross. 1990. The overconfidence effect in social prediction. *Journal of Personality and Social Psychology* 58 (4): 568–581.

Eagly, Alice H. 1987. *Sex Differences in Social Behavior: A Social-Role Interpretation.* Hillsdale, NJ: Lawrence Erlbaum.

Edwards, Kari, and Edward E. Smith. 1996. A disconfirmation bias in the evaluation of arguments. *Journal of Personality and Social Psychology* 71 (1): 5–24.

Elgin, Mehmet, and Elliott Sober. 2002. Cartwright on explanation and idealization. *Erkenntnis* 57 (3): 441–450.

Elliott, Gregory C. 1979. Some effects of deception and level of self-monitoring on planning and reacting to a self-presentation. *Journal of Personality and Social Psychology* 37 (8): 1282–1292.

Epley, Nicholas, Carey K. Morewedge, and Boaz Keysar. 2004a. Perspective taking in children and adults: Equivalent egocentrism but differential correction. *Journal of Experimental Social Psychology* 40 (6): 760–768.

Epley, Nicholas, Boaz Keysar, Leaf Van Boven, and T. Gilovich. 2004b. Perspective taking as egocentric anchoring and adjustment. *Journal of Personality and Social Psychology* 87:327–339.

Erceau, Damien, and Nicolas Guéguen. 2007. Tactile contact and evaluation of the toucher. *Social Psychology* 147 (4): 441–444.

Ervin-Tripp, Susan M. 1970. Discourse agreement: How children answer questions. In *Cognition and Language Learning*, ed. R. Hayes, 79–107. New York: Wiley.

Fadiga, L., L. Fogassi, G. Pavesi, and G. Rizzolatti. 1995. Motor facilitation during action observation: A magnetic stimulation study. *Journal of Neurophysiology* 73 (6): 2608–2611.

Felix, Sascha W. 1976. Wh-pronouns in first and second language acquisition. *Linguistische Berichte* 44 (20): 52–64.

Festinger, Leon, and James M. Carlsmith. 1959. Cognitive consequences of forced compliance. *Journal of Abnormal and Social Psychology* 58 (2): 203–210.

Fisher, J., and R. Hinde. 1949. The opening of milk bottles by birds. *British Birds* 42:347–357.

Fisher, Jeffrey D., Marvin Rytting, and Richard Heslin. 1976. Hands touching hands: Affective and evaluative effects on interpersonal touch. *Sociometry* 39:416–421.

Fiske, Susan T., and Martha G. Cox. 1979. Person concepts: The effect of target familiarity and descriptive purpose on the process of describing others. *Journal of Personality* 47 (1): 136–161.

Fiske, Susan T., and Laura E. Stevens. 1993. What's so special about sex? Gender stereotyping and discrimination. In *Gender Issues in Contemporary Society*, ed. Stuart Oskamp and Marc Costanzo, 173–196. Newbury Park, CA: Sage.

Flavell, John H., Eleanor R. Flavell, and Frances L. Green. 1987. Young children's knowledge about apparent-real and pretend-real distinctions. *Developmental Psychology* 23:816–822.

Fodor, Jerry A. 1975. *The Language of Thought*. New York: Thomas Y. Crowell.

Fodor, Jerry A. 1987. *Psychosemantics: The Problem of Meaning in the Philosophy of Mind*. Cambridge, MA: MIT Press.

Fodor, Jerry A. 1989. Making mind matter more. *Philosophical Topics* 17 (1): 59–80.

Fodor, Jerry A. 1990. *A Theory of Content and Other Essays*. Cambridge, MA: MIT Press.

Fodor, Jerry A. 1991. You can fool some of the people all of the time, everything else being equal: Hedged laws and psychological explanations. *Mind* 100 (397): 19–34.

Fodor, Jerry A. 1992. A theory of the child's theory of mind. *Cognition* 44 (3): 283–296.

Fodor, Jerry A. 1994. *The Elm and the Expert: Mentalese and Its Semantics*. Cambridge, MA: MIT Press.

Frey, Dieter. 1982. Different levels of cognitive dissonance, information seeking, and information avoidance. *Journal of Personality and Social Psychology* 43 (6): 1175–1183.

Frith, Uta, Francesca Happé, and Frances Siddons. 1994. Autism and theory of mind in everyday life. *Social Development* 3 (2): 108–124.

Gallagher, Shaun. 2001. The practice of mind: Theory, simulation, or primary interaction? *Journal of Consciousness Studies* 8 (5–7): 83–108.

Gallagher, Shaun. 2004. Understanding interpersonal problems in autism: Interaction theory as an alternative to theory of mind. *Philosophy, Psychiatry, and Psychology* 11 (3): 199–217.

Gallagher, Shaun. 2006. The narrative alternative to theory of mind. In *Radical Enactivism: Intentionality, Phenomenology, and Narrative*, ed. Richard Menary, 223–229. Amsterdam: John Benjamins.

Gallese, Vittorio, and Alvin Goldman. 1998. Mirror neurons and the simulation theory of mind-reading. *Trends in Cognitive Sciences* 2 (12): 493–501.

Gallese, Vittorio, Luciano Fadiga, Leonardo Fogassi, and Giacomo Rizzolatti. 1996. Action recognition in the premotor cortex. *Brain* 119 (2): 593–609.

Garnham, Wendy A., and Ted Ruffman. 2001. Doesn't see, doesn't know: Is anticipatory looking really related to understanding of belief? *Developmental Science* 4 (1): 94–100.

Gauker, Christopher. 2003. *Words without Meaning*. Cambridge, MA: MIT Press.

Gelman, Susan A. 1988. The development of induction within natural kind and artifact categories. *Cognitive Psychology* 20 (1): 65–95.

Gergely, György, Zoltán Nadasdy, Gergely Csibra, and Szilvia Bíró. 1995. Taking the intentional stance at 12 months of age. *Cognition* 56 (2): 165–193.

Gettier, Edmund. 1963. Is justified true belief knowledge? *Analysis* 23:121–123.

Giere, Ronald N. 1988. Laws, theories, and generalizations. In *The Limitations of Deductivism*, ed. Adolf Grünbaum and Wesley Salmon, 37–46. Los Angeles: University of California Press.

Giere, Ronald N. 1996. The scientist as adult. *Philosophy of Science* 63 (4): 538–541.

Gilbert, Daniel T., Douglas S. Krull, and Brett W. Pelham. 1988. Of thoughts unspoken: Social inference and the self-regulation of behavior. *Journal of Personality and Social Psychology* 55 (5): 685–694.

Gilbert, Daniel T., and Patrick S. Malone. 1995. The correspondence bias. *Psychological Bulletin* 117 (1): 21–38.

Glennan, Stuart. 2002. Rethinking mechanistic explanation. *Philosophy of Science* 69 (3): S342–S353.

Godfrey-Smith, Peter. 2005. Folk psychology as a model. *Philosophers' Imprint* 5 (6): 1–16.

Godfrey-Smith, Peter. 2006. The strategy of model-based science. *Biology and Philosophy* 21 (5): 725–740.

Goffman, Erving. 1979. *Gender Advertisements*. London: Macmillan.

Goldman, Alvin. 1995a. Interpretation psychologized. In *Folk Psychology*, ed. Martin Davies and Tony Stone, 74–99. Oxford: Blackwell.

Goldman, Alvin. 1995b. Empathy, mind, and morals. In *Mental Simulation: Evaluations and Applications*, ed. Martin Davies and Tony Stone, 185–208. Oxford: Blackwell.

Goldman, Alvin. 2006. *Simulating Minds: The Philosophy, Psychology, and Neuroscience of Mindreading*. New York: Oxford University Press.

Goldman, William. 2007. *The Princess Bride: S. Morgenstern's Classic Tale of True Love and High Adventure*. Orlando: Harcourt Books.

Goodall, Jane. 1971. *In the Shadow of Man*. Boston: Houghton Mifflin.

Goodall, Jane. 1986. *The Chimpanzees of Gombe: Patterns of Behavior*. Cambridge, MA: Harvard University Press.

Goodall, Jane, A. Bandora, E. Bergman, C. Busse, H. Matama, E. Mpongo, A. Pierce, and D. Riss. 1979. Intercommunity interactions in the chimpanzee population of the Gombe National Park. In *The Great Apes*, ed. David A. Hamburg and Elizabeth R. McCowen, 13–54. Menlo Park: Benjamin/Cummings.

Gopnik, Alison. 2000. Explanation as orgasm and the drive for causal knowledge: The function, evolution, and phenomenology of the theory formation system. In *Explanation and Cognition*, ed. Frank C. Keil and Robert Andrew Wilson, 299–324. Cambridge: MIT Press.

Gopnik, Alison, and Janet Wilde Astington. 1988. Children's understanding of representational change and its relation to the understanding of false belief and the appearance-reality distinction. *Child Development* 59 (1): 26–37.

Gopnik, Alison, Clark Glymour, David M. Sobel, and David Danks. 2004. A theory of causal learning in children: Causal maps and Bayes nets. *Psychological Review* 111 (1): 3–32.

Gordon, Robert. 1986. Folk psychology as simulation. *Mind and Language* 1 (2): 158–171.

Gordon, Robert. 1995a. The simulation theory: Objections and misconceptions. In *Folk Psychology*, ed. Martin Davies and Tony Stone, 100–122. Oxford: Blackwell.

Gordon, Robert. 1995b. Simulation without introspection or inference from me to you. In *Mental Simulation*, ed. Martin Davies and Tony Stone, 53–67. Oxford: Blackwell.

Gordon, Robert. 2000. Simulation and the explanation of action. In *Empathy and Agency: The Problem of Understanding in the Human Sciences*, ed. H. Kölger and K. Stuebe, 62–82. Boulder, CO: Westview Press.

Gosling, Samuel D., and Oliver P. John. 1999. Personality dimensions in non-human animals: A cross-species review. *Current Directions in Psychological Science* 8 (3): 69–75.

Graesser, Arthur C., and Cathy L. McMahen. 1993. Anomalous information triggers questions when adults solve quantitative problems and comprehend stories. *Journal of Educational Psychology* 85 (1): 136–151.

Gray, Carol. 1996. *All about Social Stories*. Videotape. Future Horizons, Inc.

Gray, Carol. 2000. *The New Social Story Book*. Arlington, TX: Future Horizons.

Grice, H. Paul. 1969. Utterer's meaning and intention. *Philosophical Review* 78 (2): 147–177.

Griffin, Dale W., David Dunning, and Lee Ross. 1990. The role of construal processes in overconfident predictions about the self and others. *Journal of Personality and Social Psychology* 59 (6): 1128–1139.

Guajardo, Jose J., and Amanda L. Woodward. 2004. Is agency skin deep? Surface attributes influence infants' sensitivity to goal-directed action. *Infancy* 6 (3): 361–384.

Guéguen, Nicolas. 2010. The effect of a woman's incidental tactile contact on men's later behavior. *Social Behavior and Personality* 38 (2): 257–266.

Hamilton, David L. 1981. Illusory correlation as a basis for stereotyping. In *Cognitive Processes in Stereotyping and Intergroup Behavior*, ed. David L. Hamilton, 115–144. Hillsdale, NJ: Lawrence Erlbaum.

Hampson, Sarah E. 1983. Trait ascription and depth of acquaintance: The preference for traits in personality descriptions and its relation to target familiarity. *Journal of Research in Personality* 17 (4): 398–411.

Happé, Francesca. 1994. *Autism: An Introduction to Psychological Theory*. Cambridge, MA: Harvard University Press.

Hare, Brian, Josep Call, Bryan Agnetta, and Michael Tomasello. 2000. Chimpanzees know what conspecifics do and do not see. *Animal Behaviour* 59 (4): 771–785.

References

Hare, Brian, Josep Call, and Michael Tomasello. 2001. Do chimpanzees know what conspecifics know? *Animal Behaviour* 61 (1): 139–151.

Harman, Gilbert. 1978. Studying the chimpanzees' theory of mind. *Behavioral and Brain Sciences* 1:576–577.

Harris, Paul L. 1992. From simulation to folk psychology: The case for development. *Mind and Language* 7 (1–2): 120–144.

Harris, Paul L., Kara Donnelly, Gabrielle R. Guz, and Rosemary Pitt-Watson. 1986. Children's understanding of the distinction between real and apparent emotion. *Child Development* 57:895–909.

Hauser, Marc D. 2006. *Moral Minds: How Nature Designed Our Universal Sense of Right and Wrong*. New York: Ecco/HarperCollins.

Heal, Jane. 1995. Replication and functionalism. In *Folk Psychology*, ed. Martin Davies and Tony Stone, 45–59. Oxford: Blackwell.

Heider, Fritz. 1958. *The Psychology of Interpersonal Relations*. New York: Wiley.

Heider, Fritz, and Marianne Simmel. 1944. An experimental study of apparent behavior. *American Journal of Psychology* 57 (2): 243–259.

Heil, John. 2004. *Philosophy of Mind: A Guide and Anthology*. New York: Oxford University Press.

Heller, Kirby A., and Thomas J. Berndt. 1981. Developmental changes in the formation and organization of personality attributions. *Child Development* 52 (2): 683–691.

Hempel, Carl G., and Paul Oppenheim. 1948. Studies in the logic of explanation. *Philosophy of Science* 15 (2): 135–175.

Heyman, Gail D., and Susan A. Gelman. 1999. The use of trait labels in making psychological inferences. *Child Development* 70 (3): 604–619.

Hickling, Anne K., and Henry M. Wellman. 2001. The emergence of children's causal explanations and theories: Evidence from everyday conversation. *Developmental Psychology* 37 (5): 668–683.

Hinde, R., and J. Fisher. 1951. Further observations on the opening of milk bottles by birds. *British Birds* 44:392–396.

Hobson, R. Peter. 2004. *The Cradle of Thought: Exploring the Origins of Thinking*. Oxford: Oxford University Press.

Hobson, R. Peter. 2007. We share, therefore we think. In *Folk Psychology Re-Assessed*, ed. Daniel D. Hutto and Matthew Ratcliffe, 41–61. Dordrecht: Springer.

Hood, Lois, and Lois Bloom. 1979. What, when, and how about why: A longitudinal study of early expressions of causality. *Monographs of the Society for Research in Child Development* 44 (6): 1–47.

Hoshino-Browne, Etsuko, Adam S. Zanna, Steven J. Spencer, Mark P. Zanna, Shinobu Kitayama, and Sandra Lackenbauer. 2005. On the cultural guises of cognitive dissonance: The case of Easterners and Westerners. *Journal of Personality and Social Psychology* 89 (3): 294–310.

Hsee, Christopher K., and Elke U. Weber. 1997. A fundamental prediction error: Self-others discrepancies in risk preference. *Journal of Experimental Psychology: General* 126 (1): 45–53.

Hudson, Judith A., Lauren R. Shapiro, and Brandi B. Sosa. 1995. Planning in the real world: Preschool children's scripts and plans for familiar events. *Child Development* 66 (4): 984–998.

Hughes, Claire. 1998. Finding your marbles: Does preschoolers' strategic behavior predict later understanding of mind? *Developmental Psychology* 34 (6): 1326–1339.

Hulme, Sarah, Peter Mitchell, and David Wood. 2003. Six-year-olds' difficulties handling intensional contexts. *Cognition* 87 (2): 73–99.

Hume, David. 1978. *A Treatise of Human Nature* (1739–1740). Oxford: Oxford University Press.

Humphrey, Nicholas K. 1976. The social function of intellect. In *Growing Points in Ethology*, ed. P. P. G. Bateson and R. A. Hinde, 303–321. Cambridge: Cambridge University Press.

Humphrey, Nicholas. 1978. Nature's psychologists. *New Scientist* 29:900–904.

Hursthouse, Rosalind. 1991. Arational actions. *Journal of Philosophy* 88 (2): 57–68.

Hutto, Daniel D. 2004. The limits of spectatorial folk psychology. *Mind and Language* 19 (5): 548–573.

Hutto, Daniel D. 2008. *Folk Psychological Narratives: The Sociocultural Basis of Understanding Reasons*. Cambridge, MA: MIT Press.

Hutto, Daniel D., and Matthew Ratcliffe, eds. 2007. *Folk Psychology Re-Assessed*. Dordrecht: Springer.

Ichheiser, Gustav. 1949. Misunderstandings in human relations: A study in false social perception. *American Journal of Sociology* 55 (S2): 1–70.

Imada, Toshie, and Shinobu Kitayama. 2010. Social eyes and choice justification: Culture and dissonance revisited. *Social Cognition* 28 (5): 589–608.

Isen, Alice M., and Kimberly A. Daubman. 1984. The influence of affect on categorization. *Journal of Personality and Social Psychology* 47 (6): 1206–1217.

Isen, Alice M., Paula M. Niedenthal, and Nancy Cantor. 1992. An influence of positive affect on social categorization. *Motivation and Emotion* 16 (1): 65–78.

Jackendoff, Ray. 2009. *Language, Consciousness, Culture: Essays on Mental Structure.* Cambridge, MA: MIT Press.

Jackson, Linda A., and Thomas F. Cash. 1985. Components of gender stereotypes: Their implications for inferences on stereotypic and nonstereotypic dimensions. *Personality and Social Psychology Bulletin* 11 (3): 326–344.

Jolly, Alison. 1966. Lemur social behavior and primate intelligence. *Science* 153:501–506.

Jones, E., and R. E. Nisbett. 1972. The actor and the observer: Divergent perceptions of the causes of behavior. In *Attribution: Perceiving the Causes of Behavior*, by Edward E. Jones, David E. Kanhouse, Harold H. Kelley, Richard E. Nisbett, Stuart Valins, and Bernard Weiner. Morristown, NJ: General Learning Press.

Judd, Charles M., Carey S. Ryan, and Bernadette Park. 1991. Accuracy in the judgment of in-group and out-group variability. *Journal of Personality and Social Psychology* 61 (3): 366–379.

Kahneman, Daniel, and Amos Tversky. 1982. The simulation heuristic. In *Judgment under Uncertainty: Heuristics and Biases*, ed. Daniel Kahneman, Paul Slovic, and Amos Tversky, 201–208. New York: Cambridge University Press.

Kalish, Charles W. 2002. Children's predictions of consistency in people's actions. *Cognition* 84 (3): 237–265.

Kamil, Alan C. 2004. Sociality and the evolution of intelligence. *Trends in Cognitive Sciences* 8 (5): 195–197.

Kaminski, Juliane, Josep Call, and Michael Tomasello. 2008. Chimpanzees know what others know, but not what they believe. *Cognition* 109:224–234.

Katz, Daniel, and Floyd H. Allport. 1931. *Students' Attitudes*. Oxford: Craftsman Press.

Keller, Harold R. 1987. Intellectual and cognitive development. In *Understanding Exceptional Children and Youth*, ed. Peter Knoblock, 98–162. New York: Little, Brown.

Kelley, Harold H. 1971. *Attribution in Social Interaction*. New York: General Learning Press.

Kelley, Harold H. 1972. Attribution in social interaction. In *Attribution: Perceiving the Causes of Behavior*, ed. Eduard E. Jones, David E. Kanouse, Harold H. Kelley, Richard E. Nisbett, Stuart Valins, and Bernard Weiner, 1–26. Morristown, NJ: General Learning Press.

Kelly, George A. 1955. *The Psychology of Personal Constructs*. New York: Norton.

Kim, Jaegwon. 2006. *Philosophy of Mind*. Boulder: Westview Press.

Király, Ildikó, Bianca Jovanovic, Wolfgang Prinz, Gisa Aschersleben, and György Gergely. 2003. The early origins of goal attribution in infancy. *Consciousness and Cognition* 12 (4): 752–769.

Kitcher, Philip. 1989. Explanatory unification and the causal structure of the world. In *Scientific Explanation*, ed. Philip Kitcher and Wesley C. Salmon, 410–505. Minneapolis: University of Minnesota Press.

Knobe, Joshua. 2003. Intentional action in folk psychology: An experimental investigation. *Philosophical Psychology* 16 (2): 309–324.

Korsgaard, Christine. 2006. Morality and the distinctiveness of human action. In *Primates and Philosophers: How Morality Evolved*, ed. Stephen Macedo and Josiah Ober, 98–119. Princeton: Princeton University Press.

Kosfeld, Michael. 2005. Rumours and markets. *Journal of Mathematical Economics* 41 (6): 646–664.

Krueger, Joachim. 1998. The bet on bias: A foregone conclusion? *Psycoloquy* 9 (46).

Krueger, Joachim, and Russell W. Clement. 1996. Inferring category characteristics from sample characteristics: Inductive reasoning and social projection. *Journal of Experimental Social Psychology* 125 (1): 52–68.

Krueger, Joachim, and Russell W. Clement. 1994. The truly false consensus effect: An ineradicable and egocentric bias in social perception. *Journal of Personality and Social Psychology* 67 (4): 596–610.

Krueger, Joachim, and Myron Rothbart. 1988. Use of categorical and individuating information in making inferences about personality. *Journal of Personality and Social Psychology* 55 (2): 187–195.

Krueger, Joachim, and Joanna S. Zeiger. 1993. Social categorization and the truly false consensus effect. *Journal of Personality and Social Psychology* 65 (4): 670–680.

Kunda, Ziva. 2002. *Social Cognition: Making Sense of People*. Cambridge, MA: MIT Press.

Labov, William, and Teresa Labov. 1977. L'Apprentissage de la syntaxe des interrogations [Learning the syntax of interrogations]. *Langue Francaise* 34 (34): 52–80.

Lakoff, George. 1987. Cognitive models and prototype theory. In *Concepts and Conceptual Development: Ecological and Intellectual Factors in Categorization*, ed. Ulric Neisser, 63–100. New York: Cambridge University Press.

Langer, Ellen J. 1975. The illusion of control. *Journal of Personality and Social Psychology* 32 (2): 311–328.

Lavelli, Manuela, and Alan Fogel. 2005. Developmental changes in the relationship between the infant's attention and emotion during early face-to-face communication: The 2-month transition. *Developmental Psychology* 41 (1): 265–280.

Lee, Yueh-Ting, Lee J. Jussim, and Clark R. McCauley, eds. 1995. *Stereotype Accuracy: Toward Appreciating Group Differences*. Washington, DC: American Psychological Association.

Legerstee, Maria, and Yarixa Barillas. 2003. Sharing attention and pointing to objects at 12 months: Is the intentional stance implied? *Cognitive Development* 18 (1): 91–110.

Leslie, Alan M. 1984. Infant perception of a manual pick-up event. *British Journal of Developmental Psychology* 2 (1): 19–32.

Leslie, Alan M. 2005. Developmental parallels in understanding minds and bodies. *Trends in Cognitive Sciences* 9 (10): 459–462.

Lewin, Kurt. 1931. *Environmental Forces in Child Behavior and Development*. Oxford: Clark University Press.

Lewis, M. M. 1938. The beginning and early functions of questions in a child's speech. *British Journal of Educational Psychology* 8:150–171.

Lewis, David. 1972. Psychophysical and theoretical identifications. *Australasian Journal of Philosophy* 50 (3): 249–258.

Lewis, David. 1994. Reduction of mind. In *A Companion to the Philosophy of Mind*, ed. Samuel Guttenplan, 412–431. Oxford: Blackwell.

Lewis, Paul T. 1995. A naturalistic test of two fundamental propositions: Correspondence bias and the actor-observer hypothesis. *Journal of Personality* 63 (1): 87–111.

Lightbown, P. M. 1978. Question form and question function in the speech of young French L2 learners. In *Aspects of Bilingualism*, ed. M. Paradis. Columbia, SC: Hornbeam Press.

Locksley, Anne, Eugene Borgida, Nancy Brekke, and Christine Hepburn. 1980. Sex stereotypes and social judgment. *Journal of Personality and Social Psychology* 39 (5): 821–831.

Loewenstein, George. 1996. Out of control: Visceral influences on behavior. *Organizational Behavior and Human Decision Processes* 65 (3): 272–292.

Lord, Charles G., Lee Ross, and Mark R. Lepper. 1979. Biased assimilation and attitude polarization: The effects of prior theories on subsequently considered evidence. *Journal of Personality and Social Psychology* 37 (11): 2098–2109.

Lorei, Theodore W. 1967. Prediction of community stay and employment for released psychiatric patients. *Journal of Consulting Psychology* 31 (4): 349–357.

Lowe, E. J. 2000. *An Introduction to the Philosophy of Mind.* Cambridge: Cambridge University Press.

Lyons, William. 2001. *Matters of the Mind.* New York: Routledge.

Mackie, Diane M., Mi Na Ahn, Arlene G. Asuncion, and Scott T. Allison. 2001. The impact of perceiver attitudes on outcome-biased dispositional inferences. *Social Cognition* 19 (1): 71–93.

Maibom, Heidi L. 2003. The mindreader and the scientist. *Mind and Language* 18 (3): 296–315.

Maibom, Heidi L. 2007. Social systems. *Philosophical Psychology* 20 (5): 557–578.

Maibom, Heidi L. 2009. In defence of (model) theory theory. *Journal of Consciousness Studies* 16 (6–8): 360–378.

Malle, Bertram F. 1999. How people explain behavior: A new theoretical framework. *Personality and Social Psychology Review* 3 (1): 23–48.

Malle, Bertram F. 2004. *How the Mind Explains Behavior: Folk Explanations, Meaning, and Social Interaction.* Cambridge, MA: MIT Press.

Malle, Bertram F. 2006a. The actor-observer asymmetry in attribution: A (surprising) meta-analysis. *Psychological Bulletin* 132 (6): 895–919.

Malle, Bertram F. 2006b. Intentionality, morality, and their relationship in human judgment. In *Folk Conceptions of Mind, Agency, and Morality*, special issue, *Journal of Cognition and Culture* 6 (1–2): 87–112.

Malle, Bertram F., Joshua Knobe, Matthew J. O'Laughlin, Gale E. Pearce, and Sarah E. Nelson. 2000. Conceptual structure and social functions of behavior explanations: Beyond person-situation attributions. *Journal of Personality and Social Psychology* 79 (3): 309–326.

Malle, Bertram F., Joshua M. Knobe, and Sarah E. Nelson. 2007. Actor-observer asymmetries in explanations of behavior: New answers to an old question. *Journal of Personality and Social Psychology* 93 (4): 491–514.

Malle, Bertram F., and Sarah E. Nelson. 2003. Judging *mens rea*: The tension between folk concepts and legal concepts of intentionality. *Behavioral Sciences and the Law* 21 (5): 563–580.

Mameli, Matteo. 2001. Mindreading, mindshaping, and evolution. *Biology and Philosophy* 16:597–628.

Marcus, Ruth Barcan. 1990. Some revisionary proposals about belief and believing. *Philosophy and Phenomenological Research* 50:133–153.

Marks, Gary, and Norman Miller. 1987. Ten years of research on the false-consensus effect: An empirical and theoretical review. *Psychological Bulletin* 102 (1): 72–90.

Marler, Peter, and Miwako Tamura. 1964. Culturally transmitted patterns of vocal behavior in sparrows. *Science* 146:1483–1486.

Martin, Carol Lynn. 2000. Cognitive theories of gender development. In *The Developmental Social Psychology of Gender*, ed. Thomas Eckes and Hanns Martin Trautner, 91–121. Mahwah, NJ: Lawrence Erlbaum.

Matsuzawa, Tetsuro. 2006. Evolutionary origins of the human mother-infant relationship. In *Cognitive Development in Chimpanzees*, ed. T. Matsuzawa, M. Tomonaga, and M. Tanaka, 127–141. Tokyo: Springer.

McCabe, Allyssa, and Carole Peterson. 1988. A comparison of adults' versus children's spontaneous use of "because" and "so." *Journal of Genetic Psychology* 149 (2): 257–268.

McCauley, Clark R. 1995. Are stereotypes exaggerated? A sampling of racial, gender, academic, occupational, and political stereotypes. In *Stereotype Accuracy: Toward Appreciating Group Differences*, ed. Yueh-Ting Lee, Lee J. Jussim, and Clark R. McCauley, 215–243. Washington, DC: American Psychological Association.

McGeer, Victoria. 2007. The regulative dimension of folk psychology. In *Folk Psychology Re-Assessed*, ed. Daniel D. Hutto and Matthew Ratcliffe, 137–156. Dordrecht: Springer.

McGrew, William C. 1992. *Chimpanzee Material Culture: Implications for Human Evolution*. Cambridge: Cambridge University Press.

McGrew, William C. 2009. Ten dispatches from the chimpanzee culture wars, plus revisiting the battlefronts. In *The Question of Animal Culture*, ed. B. G. Galef and K. N. Laland. Cambridge, MA: Harvard University Press.

McGrew, William C., and C. E. G. Tutin. 1978. Evidence for a social custom in wild chimpanzees? *Man* 13 (2): 234–251.

McHoskey, John W., and Arthur G. Miller. 1994. Effects of constraint identification, processing mode, expectancies, and intragroup variability on attributions toward group members. *Personality and Social Psychology Bulletin* 20 (3): 266–276.

Melis, Alicia P., Josep Call, and Michael Tomasello. 2006. Chimpanzees conceal visual and auditory information from others. *Journal of Comparative Psychology* 120:154–162.

Meltzoff, Andrew N. 1990. Foundations for developing a concept of self: The role of imitation in relating self to other and the value of social mirroring, social modeling, and self practice in infancy. In *The Self in Transition: Infancy to Childhood*, ed. Dante Cicchetti and Marjorie Beeghly, 139–164. Chicago: University of Chicago Press.

Meltzoff, Andrew N., and Keith M. Moore. 1977. Imitation of facial and manual gestures by human neonates. *Science* 198 (4312): 75–78.

Milgram, Stanley. 1963. Behavioral study of obedience. *Journal of Abnormal and Social Psychology* 67 (4): 371–378.

Miller, Geoffrey, Joshua M. Tybur, and Brent D. Jordan. 2007. Ovulatory cycle effects on tip earnings by lap dancers: Economic evidence for human estrus? *Evolution and Human Behavior* 28 (6): 375–381.

Miller, Joan G. 1984. Culture and the development of everyday social explanation. *Journal of Personality and Social Psychology* 46 (5): 961–978.

Miller, Patricia H., and Patricia A. Aloise. 1989. Young children's understanding of the psychological causes of behavior: A review. *Child Development* 60 (2): 257–285.

Miller, Dale T., Stephen A. Norman, and Edward Wright. 1978. Distortion in person perception as a consequence of the need for effective control. *Journal of Personality and Social Psychology* 36 (6): 598–607.

Minsky, Marvin. 1981. A framework for representing knowledge. In *Mind Design*, ed. John Haugeland, 95–128. Cambridge, MA: MIT Press.

Mischel, Walter. 1972. Direct versus indirect personality assessment: Evidence and implications. *Journal of Consulting and Clinical Psychology* 38 (3): 319–324.

Mischel, Walter, Katharine M. Jeffery, and Charlotte J. Patterson. 1974. The layman's use of trait and behavioral information to predict behavior. *Journal of Research in Personality* 8 (3): 231–242.

Mitani, John C., David P. Watts, and Martin N. Muller. 2002. Recent developments in the study of wild chimpanzee behavior. *Evolutionary Anthropology* 11 (1): 9–25.

Mitchell, Peter. 1994. Realism and early conception of mind: A synthesis of phylogenetic and ontogenetic issues. In *Children's Early Understanding of Minds: Origins and Development*, ed. Charlie Lewis and Peter Mitchell, 19–46. Hillsdale, NJ: Lawrence Erlbaum.

Mitchell, Peter, and Hazel Lacohée. 1991. Children's early understanding of false belief. *Cognition* 39 (2): 107–127.

Mithen, Steven. 2000. Paleoanthropological perspectives on theory of mind. In *Understanding Other Minds*, ed. Simon Baron-Cohen, Helen Tager-Flusberg, and Donald J. Cohen. Oxford: Oxford University Press.

Mithen, Steven. 2002. Human evolution and the cognitive basis of science. In *The Cognitive Basis of Science*, ed. Peter Carruthers, Stephen P. Stich, and Michael Siegal, 23–40. Cambridge: Cambridge University Press.

Moll, Henrike, and Michael Tomasello. 2007. How 14- and 18-month-olds know what others have experienced. *Developmental Psychology* 43 (2): 309–317.

Moore, Don A. 2005. Myopic biases in strategic social prediction: Why deadlines put everyone under more pressure than everyone else. *Personality and Social Psychology Bulletin* 31 (5): 668–679.

Morris, Michael W., Tanya Menon, and Daniel R. Ames. 2001. Culturally conferred conceptions of agency: A key to social perception of persons, groups, and other actors. *Personality and Social Psychology Review* 5 (2): 169–182.

Morris, Michael W., and Kaiping Peng. 1994. Culture and cause: American and Chinese attributions for social and physical events. *Journal of Personality and Social Psychology* 67 (6): 949–971.

Morton, Adam. 2003. *The Importance of Being Understood: Folk Psychology as Ethics*. London: Routledge.

Moses, Louis J., and John H. Flavell. 1990. Inferring false beliefs from actions and reactions. *Child Development* 61 (4): 929–945.

Mullen, Brian, Jennifer L. Atkins, Debbie S. Champion, Cecelia Edwards, Dana Hardy, John E. Story, and Mary Vanderklok. 1985. The false consensus effect: A meta-analysis of 115 hypothesis tests. *Journal of Experimental Social Psychology* 21 (3): 262–283.

Myowa-Yamakoshi, Masako, and Tetsuro Matsuzawa. 2000. Imitation of intentional manipulatory actions in chimpanzees (Pan troglodytes). *Journal of Comparative Psychology* 114 (4): 381–391.

Newman, Leonard S. 1996. Trait impressions as heuristics for predicting behavior. *Personality and Social Psychology Bulletin* 22 (4): 395–411.

Newman, Leonard S., and James S. Uleman. 1993. When are you what you did? Behavior identification and dispositional inference in person memory, attribution, and social judgment. *Personality and Social Psychology Bulletin* 19 (5): 513–525.

Nichols, Shaun, and Stephen Stich. 2003. *Mindreading: An Integrated Account of Pretence, Self-Awareness, and Understanding Other Minds*. Oxford, UK: Oxford University Press.

Nichols, Shaun, Stephen Stich, Alan Leslie, and David Klein. 1996. Varieties of offline simulation. In *Theories of Theories of Mind*, ed. Peter Carruthers and Peter K. Smith, 39–74. Cambridge: Cambridge University Press.

Nielsen, Mark, Emma Collier-Baker, Joanne M. Davis, and Thomas Suddendorf. 2005. Imitation recognition in a captive chimpanzee (Pan troglodytes). *Animal Cognition* 8:31–36.

Nisbett, Richard E. 1987. Lay personality theory: Its nature, origin, and utility. In *A Distinctive Approach to Psychological Research: The Influence of Stanley Schachter*, ed. Neil E. Grunberg, Richard E. Nisbett, Judith Rodin, and Jerome E. Singer, 87–117. Hillsdale, NJ: Lawrence Erlbaum.

Nisbett, Richard E. 2003. *The Geography of Thought: How Asians and Westerners Think Differently . . . and Why*. New York: Free Press.

Nisbett, Richard E., and Lee Ross. 1980. *Human Inference: Strategies and Shortcomings of Social Judgment*. Englewood Cliffs, NJ: Prentice-Hall.

Nisbett, Richard E., Craig Caputo, Patricia Legant, and Jeanne Marecek. 1973. Behavior as seen by the actor and as seen by the observer. *Journal of Personality and Social Psychology* 27 (2): 154–164.

Norenzayan, Ara, Incheol Choi, and Richard E. Nisbett. 2002. Cultural similarities and differences in social inference: Evidence from behavioral predictions and lay theories of behavior. *Personality and Social Psychology Bulletin* 28 (1): 109–120.

Olson, James M., Neal J. Roese, and Mark P. Zanna. 1996. Expectancies. In *Social Psychology: Handbook of Basic Principles*, ed. Eduard Tory Higgins and Arie W. Kruglanski, 211–238. New York: Guilford Press.

Onishi, Kristine H., and Renée Baillargeon. 2005. Do 15-month-old infants understand false beliefs? *Science* 308:255–258.

Ozonoff, Sally, and Judith N. Miller. 1995. Teaching theory of mind: A new approach to social skills training for individuals with autism. *Journal of Autism and Developmental Disorders* 25 (20): 415–433.

Park, Bernadette. 1986. A method for studying the development of impressions of real people. *Journal of Personality and Social Psychology* 51 (5): 907–917.

Parr, Lisa A. 2003. The discrimination of facial expressions and their emotional content by chimpanzees (Pan troglodytes). In *Emotions Inside Out: 130 Years after Darwin's "The Expression of the Emotions in Man and Animals,"* vol. 100, ed. Paul Ekman, Joseph J. Campos, Richard J. Davidson, and Frans B. M. de Waal, 56–78. New York: Annals of the New York Academy of Sciences.

Payne, B. Keith. 2001. Prejudice and perception: The role of automatic and controlled processes in misperceiving a weapon. *Journal of Personality and Social Psychology* 81 (2): 181–192.

Pendry, Louise F., and C. Neil Macrae. 1996. What the disinterested perceiver overlooks: Goal-directed social categorization. *Personality and Social Psychology Bulletin* 22 (3): 249–256.

Perner, Josef. 1991. *Understanding the Representational Mind*. Cambridge, MA: MIT Press.

Perner, Josef. 1996. Simulation as explicitation of predication-implicit knowledge about the mind: Arguments for a simulation-theory mix. In *Theories of Theories of Mind*, ed. Peter Carruthers and Peter K. Smith, 90–104. Cambridge University Press.

Perner, Josef, Birgit Lang, and Daniela Kloo. 2002. Theory of mind and self-control: More than a common problem of inhibition. *Child Development* 73 (3): 752–767.

Perner, Josef, and Ted Ruffman. 2005. Infants' insight into the mind: How deep? *Science* 308 (5719): 214–216.

Perry, Susan, Mary Baker, Linda Fedigan, Julie Gros-Louis, Katherine Jack, Katherine C. MacKinnon, Joseph H. Manson, Melissa Panger, Kendra Pyle, and Lisa Rose. 2003. Social conventions in wild white-faced capuchin monkeys: Evidence for traditions in a neotropical primate. In *Divergences and Commonalities within Taxonomic and Political Orders*, special issue, *Current Anthropology* 44 (2): 241–268.

Peterson, Christopher, and Martin E. Seligman. 1984. Causal explanations as a risk factor for depression: Theory and evidence. *Psychological Review* 91 (3): 347–374.

Peterson, Christopher, Dawn Colvin, and Emily H. Lin. 1992. Explanatory style and helplessness. *Social Behavior and Personality* 20 (1): 1–13.

Piaget, Jean. 1936/1952. *The Origins of Intelligence in Children*. Trans. M. Cook. New York: International Universities Press.

Peirce, Charles S. 1877. The fixation of belief. *Popular Science Monthly* 12:1–15.

Pietromonaco, Paula, and Richard E. Nisbett. 1982. Swimming upstream against the fundamental attribution error: Subjects' weak generalizations from the Darley and Batson study. *Social Behavior and Personality* 10:1–4.

Plooij, F. X. 1978. Some basic traits of language in wild chimpanzees? In *Action, Gesture, and Symbol: The Emergence of Language*, ed. A. Lock, 111–131. New York: Academic Press.

Povinelli, Daniel J., and John G. H. Cant. 1995. Arboreal clambering and the evolution of self-conception. *Quarterly Review of Biology* 70 (4): 393–421.

Povinelli, Daniel J., and Sarah Dunphy-Lelii. 2001. Do chimpanzees seek explanations? Preliminary comparative investigations. *Canadian Journal of Experimental Psychology* 55 (2): 185–193.

Povinelli, Daniel J., and Timothy J. Eddy. 1996. What young chimpanzees know about seeing. *Monographs of the Society for Research in Child Development* 61 (3): 1–152.

Povinelli, Daniel J., and Jennifer Vonk. 2003. Chimpanzee minds: Suspiciously human? *Trends in Cognitive Sciences* 7 (4): 157–160.

Povinelli, Daniel J., and Jennifer Vonk. 2004. We don't need a microscope to explore the chimpanzee's mind. *Mind and Language* 19 (1): 1–28.

Premack, David. 1988. "Does the chimpanzee have a theory of mind?" revisited. In *Machiavellian Intelligence: Social Expertise and the Evolution of Intellect in Monkeys, Apes, and Humans*, ed. Richard Byrne and Andrew Whiten, 160–179. New York: Oxford University Press.

Premack, David. 1990. Words: What are they, and do animals have them? *Cognition* 37 (3): 197–212.

Premack, David, and Ann James Premack. 2003. *Original Intelligence: Unlocking the Mystery of Who We Are*. New York: McGraw-Hill.

Premack, David, and Guy Woodruff. 1978. Does the chimpanzee have a theory of mind? *Behavioral and Brain Sciences* 1 (4): 515–526.

Prinstein, Mitchell J., and Shirley S. Wang. 2005. False consensus and adolescent peer contagion: Examining discrepancies between perceptions and actual reported levels of friends' deviant and health risk behaviors. *Journal of Abnormal Child Psychology* 33 (3): 293–306.

Quattrone, George A. 1982. Overattribution and unit formation: When behavior engulfs the person. *Journal of Personality and Social Psychology* 42 (4): 593–607.

Ramsey, Grant, Meredith L. Bastian, and Carel van Schaik. 2007. Animal innovation defined and operationalized. *Behavioral and Brain Sciences* 30 (4): 393–407.

Reader, Simon. 2003. Innovation and social learning: Individual variation and brain evolution. *Animal Biology* 53 (2): 147–158.

Reader, Simon M., and Kevin N. Laland. 2002. Social intelligence, innovation, and enhanced brain size in primates. *Proceedings of the National Academy of Sciences of the United States* 99 (7): 4436–4441.

Reader, Simon M., and Kevin N. Laland, eds. 2003. *Animal Innovation*. New York: Oxford University Press.

Rendell, Luke, and Hal Whitehead. 2001. Culture in whales and dolphins. *Behavioral and Brain Sciences* 24:309–382.

Repacholi, Betty M., and Alison Gopnik. 1997. Early reasoning about desires: Evidence from 14- and 18-month-olds. *Developmental Psychology* 33 (1): 12–21.

Rescorla, Michael. 2009. Chrysippus' dog as a case study in non-linguistic cognition. In *The Philosophy of Animal Minds*, ed. Robert Lurz. New York: Cambridge University Press.

Rholes, William S., Leonard S. Newman, and Diane N. Ruble. 1990. Understanding self and other: Developmental and motivational aspects of perceiving persons in terms of invariant dispositions. In *Handbook of Motivation and Cognition: Foundations of Social Behavior*, vol. 2, ed. E. Tory Higgins and Richard M. Sorrentino, 369–407. New York: Guilford Press.

Rholes, William S., and Diane N. Ruble. 1984. Children's understanding of dispositional characteristics of others. *Child Development* 55 (2): 550–560.

Riggs, Kevin J., Donald M. Peterson, Elizabeth J. Robinson, and Peter Mitchell. 1998. Are errors in false belief tasks symptomatic of a broader difficulty with counterfactuality? *Cognitive Development* 13 (1): 73–90.

Rizzolatti, Giacomo, Luciano Fadiga, Vittorio Gallese, and Leonardo Fogassi. 1996. Premotor cortex and the recognition of motor actions. *Brain Research: Cognitive Brain Research* 3 (2): 131–141.

Robinson, Elizabeth J. 1994. What people say, what they think, and what is really the case: Children's understanding of utterances as sources of knowledge. In *Children's Early Understanding of Minds: Origins and Development*, ed. Charlie Lewis and Peter Mitchell, 355–381. East Sussex: Lawrence Erlbaum.

Robinson, Elizabeth J., and Peter Mitchell. 1995. Masking of children's early understanding of the representational mind: Backwards explanation versus prediction. *Child Development* 66 (4): 1022–1039.

Robison, John Elder. 2008. *Look Me in the Eye: My Life with Asperger's*. 2nd ed. New York: Three Rivers Press.

Rosch, Eleanor. 1973. Natural categories. *Cognitive Psychology* 4:328–350.

Ross, Lee. 1977. The intuitive psychologist and his shortcomings: Distortions in the attribution process. In *Advances in Experimental Social Psychology*, vol. 10, ed. Leonard Berkowitz, 174–221. New York: Academic Press.

Ross, Lee, David Greene, and Pamela House. 1977. The "false consensus effect": An egocentric bias in social perception and attribution processes. *Journal of Experimental Social Psychology* 13 (3): 279–301.

Ross, Lee, and Richard E. Nisbett. 1991. *The Person and the Situation: Perspectives of Social Psychology*. Philadelphia: Temple University Press.

Ross, Michael, and Fiore Sicoly. 1979. Egocentric biases in availability and attribution. *Journal of Personality and Social Psychology* 37 (3): 322–336.

Roth, Daniel, and Alan M. Leslie. 1998. Solving belief problems: Toward a task analysis. *Cognition* 66 (1): 1–31.

Roth-Hanania, Ronit. 2002. The role of self-concept development in the development of empathic concern during infancy. *Dissertation Abstracts International: Section B: The Sciences and Engineering* 62 (12 B).

Rothbart, Myron, and Bernadette Park. 1986. On the confirmability and disconfirmability of trait concepts. *Journal of Personality and Social Psychology* 50 (1): 131–142.

Russell, James. 1987. "Can we say . . . ?" Children's understanding of intensionality. *Cognition* 25 (3): 289–308.

Russon, Anne, and Kristin Andrews. 2010. Orangutan pantomime: Elaborating the message. *Biology Letters*. Published online before print, August 11, 2010. DOI 0.1098/rsbl.2010.0564.

Ryan, Carey S. 1996. Accuracy of black and white college students' in-group and outgroup stereotypes. *Personality and Social Psychology Bulletin* 22 (11): 1114–1127.

Sabbagh, Mark A., and Maureen A. Callanan. 1998. Metarepresentation in action: 3-, 4-, and 5-year-olds' developing theories of mind in parent-child conversations. *Developmental Psychology* 34 (3): 491–502.

Safer, Martin A. 1980. Attributing evil to the subject, not the situation: Student reaction to Milgram's film on obedience. *Personality and Social Psychology Bulletin* 6 (2): 205–209.

Salmon, Wesley C. 1971. *Statistical Explanation and Statistical Relevance*. Pittsburgh: University of Pittsburgh Press.

Salmon, Wesley C. 1984. *Scientific Explanation and the Causal Structure of the World*. Princeton, NJ: Princeton University Press.

Salmon, Wesley C. 1994. Causality without counterfactuals. *Philosophy of Science* 61:297–312.

Saltmarsh, Rebecca, Peter Mitchell, and Elizabeth J. Robinson. 1995. Realism and children's early grasp of mental representation: Belief-based judgments in the state change task. *Cognition* 57 (3): 297–325.

Savage-Rumbaugh, Sue, Stuart G. Shanker, and Talbot J. Taylor. 1998. *Apes, Language, and the Human Mind*. New York: Oxford University Press.

Schneider, David J. 2004. *The Psychology of Stereotyping*. New York: Guilford Press.

Schult, Carolyn A. 2002. Children's understanding of the distinction between intentions and desires. *Child Development* 73 (6): 1727–1747.

Schwitzgebel, Eric. 1999. Children's theories and the drive to explain. *Science and Education* 8 (5): 457–488.

Schwitzgebel, Eric. 2002. A phenomenal, dispositional account of belief. *Noûs* 36 (2): 249–275.

Scott, Rose M., and Renée Baillargeon. 2009. Which penguin is this? Attributing false beliefs about object identity at 18 months. *Child Development* 80 (4): 1172–1196.

Sehon, Scott. 2005. *Teleological Realism: Mind, Agency, and Explanation.* Cambridge, MA: MIT Press.

Sellars, Wilfred. 1956. *Empiricism and the Philosophy of Mind.* Cambridge, MA: Harvard University Press.

Siegal, Michael, and Candida C. Peterson. 1996. Breaking the mold: A fresh look at questions about children's understanding of lies and mistakes. *Developmental Psychology* 32:322–334.

Siegal, Michael, and Candida C. Peterson. 1998. Children's understanding of lies and innocent and negligent mistakes. *Developmental Psychology* 34:332–343.

Silk, Joan B., Susan C. Alberts, and Jeanne Altmann. 2003. Social bonds of female baboons enhance infant survival. *Science* 302 (5648): 1231–1234.

Small, Kim H., and John L. Peterson. 1981. The divergent perceptions of actors and observers. *Journal of Social Psychology* 113 (1): 123–132.

Song, Hyun-joo, Kristine H. Onishi, Renée Baillargeon, and Cynthia Fisher. 2008. Can an agent's false belief be corrected through an appropriate communication? Psychological reasoning in 18-month-old infants. *Cognition* 109:295–315.

Song, Hyun-joo, and Renée Baillargeon. 2008. Infants' reasoning about others' false perceptions. *Developmental Psychology* 44 (6): 1789–1795.

Southgate, Victoria, Atsushi Senju, and Gergely Csibra. 2007. Action anticipation through attribution of false belief by 2-year-olds. *Psychological Science* 18 (7): 587–592.

Spencer-Rodgers, Julie, Helen C. Boucher, Sumi C. Mori, Lei Wang, and Kaiping Peng. 2009. The dialectical self-concept: Contradiction, change, and holism in East Asian cultures. *Personality and Social Psychology Bulletin* 35 (1): 29–44.

Spirtes, Peter, Clark N. Glymour, and Richard Scheines. 1993. *Causation, Prediction, and Search.* New York: Springer.

Spragg, S. D. S. 1940. Morphine addiction in chimpanzees. *Comparative Psychology Monographs* 15:1–132.

Sproull, Lee, and Sara Kiesler. 1986. Reducing social context cues: Electronic mail in organizational communication. *Management Science* 32 (11): 1492–1512.

Stangor, Charles, Laurie Lynch, Changming Duan, and Beth Glass. 1992. Categorization of individuals on the basis of multiple social features. *Journal of Personality and Social Psychology* 62 (2): 207–218.

Steward, A. Lee, and Michael Lupfer. 1987. Touching as teaching: The effect of touch on students' perceptions and performance. *Journal of Applied Social Psychology* 17 (9): 800–809.

Stich, Stephen P. 1979. Do animals have beliefs? *Australasian Journal of Philosophy* 57 (1): 15–28.

Stich, Stephen P., and Shaun Nichols. 1995. Second thoughts on simulation. In *Mental Simulation: Evaluations and Applications*, ed. Martin Davies and Tony Stone, 87–108. Oxford: Blackwell.

Stich, Stephen, and Shaun Nichols. 1996. How do minds understand minds? Mental simulation versus tacit theory. In *Deconstructing the Mind*, ed. Stephen P. Stich, 136–167. Oxford: Oxford University Press.

Stich, Stephen P., and Ian Ravenscroft. 1996. What is folk psychology? In *Deconstructing the Mind*, ed. Stephen P. Stich, 115–135. Oxford: Oxford University Press.

Steward, A. Lee, and Michael Lupfer. 1987. Touching as teaching: The effect of touch on students' perceptions and performance. *Journal of Applied Social Psychology* 17 (9): 800–809.

Stocker, Michael. 1997. The schizophrenia of modern ethical theories. In *Virtue Ethics*, ed. Roger Crisp and Michael Slote. New York: Oxford University Press.

Suppe, Frederick R. 1972. What's wrong with the received view on the structure of scientific theories. *Philosophy of Science* 39:1–19.

Surian, Luca, Stefania Caldi, and Dan Sperber. 2007. Attribution of beliefs to 13-month-old infants. *Psychological Science* 18:580–586.

Swann, William B., Jr. 1984. Quest for accuracy in person perception: A matter for pragmatics. *Psychological Review* 91 (4): 457–477.

Swann, William B., Jr., Blair Stephenson, and Thane S. Pittman. 1981. Curiosity and control: On the determinants of the search for social knowledge. *Journal of Personality and Social Psychology* 40 (4): 635–642.

Swim, Janet K. 1993. In search of gender bias in evaluations and trait inferences: The role of diagnosticity and gender stereotypicality of behavioral information. *Sex Roles* 29 (3–4): 213–237.

Tammet, Daniel. 2006. *Born on a Blue Day*. London: Hodder & Stoughton.

Taylor, Marjorie, Bonnie M. Esbensen, and Robert T. Bennett. 1994. Children's understanding of knowledge acquisition: The tendency for children to report that they have always known what they have just learned. *Child Development* 65 (6): 1581–1604.

Taylor, Shelley E. 1981. A categorizing approach to stereotyping. In *Cognitive Processes in Stereotyping and Intergroup Behavior*, ed. David L. Hamilton, 83–114. Hillsdale, NJ: Lawrence Erlbaum.

Taylor, Shelley E., and Jennifer Crocker. 1981. Schematic bases of social information processing. In *Social Cognition*, ed. E. Tory Higgins, C. Peter Herman, and Mark P. Zanna, 89–134. Hillsdale, NJ: Lawrence Erlbaum.

Taylor, Shelley E., and Judith H. Koivumaki. 1976. The perception of self and others: Acquaintanceship, affect, and actor-observer differences. *Journal of Personality and Social Psychology* 33 (4): 403–408.

Terkel, Studs. 2003. *Hope Dies Last: Keeping the Faith in Difficult Times*. New York: New Press.

Thelen, Esther, and Linda B. Smith. 1994. *A Dynamic Systems Approach to the Development of Cognition and Action*. Cambridge, MA: MIT Press.

Thompson, Evan. 2007. *Mind in Life: Biology, Phenomenology, and the Sciences of Mind*. Cambridge, MA: Belknap Press of Harvard University Press.

Thompson, Roger K., David L. Oden, and Sarah T. Boysen. 1997. Language-naïve chimpanzees (Pan troglodytes) judge relations between relations in a conceptual matching-to-sample task. *Journal of Experimental Psychology: Animal Behavior Processes* 23 (1): 31–42.

Tomasello, Michael, and Katharina Haberl. 2003. Understanding attention: 12- and 18-month-olds know what is new for other persons. *Developmental Psychology* 39 (5): 906–912.

Tomasello, Michael, Josep Call, and Brian Hare. 2003a. Chimpanzees understand psychological states—the question is which ones and to what extent. *Trends in Cognitive Sciences* 7 (4): 153–156.

Tomasello, Michael, Josep Call, and Brian Hare. 2003b. Chimpanzees versus humans: It's not that simple. *Trends in Cognitive Sciences* 7 (6): 239–240.

Tomasello, Michael, and Malinda Carpenter. 2005. The emergence of social cognition in three young chimpanzees. *Monographs of the Society for Research in Child Development* 70 (1): 1–131.

Träuble, Birgit, Vesna Marinović, and Sabina Pauen. 2010. Early theory of mind competencies: Do infants understand others' beliefs? *Infancy* 15 (4): 434–444.

Trevarthen, Colwyn. 1977. Descriptive analyses of infant communicative behavior. In *Studies in Mother-Infant Interaction*, ed. H. R. Schaffer, 227–270. London: Academic Press.

Trevarthen, Colwyn. 1979. Communication and cooperation in early infancy: A description of primary intersubjectivity. In *Before Speech: The Beginning of Interpersonal Communication*, ed. Margaret Bullowa, 321–347. Cambridge: Cambridge University Press.

Triandis, Harry C., and Vasso Vassiliou. 1967. Frequency of contact and stereotyping. *Journal of Personality and Social Psychology* 7 (3): 316–328.

Uleman, James S., Alex Hon, Robert J. Roman, and Gordon B. Moskowitz. 1996. Online evidence for spontaneous trait inferences at encoding. *Personality and Social Psychology Bulletin* 22 (4): 377–394.

Uller, Claudia. 2004. Disposition to recognize goals in infant chimpanzees. *Animal Cognition* 7 (3): 154–161.

Vallone, Robert P., Dale W. Griffin, Sabrina Lin, and Lee Ross. 1990. Overconfident prediction of future actions and outcomes by self and others. *Journal of Personality and Social Psychology* 58 (4): 582–592.

van Fraassen, Bas. 1980. *The Scientific Image*. Oxford: Oxford University Press.

Van Gelder, Tim. 1995. What might cognition be, if not computation? *Journal of Philosophy* 92 (7): 345–381.

Van Schaik, Carel P., Marc Ancrenaz, Gwendolyn Borgen, Birute Galdikas, Cheryl D. Knott, Ian Singleton, Akira Suzuki, Sri Suci Utami, and Michelle Merrill. 2003. Orangutan cultures and the evolution of material culture. *Science* 299 (5603): 102–105.

Velleman, David J. 2003. Narrative explanation. *Philosophical Review* 112 (1): 1–25.

Verbeek, Monica E. M., Piet J. Drent, and Piet R. Wiepkema. 1994. Consistent individual differences in early exploratory behavior of male great tits. *Animal Behaviour* 48 (5): 1113–1121.

Von Eckardt, Barbara. 1995. The notion of accuracy in current social perception research. *Proceedings of the Biennial Meetings of the Philosophy of Science Association* 2:35–46.

Vonk, Jennifer, and Francys Subiaul. 2009. Do chimpanzees know what others can and cannot do? Reasoning about "capability." *Animal Cognition* 12 (2): 267–286.

Voss, Hans-Georg, and Heidi Keller. 1986. Curiosity and exploration: A program of investigation. *German Journal of Psychology* 10 (4): 327–337.

de Waal, Frans. 1982. *Chimpanzee Politics: Power and Sex among Apes*. London: Jonathan Cape.

de Waal, Frans. 1996. *Good Natured: The Origins of Right and Wrong in Humans and Other Animals*. Cambridge, MA: Harvard University Press.

Warneken, Felix, and Michael Tomasello. 2006. Altruistic helping in infants and young chimpanzees. *Science* 311 (5765): 1301–1303.

Wason, Peter C. 1968. Reasoning about a rule. *Quarterly Journal of Experimental Psychology* 20 (3): 273–281.

Watts, David P., Martin Muller, Sylvia J. Amsler, Godfrey Mbabazi, and John C. Mitani. 2006. Lethal intergroup aggression by chimpanzees in Kibale National Park, Uganda. *American Journal of Primatology* 68:161–180.

Weinstein, Tamara A. R., and John P. Capitanio. 2008. Individual differences in infant temperament predict social relationships of yearling rhesus monkeys, Macaca mulatta. *Animal Behaviour* 76 (2): 455–465.

Weinstein, Tamara A. R., John P. Capitanio, and Samuel D. Gosling. 2008. Personality in animals. In *Handbook of Personality: Theory and Research*, 3rd ed., ed. Oliver P. John, Richard W. Robins, and Lawrence A. Pervin, 328–350. New York: Guilford Press.

Wellman, Henry M. 1990. *The Child's Theory of Mind*. Cambridge, MA: MIT Press.

Wellman, Henry M. 2010. Developing a theory of mind. In *The Wiley-Blackwell Handbook of Childhood Cognitive Development*, 2nd ed., ed. Usha Goswami. Malden, MA: Blackwell.

Wellman, Henry M., Michelle Hollander, and Carolyn A. Schult. 1996. Young children's understanding of thought bubbles and of thoughts. *Child Development* 67 (3): 768–788.

Wellman, Henry M., David Cross, and Julanne Watson. 2001. Meta-analysis of theory of mind development: The truth about false belief. *Child Development* 72 (3): 655–684.

Whiten, Andrew. 2007. Cultural panthropology. Paper presented at the Understanding Chimpanzees: The Mind of the Chimpanzee conference. Lincoln Park Zoo, Chicago, Illinois, 2007.

Whiten, Andrew, and Richard W. Byrne. 1988. The Machiavellian intellect hypotheses. In *Machiavellian Intelligence*, ed. Richard W. Byrne and Andrew Whiten, 1–9. Oxford: Oxford University Press.

Whiten, Andrew, Jane Goodall, William C. McGrew, Toshisada Nishida, V. Reynolds, Y. Sugiyama, C. E. G. Tutin, R. W. Wrangham, and Christophe Boesch. 1999. Cultures in chimpanzees. *Nature* 399 (6737): 682–685.

Wilkes, Kathleen V. 1981. Functionalism, psychology, and the philosophy of mind. *Philosophical Topics* 12 (1): 147–167.

Wilkes, Kathleen V. 1984. Pragmatics in science and theory in common sense. *Inquiry* 27 (4): 339–361.

Williamson, Timothy. 2000. *Knowledge and Its Limits*. New York: Oxford University Press.

Wilson, David S., Kristine Coleman, Anne B. Clark, and Laurence Biederman. 1993. Shy-bold continuum in pumpkinseed sunfish (Lepomis gibbosus): An ecological study of a psychological trait. *Journal of Comparative Psychology* 107 (3): 250–260.

Wilson, Timothy D., and Daniel T. Gilbert. 2005. Affective forecasting: Knowing what to want. *Current Directions in Psychological Science* 14 (3): 131–134.

Wilson, Timothy D., and Suzanne J. LaFleur. 1995. Knowing what you'll do: Effects of analyzing reasons on self-prediction. *Journal of Personality and Social Psychology* 68 (1): 21–35.

Wimmer, Heinz J., and Heinz Mayringer. 1998. False belief understanding in young children: Explanations do not develop before predictions. *International Journal of Behavioral Development* 22 (2): 403–422.

Wimmer, Heinz J., and Josef Perner. 1983. Beliefs about beliefs: Representation and constraining function of wrong beliefs in young children's understanding of deception. *Cognition* 13 (1): 103–128.

Wimmer, Heinz J., and Viktor Weichbold. 1994. Children's theory of mind: Fodor's heuristics examined. *Cognition* 53 (1): 45–57.

Woodward, Amanda L. 1998. Infants selectively encode the goal object of an actor's reach. *Cognition* 69 (1): 1–34.

Woodward, James. 2003. *Making Things Happen: A Theory of Causal Explanation*. New York: Oxford University Press.

Worth, Leila T., Scott T. Allison, and David M. Messick. 1987. Impact of a group decision on perception of one's own and others' attitudes. *Journal of Personality and Social Psychology* 53 (4): 673–682.

Wrangham, Richard. 2009. *Catching Fire: How Cooking Made Us Human*. New York: Basic Books.

Wright, Jack C., and Walter Mischel. 1987. A conditional approach to dispositional constructs: The local predictability of social behavior. *Journal of Personality and Social Psychology* 53 (6): 1159–1177.

Xu, Fei, and Vashti Garcia. 2008. Intuitive statistics by 8-month-old infants. *Proceedings of the National Academy of Sciences of the United States of America* 105 (13): 5012–5015.

Yuill, Nicola. 1984. Young children's coordination of motive and outcome in judgments of satisfaction and morality. *British Journal of Developmental Psychology* 2:73–81.

Yuill, Nicola, and Anna Pearson. 1998. The development of bases for trait attribution: Children's understanding of traits as causal mechanisms based on desire. *Developmental Psychology* 34 (3): 574–586.

Yuill, Nicola, Josef Perner, Anna Pearson, Denise Peerbhoy, and Joanne Van den Ende. 1996. Children's changing understanding of wicked desires: From objective to subjective to moral. *British Journal of Developmental Psychology* 14:457–475.

Zárate, Michael A., James S. Uleman, and Corrine I. Voils. 2001. Effects of culture and processing goals on the activation and binding of trait concepts. *Social Cognition* 19 (3): 295–323.

Zawidzki, Tadeusz W. 2008. The function of folk psychology: Mind reading or mind shaping? *Philosophical Explorations* 11 (3): 193–210.

Zimmer, Carl. 2006. Devious butterflies, full-throated frogs, and other liars. *New York Times*, December 26.

Zuckerman, Miron. 1979. Attribution of success and failure revisited, or The motivational bias is alive and well in attribution theory. *Journal of Personality* 47 (2): 245–287.

Index

Affective state. *See* Mood
Affective tension. *See* Curiosity state
Animal culture, 255–229, 247
Anomalous behavior, 110, 154, 220–222, 224, 240–242
    innovative, 225–229
Ape mindreading. *See* Critter psychology; Mindreading in critters
Apperly, Ian, 170–171
Arational action, 176–177, 194–195, 199, 202–204
Aristotle, 14–16, 19
Atance, Cristina, 152
Attributing propositional attitudes. *See* Mindreading
Attributing mental content. *See* Mindreading
Autism, 101–102, 119, 166–167, 187–189, 192–193, 196–197, 208–209. *See also* False-belief tasks and autism; Mindblindness; Mindreading and autism

Baillargeon, Renee, 25–28
Behavioral generalizations. *See* Heuristics
Belief-desire psychology, 14–15, 52–54, 95, 99–112, 131–133, 153, 217, 221, 243. *See also* Representational nature of belief

Bloom, Harold, 79–80, 151–152
Boesch, Christophe, 237–238
Bromberger, Sylvan, 41, 118–119
Buttleman, Frederick, 28–29
Byrne, Richard, 218

Call, Josep, 232, 243
Callanan, Maureen, 149–150
Camp, Elisabeth, 165
Cartwright, Nancy, 140–141
Ceteris paribus clauses, 56–60
Chimpanzee psychology. *See* Critter psychology; Mindreading in critters
Chouinard, Michelle, 148–150
Churchland, Paul, 40, 50, 58–59, 129, 186
Cognitive dissonance, 120, 122, 145, 153–154
Cognitive penetrability, 61, 63
Cohen, Adam, 171–172
Confabulation, 174, 229
Confirmation bias, 107–108, 124
Coordinating behavior. *See* Folk psychological practices, other
Correspondence bias. *See* Fundamental attribution error
Covering law explanation. *See* Deductive-nomological explanation

Critter psychology, 12, 197, 234–248. *See also* Mindreading in critters
  explaining behavior, 240–243
  mindreading, 231–235, 243–248
  predicting behavior, 237–240
Curiosity state, 120–124, 126–128, 145–146, 148, 220, 222, 240–243. *See also* Explanation seeking; Folk psychological explanation
Currie, Gregory, 199

Davidson, Donald, 17–18, 21–22, 103, 131, 135, 157, 165–167, 176
Deception. *See* Folk psychological practices, other
Deductive-nomological explanation, 39–40, 119, 129–131, 138; *See also* Scientific explanation
Dennett, Daniel, 16, 18, 20–21, 49, 54–55, 106–107
De re and *de dicto* belief, 160
de Waal, Frans, 216, 242, 245
Dispositional nature of belief, 22, 30–33, 204. *See also* Representational nature of belief
Dunbar, Robin, 129

Egocentric bias, 76–81
Elgin, Mehmet, 141
Emotional action. *See* Arational action
Epley, Nicholas, 80
Explaining behavior. *See* Folk psychological explanation
Explanation seeking, 12, 119–124, 127–128, 135, 145–146, 152–153, 220–22, 228. *See also* Curiosity state; Folk psychological explanation; Why-questions
  causal, 149–151
  in chimpanzees, 232–233, 240–243, 247–248
Exploratory behavior. *See* Explanation seeking

False-belief tasks, 6, 10, 20–29, 31–35, 43, 185–187, 189, 244. *See also* Mindblindness; Mindreading; Standard Folk Psychology
  and autism, 189
  and children, 14, 21–24, 33–35, 79, 103, 136, 152, 172
  and critters, 20–21, 172
  and infants, 25–29, 31–31
False-consensus effect. *See* Egocentric bias
Fodor, Jerry, 16–18, 21, 50, 55, 57, 129, 165
Folk causation, 157–161, 175–178, 185, 193–195, 219, 221. *See also* Folk psychological explanation
Folk psychological explanation, 6–17, 20, 32, 24–44, 57–59, 71–73, 94, 111–112, 115–178, 183–187, 189–192, 194–195, 197–201, 203–211, 216, 220–222, 224–230, 232, 239–248. *See also* Curiosity state; Explanation seeking; Folk causation; Scientific explanation; Why-questions
  from causal histories, 157–159, 161, 221 (*see also* Folk causation)
  from enabling factors, 157, 159–162, 168, 173, 175, 221 (*see also* Folk causation)
  generating, 121–122, 124, 127, 145, 151
  nonverbal, 163–168
  quotidian, 42
  from reasons, 157–159, 161, 167, 175, 221 (*see also* Folk causation)
  from situations, 131, 151, 156, 159–162, 168, 173
  from stereotypes, 126, 221
  from trait attribution, 128, 131, 156–157, 160–162, 164, 168–169, 173–178, 195, 221

Folk psychological practices, other, 6,
    11–12, 183–187, 197–211, 216, 234.
    See also Folk psychological
    explanation; Folk psychological
    prediction; Heuristics
  automaticity of, 202–203, 205–206
  coordinating, 237, 239
  deceiving, 217–220
Folk psychological prediction, 6–16,
    18–21, 23–24, 32–38, 42–44, 47–112,
    115, 126–128, 138–140, 152, 161,
    170, 173–174, 179, 183–192,
    194–195, 197–201, 203–211,
    216–220, 222, 224, 230–234,
    236–240, 243–248
  in anomalous situations, 50–51,
    110–111, 220–222 (*see also*
    Anomalous behavior)
  prognosticating, 68, 72, 74, 115, 210
  quotidian, 10, 50–51, 67–68, 72, 74,
    99, 115, 192, 208, 210, 220
  from self, 68–69, 75–81, 105
  from situations, 68–76, 96, 105, 191
  from stereotypes, 51, 68–70, 72, 79,
    81–88, 96, 198, 220
  from trait attribution, 68–70, 83,
    88–93, 96, 101–106, 191–198, 220
Folk psychological styles, 191–193, 211.
    See also Pluralistic Folk Psychology
Frith, Uta, 187
Fundamental attribution error, 71, 92,
    106, 108, 155–156

Gallese, Vittorio, 190
General rules. *See* Heuristics
Gergely, György, 147
German, Tamsin, 171–172
Giere, Ron, 58–59, 138
Gilbert, Daniel, 108
Godfrey-Smith, Peter, 60, 138–140,
    142, 195, 201, 203–205
Goldman, Alvin, 7, 40–41, 48, 51, 60,
    132–135, 137, 194–195, 199

Gopnik, Alison, 121–122
Gordon, Robert, 40–41, 60, 135–138,
    159–160
Grice, Paul, 103

Happé, Francesca, 187
Hare, Brian, 232, 245
Heider, Fritz, 65–67, 71, 108, 116–117,
    147
Hempel, Carl, 39, 117, 185
Heuristics, 48, 54–56, 64, 68–97, 108,
    110, 161–162, 175, 187, 198,
    206–207, 217–218. *See also* Folk
    psychological prediction, quotidian,
    from self, from situations, from
    stereotypes; Social norms
  "people generally do what they say,"
    52, 55, 103–104
  "people keep their easy-to-keep
    promises," 54
  "people look for objects where they
    left them," 33
Hobbes, Thomas, 19, 121
Hobson, Peter, 186, 197
Hood, Bruce, 151–152
Hume, David, 15–17, 19, 121–122
Humphrey, Nicholas, 19, 215–217, 219,
    224
Hursthouse, Rosalind, 176–177, 194
Hutto, Daniel, 186
Hybrid theories, 6–7, 9, 199–200. *See
    also* Simulation theory; Standard Folk
    Psychology; Theory theory
  and explanation, 132–135, 137
  and prediction, 48, 51, 63

Inductive rules. *See* Heuristics
Information seeking, 242
In-group/out-group psychology, 49,
    68–69, 78–79, 81, 156, 207–208, 221,
    228
Innovative behavior. *See* Anomalous
    behavior

Intentional agents, 10–12, 22, 103–104, 143, 146–147, 178, 183–185, 191, 196–211, 233–237, 239, 248. *See also* Person reading; Pluralistic Folk Psychology
Intentionality, 7, 11, 54, 65–68, 71, 167–168, 175–178, 194, 234–237
Intentional stance, 54, 106–107

Jolly, Alison, 19, 215–216, 224

Kahneman, Daniel, 73, 76, 79
Kanner, Leo, 196–197
Kanzi, 232, 248
Knobe, Joshua, 175–176
Knowledge how and knowledge that, 31–32, 224
Korsgaard, Christine, 229

LaFleur, Suzanne, 107
Langer, Ellen, 61–62
 Langer effect, 62–63
Language of thought, 165
Leslie, Alan, 22
Lewin, Kurt, 71
Lewis, David, 16, 40, 129, 165
Logical empiricism, 39, 117, 130, 185

Machiavellian Intelligence Hypothesis. *See* Social Intelligence Hypothesis
Maibom, Heidi, 60, 138, 201, 203
Malle, Bertram, 71, 111, 157–160
Malone, Patrick, 108
Marcus, Ruth Barcan, 30
Mental maps, 165–166
Metacognition. *See* Representational nature of belief
Metaphysics of belief. *See* Dispositional nature of belief; Representational nature of belief
Milgram obedience experiments, 71, 91
Mindblindness, 15–16, 109, 166, 197, 209, 219–220. *See also* Autism

Mindreading, 4–10, 12–29, 31–44, 47–68, 93–96, 99–112, 115–116, 125–137, 143, 145, 148–149, 151–152, 154–157, 160–179, 187–211, 215–222, 224–225, 229–233, 250–252. *See also* False belief tasks; Hybrid theories; Model theory; Representational nature of belief; Simulation theory; Standard Folk Psychology; Theory theory
 adaptive function of, 224–229
 and autism, 101, 109, 166, 197, 209 (*see also* Autism; Mindblindness)
 automatic, 168–173
 in children, 14, 21–24, 33–35, 79–80, 103, 110
 in critters, 19–21, 44, 94, 104, 196, 211, 231–233, 235, 243–248 (*see also* Critter psychology, mindreading)
 in infants, 14, 25–29, 31–32, 104, 127, 148
Mirror neurons, 190, 195
Mitani, John, 238
Model theory, 195, 201–205
 and explanation, 128–129, 132, 138–142
 and prediction, 60
Mood, 94–95, 160–162, 204–205
Moral sense, 218, 228–230. *See also* Social norms
Myth of the Given, 15

Nature of belief. *See* Dispositional nature of belief; Representational nature of belief
Nichols, Shaun, 7, 61–63, 194, 199
Nielsen, Mark, 235, 240
Nisbett, Richard, 89–90, 92–93, 106
Nozick, Robert, 54

Oakes, Lisa, 149–150
O'Neill, Daniela, 152
Onishi, Kristine, 25
Oppenheim, Paul, 39

Index

Parr, Lisa, 241
Payne, Keith, 84
Peirce, Charles Sanders, 121
Perner, Josef, 21–23, 199
Perry, Susan, 223
Person reading, 10–12, 22, 64, 103–104, 143, 147, 178, 179, 183–185, 191, 196–198, 206–211, 233–237, 239, 248, 250. *See also* Intentional agents; Pluralistic Folk Psychology
Persons. *See* Intentional agents
Piaget, Jean, 79, 123, 146
Pluralistic Folk Psychology, 5–6, 9–12, 162, 164, 178–179, 183–211, 220, 232, 234, 248, 251–252. *See also* Folk psychological practices, other; Folk psychological styles; Person reading
cognitive mechanisms involved, 184–187, 198, 208–211
principles of, 11–12, 184–194
as a social competence, 184–187, 198, 208–211
Povinelli, Daniel, 232
Predicting behavior. *See* Folk psychological prediction
Premack, David, 19–21, 44, 231–232, 235, 243
Princeton Seminary experiment, 72, 91

Radenovic, Ljiljana, 166
Ravenscroft, Ian, 199
Representational nature of belief, 10, 12, 16–18, 21–22, 123, 165–167, 199, 220, 251. *See also* Belief-desire psychology; Dispositional nature of belief; Mindreading
and autism, 166–167
children's understanding of, 14, 24, 28–35, 103, 105, 152–153, 159, 166, 169, 172, 204
critters' understanding of, 104–105, 172, 232–233
Rizzolatti, Giacomo, 190

Robison, John Elder, 188–189, 209
Ross, Lee, 77, 80, 89–90, 92–93, 106
Rylean ancestors, 15–16, 109–110

Salmon, Wesley, 118
Savage-Rumbaugh, Sue, 232, 248
Schwitzgebel, Eric, 30, 121, 204
Scientific explanation, 39–41, 58–59, 116–120, 129–130, 145. *See also* Deductive-nomological explanation; Folk psychological explanation
Scott, Rose, 26–27
Seeing the whole person. *See* Person reading
Sellars, Wilfrid, 15–16, 19, 65–67, 109
Simulation theory, 6–7, 9, 27, 40–41, 194–195, 198–201. *See also* Hybrid theories; Standard Folk Psychology
and explanation, 116, 128–129, 132–139
and prediction, 48, 51–52, 59–61, 63, 73, 75–76, 95
Situation. *See* Folk psychological explanation from situation; Folk psychological prediction from situation; Fundamental attribution error
Sober, Elliott, 141
Social Intelligence Hypothesis, 12, 19, 215–217, 219–220, 224–225
Social learning, 224–229
Social norms, 94, 198, 205, 220–230, 247. *See also* Heuristics
Standard Folk Psychology, 5–10, 13, 32, 48, 52, 55, 63–64, 67, 99–100, 105, 111, 133–134, 167, 173, 175, 179, 183–185, 194, 197–200, 204, 206, 210, 243, 250–251. *See also* Hybrid theories; Mindreading; Representational nature of belief; Simulation theory; Symmetry thesis; Theory theory
principles of, 7–9, 19, 37–43, 184

Statistical generalizations. *See* Heuristics
Stereotypes. *See* Folk psychological explanation, from stereotypes; Folk psychological prediction, from stereotypes
Stich, Stephen, 7, 165, 194, 199
Stocker, Michael, 251
Swann, William, 87–88
Symmetry Thesis, 8, 10, 36–44, 47, 127–128, 131, 140, 200, 205, 232–233

Theory of mind. *See* Mindreading
Theory theory, 6–7, 9, 40, 194, 199–201. *See also* Hybrid theories; Standard Folk Psychology
and explanation, 116, 128–135, 137–139
and prediction, 51–52, 56, 59–60, 63, 65, 76, 95
Tomasello, Michael, 104, 232, 243
Traits. *See* Folk psychological explanation from trait attribution; Folk psychological prediction from trait attribution
Tversky, Amos, 73, 76, 79

Vallone, Robert, 72
van Frassen, Bas, 39, 118–119
Velleman, David, 122

Warneken, Felix, 104
Watts, David, 239
Wellman, Henry, 28
Whiten, Andrew, 218
Whole persons. *See* Intentional agents
Why-questions, 39, 42–44, 115, 117–120, 125, 128, 140, 146, 149–151. *See also* Explanation seeking
Wilson, Timothy, 107
Wimmer, Hans, 21, 23

Wondering why. *See* Explanation seeking
Woodruff, Guy, 19–20, 44, 231, 243
Woodward, Amanda, 147–148

Zawidzk, Tadeusz, 186